Putting Together The Puzzle Pieces of Full Eating Disorder Recovery

Catherine Wilson Gillespie, Ph.D.

ISBN: 9781980815280

TABLE OF CONTENTS

INTRODUCTION

This is the book that I would like to have read 20 to 30 years ago: a thoughtful consideration of full eating disorder recovery, peppered with both academic research and personal experience. I am an academic – I have a Ph.D. in Child Development and have worked in academia since 1995, first as a professor for 17 years and now as a university administrator. And I definitely have personal experience with eating disorders. I have told my story elsewhere (Gillespie, 2013 and Gillespie, 2016) so I will not go into all the details here, but throughout this book I use personal stories from living with an eating disorder from age 11 to 23, and from being in recovery (including relapse) since 1985. My personal stories illustrate what I have learned from reading hundreds of articles and books about eating disorder recovery. I do my best to present research studies so that others can form their own opinion. This book is partly my story, but mostly it is meant to be a resource for others. It does not present one clear-cut solution (darn it!) but rather offers a variety of research-based options and personal insights that hopefully will turn out to be useful on the journey to full recovery.

For a person concerned about possibly having an eating disorder, there are many great resources available. First, consider contacting a counselor. The National Eating Disorders Association (NEDA) is a great resource https://www.nationaleatingdisorders.org/. NEDA offers a help line at 800-931-2237 that is available from 9 am to 9 pm eastern time Mondays through Thursdays and from 9 am to 5 pm on Fridays.

Another resource, referred to fairly frequently in the research articles reviewed throughout this manuscript, is the Eating Disorder Examination Questionnaire (Fairburn & Belgin, 2008), which is included as Appendix A. It is broken down into the following areas are most frequently experienced by people with eating disorders: eating restraint, eating concern, shape concern, and weight concern. Higher scores indicate more eating disorder symptoms. Community samples of people without eating disorders score on average around 1-2 on the subcales (Mond, Hay, Rogers & Owen, 2006). Higher scores indicate more concern.

There is no doubt that eating disorders are serious. They can lead to years of frustration and even death. But with effort and support, it is possible to fully recover from an eating disorder. This book aims to help people who have started on that journey to find a path to full recovery.

As someone who has devoted an immense amount of attention to my own recovery since I first took action in 1985 to find relief from my eating disorder, I have found that there are many resources out there to help a person begin eating disorder recovery. What seems to be missing are resources that might help a person get from the middle stages of recovery all the way to a place of full recovery. I remember one time asking a friend who is a counselor: "how are people who have struggled with eating disorders doing?" and I also remember the disappointment and frustration in her voice when she said, "not very well, for the most part." She did not elaborate and it was certainly not my business to ask or learn about any of her clients' level of wellbeing or lack thereof, but her comment did affirm for me my sense that after Herculean efforts to extricate themselves from the worst throes of an eating disorder, many people get stalled. Or maybe "stalled" is not the best analogy – maybe it feels more like banging one's head against a wall, or maybe it feels more like engaging in Sisyphus's eternal task of pushing a rock up a hill, only to have it come rolling back down, over and over again. Whatever one's frustrations, there are answers out there, but the answers are not well organized into one resource. Research articles abound, but they are published in a diverse set of journals that are released every few months, and are not available for free to the general public. It's hard to keep track, even for someone like me who has access to these journals. In this book, I have attempted to collect as many answers as I can find. Not every person has the same roadblocks (to continue the varied analogies!) but there are likely to be similar themes. I hope this book will be a useful resource to those who are working on their own recovery as well as to those who might be assisting others on their path to full recovery from eating disorders.

Full recovery is an important and worthy goal. It can positively affect not just one person, but possibly the whole family. One might think that family climate is related to adolescents' eating disorders, and indeed that is the case, but not in the way that the average person might predict. Researchers who studied 102 Swedish adolescents with eating disorders found that their recovery improved family climate, rather than family climate improving recovery (Nilsson, Engstrom & Hagglof, 2012). In other words, only after adolescents recovered from their eating disorders did their family climates become closer, less distant, and less chaotic. This makes sense to most parents – whenever any member of a family is struggling, the whole family is affected. It is also something to take to heart. If mom thinks that her eating disorder does not affect her family, she is likely wrong. The family climate is likely suffering, but is also likely to improve with recovery.

Causes of eating disorders

It is beyond the scope of this book to determine why people develop eating disorders, but it is worth noting that there appears to be general agreement that eating disorders have both genetic and environmental components. Analyzing the Minnesota Twin Study data, researchers determined that the contribution of genetics is strong, even to something as apparently environmentally-driven as body image (O'Connor, Klump, VanHuysse, McGue & Iacono, 2016). There is not one simple reason to explain why I developed an eating disorder. There are many contributing factors, the strongest of which I suspect is an underlying genetic predisposition. It is not that I was born with an eating disorder, but rather that I was an eating disorder waiting to happen. Add societal influences and presto there you have a full-blown eating disorder. "It is important to avoid simplifying the issues as the etiology of eating disorders is complex; while we strive to reduce dieting and body dissatisfaction in many of our prevention programs, any parent of a child with anorexia nervosa can rightfully attest to the fact that this illness is not just a diet gone astray" (Neumark-Sztainer, 2016, p. 31).

This book is not about causes of eating disorders. This book is aimed at people who want to take steps in eating disorder recovery toward full recovery. I review a lot of research and also share my own experiences and opinions. All of what I write is an attempt to bring together resources that I had a hard time finding when I was wanting information about full recovery. What is found in these pages is an offering and hopefully a blessing but it is not intended to replace or supplant other forms of treatment for eating disorders. Rather, this book is intended to supplement and complement other forms of eating disorder treatment. Hopefully it provides information and food for thought along the journey.

Of all of the possible immediate causes of eating disorders, weight loss dieting has been shown to lead to eating disorders, binge eating, body dissatisfaction, and low self-esteem (Ulian, et al., 2015). Let nobody say "diets don't work." Diets definitely work, it's just that they work in unanticipated ways. Most people go on a diet to lose weight – dieters did not realize that they were signing up for an eating disorder, binge eating, body dissatisfaction, or low self-esteem as a result of all their rigid control. To go on a diet is to take a risk. Not everybody who goes on a diet develops and eating disorder, and not everybody who rides a motorcycle on the highway without a helmet dies in a motor vehicle accident, but neither seem like a good idea, not given the research that I review in this book. But if someone is looking for an eating disorder, binge eating, body dissatisfaction or low self-esteem, then a diet is definitely the way to go!

Functions of eating disorders

Rather than pondering the possible cause(s) of eating disorders, I find it much more useful to consider the function of my eating disorder. How is it helping me, what is it doing for me? For the longest time, I could not break down the function of my eating disorder into its component parts. It all seemed like one big tornado of craving, obsession, and compulsion that controlled me and caused me to do things that my better self-did not really want to do. I saw my eating disorder as separate from myself but in fact, it was part of me and when I saw that I used it to my benefit in certain ways, it was easier for me to let go of it. Certainly, I suffered from the negative consequences of my eating disorder behaviors, but they also served me in the following ways:

Stress relief,

Anxiety reduction,

An excuse to avoid whatever it was that I didn't want to do,

Confirmation of my negative self-concept (see, there really is something wrong with me!).

Maintaining factors

One research article opens with this rather depressing introduction: "The fact that more than half of those who receive our best available treatments for eating disorders do not experience remission by the end of treatment and an additional portion relapse, suggests that current treatments are not adequately addressing maintaining factors in many individuals. To make a substantial gain in improving eating disorder treatment outcomes, we need to identify, investigate, and address potential maintaining factors" (Trottier, Wonderlich, Monson, Crosby & Olmsted, 2016, p. 455). The authors distinguish between risk factors for eating disorders and maintaining factors. Risk factors are not necessarily direct causes of eating disorders, but they do increase the probability that a person could develop an eating disorder. The more risk factors a person experiences, the more likely she will develop an eating disorder. Maintaining factors, however, are situations or ways of thinking or personality characteristics that keep the eating disorder alive. These scholars argue that post-traumatic stress disorder could be not just a risk factor, but also a maintaining factor for eating disorders. They argue that "Eating disorder behaviors such as severe food restriction, binge eating, and purging have the strong potential to facilitate escape and avoidance of distressing memories, thoughts, and feelings and to decrease the hyperarousal symptoms of post-traumatic stress disorder. Any degree of successful avoidance of trauma-related thoughts, feelings and memories is reinforcing and promotes maintenance of the eating disorder. Although eating disorder behaviors may attenuate post-traumatic symptoms in the short term, this behavioral pattern promotes the maintenance of both disorders" (Trottier, Wonderlich, Monson, Crosby & Olmsted, 2016, p. 455-456). Attenuate means to reduce the force or effect. I think this is a very important argument for people who are working on achieving full recovery from an eating disorder and finding it difficult. It may be useful to consider maintaining factors. There are an unlimited number of possible maintaining factors, but each person only has a limited number. The tricky thing with maintaining behaviors is that they actually work in the short run. They help a person feel better. But in the long run, they keep the problem alive instead of helping the person to let it go.

Maintaining factors are also present in anxiety disorders, and, interestingly enough, eating disorders are sometimes conceptualized as anxiety disorders. A person with anxiety usually has behaviors to use in order to reduce anxiety, and these are called safety, or maintaining, behaviors. Examples of safety behaviors include: double-checking, monitoring, making sure, being very careful, and avoiding. "Intended to avert threat and relieve anxiety, such behaviors are ultimately counter-productive, serving to maintain anxiety in the long term" (Waller & Marcoulides, 2013, p. 257). Not only do safety behaviors maintain anxiety in the long term, but they also can maintain eating disorders. Safety behaviors among people with eating disorders can vary, but might include body checking, frequent self-weighing, double-checking nutritional values, monitoring food intake or weight, being very careful about food ingredients, and avoiding activities such as eating at restaurants or eating in social situations or eating alone.

For me, self-weighing was a safety, or maintaining, behavior. I weighed myself in order to relieve anxiety, to reassure myself that my weight was still okay and by extension that I was still okay as a human being. No matter what the result on the scale, it did not help. It took me a long time to figure out that the reason it could not help was that my motivation is to relieve anxiety, however, by their very nature safety behaviors actually serve to maintain anxiety. They maintain anxiety because they do not consider the cause of the anxiety, but instead just address the symptoms. I was worried about my own sense of self-worth and well-being and no number on the scale was going to get me to where I wanted to be. As researchers concluded regarding safety behaviors such as taking deep breaths before going into a social situation, "It can be hypothesized that socially oriented safety behaviours serve to reduce the immediate experience of social anxiety among such patients but that they result in the original cognitions and emotions remaining unchallenged" (p. 260). Later in this book I include an excerpt from my journal when I conducted what I call my "no weigh" experiment. I journaled until I accumulated 30 days of not weighing myself (note that this took me 38 days!) after which time, well, stay tuned for the details in the section entitled "to weigh or not to weigh."

Body distrust was another maintaining factor for me. It may be an exaggeration to call my anxiety "terror," as terror has so many other contemporary meanings, but the whole idea of accepting my body as it is, trusting it fully, eating to satisfaction, and so forth, struck terror in my heart. But it did not strike terror in my soul. My soul sang for joy and then sighed with relief. My heart clenched and "knew" that I was not up to the task. There was some part of me (the eating disorder part?) that was quite sure that if I allowed myself to eat some of the cake batter the way I wanted to, that my binge engine would rev me up and I would be like a racing car, careening out of control until I hit a wall and exploded. But I am living proof that this does not happen. I do remember a time when I was restricting and binge eating that I ate an entire box of cake batter. It was so many years ago that I do not remember if I added the wet ingredients, but I must have because how else could I have choked it all down? I also remember that my response to eating an entire box of raw cake batter was to go on a low carbohydrate diet. And I also remember that my low carb kick lasted about five days, until I had my annual doctor's appointment at which I weighed in at a weight that I could live with, and then my eating was off to the races again. More recently, after many years and much more recovery, about three hours after dinner, and I was hungry for a snack. Normally I would not have a sweet at that time, but I was thinking "we have that cake mix; I would sure like some of that, and actually what I want is some of the cake batter." I made up the cake mix and poured cupcakes for the oven and ate about a cupcake or a little bit more of the batter. It was perfect. It hit the spot. It was indulgent and exactly what I wanted. I was satisfied and I did not want to eat any more. Once again, I was truly amazed. My body really is completely trustworthy. All of our bodies are completely trustworthy. If I had given into my fear of being out of control, I would not have walked through the anxiety of eating what I wanted, and I would have stayed stuck in my thinking that my body was untrustworthy. This is how body distrust serves to be a maintaining factor in my eating disorder and how being courageous to trust my body is the way out. I had to engage in a little bit of mind-body battle before I decided to go to the kitchen and prepare the cake batter. The debate went something like this:

Body: Mmm….sweet…smooth…cake batter…that would really hit the spot right now.

Mind: Yeah, right. That's what you say now, but a few licks of cake batter and you will be cruising the kitchen looking for more trouble.

Body: I just want something sweet and rich.

Mind: Sweet and Rich is like saying Risky and More Risky. I honestly think it would be better to have, say, a frozen banana. You love frozen bananas, don't you?

Body: Right now, cake batter would be great, not a frozen banana (although I do love them, I don't want one right now)

Mind: For crying out loud. Fine. But don't say I didn't tell you so. Go for it. But don't think I trust you for a minute. You are a trickster and a liar. And I know it. But I'm not going to stop you, so just do it and then I'll be the one who knew better in the end.

Body: Thank you ma'am.

And the way it unfolded of course was not the way my mind feared. As I was putting things away in the kitchen after enjoying my cake batter and while waiting for the cupcakes to cook, I opened a cabinet that contains sugary cereal that would have been a binge food for me in the past. I looked at that cereal and thought, "Amazing! I don't want it! I am not bingeing!! I don't even want to binge. I had what I wanted and I don't want anything else." Despite many experiences like this, each time it is still amazing to me. I feel like I am taking a huge risk when I trust my body and yet the truth is that I am truly taking a huge risk when I do not trust my body. When I do not eat the foods I want, when I eat foods I do not want, when I stop myself from eating enough to be satisfied – all of those are instances of unnecessary risk taking. All of those attempts at restricting or controlling my food intake according to my mind's view of what my eating should look like ends up backfiring. Not that there is a problem with the Mind's question, "I honestly think it would be better to have, say, a frozen banana. You love frozen bananas, don't you?" because I really do love frozen bananas (and so easy to make – just peel a banana and put it in a plastic container in the freezer for later eating) and it's a great sweet option when I am not looking for an indulgent dessert. It's one of my daily "go-to" foods. Cake batter is not a daily thing for me. But if and when I want it, it's much wiser to just go ahead and have it than to eat a few frozen bananas before moving on to something else that I don't want and then ending up either with cake batter or some other sweet, rich treat that hopefully in the end might satisfy although by that time I would have put a dent in the pleasure and satisfaction that I could have gotten out of it. I am glad that I trusted my body in that situation and I look forward to many other opportunities to do so. I also know that I don't have to seek out opportunities. My body will tell me. There are some foods that I know I like and that feel good in my body. When I am hungry for a meal or snack, I can generally go with one of the foods I like and be quite satisfied. Each meal and snack is not a big deal. The big deals come for me in the slightly unusual situations, where I am reminded once again how blessedly trustworthy my body is.

Research studies

In addition to my own experiences and the findings of many other scholars' work in the area of eating disorders and recovery, I have included data from two research studies that I conducted with colleagues at Drake University in Des Moines, Iowa. Study 1 includes unpublished data from seven women who struggled with an eating disorder at some point in their lives. The initial data analysis of Study 1 was a collaborative effort between myself and a colleague, Dr. Bengu Erguner-Tekinalp, with whom I collaborated with on another study related to eating disorders (Ergruner-Tekinalp & Gillespie, 2010). I am very grateful for Dr. Erguner-Tekinalp's collaboration and insight into these data, but we never published our findings. For this book, I re-analyzed the data, looking specifically at participants' responses regarding their recovery. Study 2 consisted of face-to-face interviews with five women who identified as recovering or recovered from an eating disorder that I conducted with a student who is now an eating disorder counselor. These data have been published elsewhere (Fee & Gillespie, 2014) but I also re-analyzed a portion of the data for this book, focusing on participants' recovery.

Participants' pseudonyms and eating challenges are listed below.

Research Participants' pseudonyms and eating challenges

Study Number	Participant Number	Pseudonym	Eating Challenge
1	1	Abby	Restricting
1	2	Beth	Restricting
1	3	Caroline	Restricting
1	4	Debbie	Restricting
1	5	Ella	Binge
1	6	Francesca	Binge/Purge
1	7	Georgia	Binge/Purge
2	8	Cathy	Restricting
2	9	Natalie	Binge
2	10	Alex	Binge/Purge
2	11	Alice	Restricting
2	12	Maria	Binge

Study 1 included the first seven participants, all of whom responded to the following writing prompt: "Describe your experience of living with an eating disorder over the years, as well as how you cope and have coped with it over time." We made no assumption in Study 1 about whether complete recovery from an eating disorder was even possible, or whether eating disorders are a chronic condition. That is why we chose the wording "living with an eating disorder" instead of "recovering from an eating disorder." We did not want to put ideas in their heads that were different than their actual lived experiences. Study 2 included five participants (numbered 8-12 in the table above) who were interviewed as part of the research project reported in Fee and Gillespie (2014). As these data have been reported elsewhere, in addition to data already published, answers to these two interview questions were re-analyzed and are woven into this book: (1) If someone were to ask whether or not you are recovered from the eating disorder, what would your response be? (2) What would you constitute as full recovery in terms of an eating disorder?

In case anyone is concerned about human subjects' protection in research, please know that only women over age 18 and over who had (at some point in their lives) an eating disorder were eligible to participate in Study 1. The same criteria applied to Study 2, although in the case of Study 2, participation was further limited to women who saw themselves as either recovering or recovered from an eating disorder. No race, ethnicity or other demographic variables were collected other than to verify that each participant was a woman age 18 or over. Both studies were approved by Drake University's Institutional Research Board and all the women signed and submitted written informed consent forms. They did not receive anything in return. Study 1 participants' submissions were in writing and anonymous and it is not known where each of the seven participants learned of the study, although the venues where the study was publicized are listed below. These submissions were received through the U.S. mail and through email. Study 2 participants were interviewed face-to-face at Drake University in Des Moines, Iowa. These participants responded to flyers and verbal announcements in college classes regarding the second study.

In order to encourage participation in Study 1, we tried many ways to advertise the study. A local therapist specializing in eating disorders was given informed consent forms to hand out to her clients who might be interested in participating. Informed consent forms were also mailed and emailed to therapists in other states and students in undergraduate and graduate classes in counseling and human development were given informed consent forms to use themselves or to pass along to friends or family who might be interested in participating. An article about the study appeared in the university newspaper and an announcement of the study was posted on the National Eating Disorders Association website in their research study section, as well as on the Academy for Eating Disorders list serve.

Data from both research studies are included in this book in a variety of sections. The data provide depth and a snapshot of real women who have been there, living with and beyond eating disorders. Here is a brief preview of what to expect. In terms of the function of their eating disorders, participants emphasized the functions of their eating disorders. Ella stated, *"I see the eating disorder as a coping tool – not a great one, but sometimes the best one I have in my limited tool bag. My overeating, eating foods that make my body sluggish rather than powerful – it's all an attempt to take care of myself and cope with a life that feels unmanageable."* For Georgia, her eating disorder provided *"comfort and control in a world that just went crazy around me."*

The process of recovery was not without its struggles for participants, but it was also full of hope. Although women had found a variety of levels of relief from their eating disorders, they had all survived and they were making sense of their experiences. For instance, Debbie said, *"I have done the hardest thing I have ever done in my life – recovering from my eating disorder…It wasn't as scary as I thought it would be….Since that time, I have nourished and carried a healthy baby boy to full term. I never thought that I would be brave enough or healthy enough to have a child. I am thankful for my journey."* That is a strong statement of hope that I believe is carried through the remainder of the pages of this book. Full eating disorder recovery IS possible.

Preview

There is a lot of detail in this book about my own eating disorder recovery experiences and about what research from a variety of perspectives and disciplines has found by studying people in recovery as well as by studying human nature. I personally find the research compelling and convincing. And I find that I am not very likely to stick with anything unless I am convinced. So please read what I hope are convincing arguments that support the to-do list below. But for those who want to know what they might learn in this book, for those who don't have time today to sit down and slog through all the details, here is preview of upcoming attractions in this book. Below is a distillation of the high points of my personal recommendations, based on my experience and my own and others' research, of how to proceed with eating disorder recovery beyond the first initial stages, when the goal is full recovery.

First, make sure to establish solid recovery:

1. Make sure to eat regularly (three meals and two to three snacks, separated by two to four hours each; or, more simply, eat approximately every three hours).

2. Make sure to eat to satisfaction. Eating enough is really important.

Next, to make progress toward full recovery:

3. Truly believe that full recovery is possible. Learn about what full recovery from an eating disorder really is, and that it is truly possible.

4. Practice body acceptance and appreciation. Each person only gets one body – we might as well accept it. And everybody's body does some pretty amazing things! Take time to appreciate all the things the body does.

5. Practice Body-led eating. Let the body take the lead with regarding eating. Trust and respond to its signals of hunger and satisfaction.

6. Stop thinking so much about food, eating, body, or weight.

7. Start thinking about other aspects of life besides food eating, body or weight.

8. Get in the zone. Find healthy ways to disconnect mentally such as meditation, reading a really good book, or any other activity that is

completely mentally absorbing, including physical or creative activities. Do this daily, or at least regularly.

9. Review possible maintaining factors as needed. When (not if) things aren't going as well as they might, consider what personal maintaining factors may be at play. What might be decreased (such as self-weighing, over-planning, or perfectionism) and what might be increased (such as support, sleep, movement, self-compassion, down time, or mentally engaging activities) to foster a greater sense of personal integration, connection, and/or coherence?

10.   Move on. Keep a hand in recovery by helping someone else or making the world a better place for all bodies, but make commitments in other areas of life; pursue other interests.

CHAPTER 1
Make sure to eat regularly

Three meals and two to three snacks, separated by two to four hours each; or, more simply, eat approximately every three hours.

Start here: Regular Eating

When in doubt, start with regular eating. For chaotic eaters, whether someone is underweight, overweight or anywhere in between, especially for constant hunger or binge eating, regular eating is the place to start in order to start feeling more sane around food. When I first heard the term "regular eating," I thought "regular" meant "normal" as in "eat a bowl of cereal with milk for breakfast" or "have a peanut butter and jelly sandwich and chips for lunch." But I learned that "regular" in this case meant "following a predictable pattern," more like the regularity of a metronome than the regularity of normalcy. The regular eating intervention, popularized by psychiatrist and eating disorder expert extraordinaire Dr. Christopher Fairburn (Fairburn, Cooper, Shafran, Bohn, Hawker, Murphy, & Straebler, 2008) as part of a cognitive behavior therapy approach to treating eating disorders, translates to eating a meal or snack every two to four hours. Regular eating is powerful, both surprisingly difficult at first and then thankfully easier and easier over time. Most normal eaters follow this basic eating pattern. It also fits well with both the needs of the human body and with social norms, so it's a win-win-win. One can eat in rhythm with what one's body wants and needs as well as join in with others in social eating opportunities. I know that may sound completely out of reach to someone who feels chaotic, but I highly recommend it as a starting place. I went from feeling crazy and in need of in-patient treatment to much less crazy and possibly even trustworthy in the matter of a few days of eating breakfast at 6 am, a snack at 9 am, lunch at noon, a snack at 3 pm, dinner at 6 pm and a final snack at 9 pm. The "eat every three hours" that is implied here is useful to me, as I didn't have to calculate and re-calculate the "eat every two to four hours" and it also gave me an hour-long window of flexibility on either side of a social meal or snack in case something was early or delayed so I didn't have to worry about being exactly on time, but had a little bit of built-in flexibility. In other words, if I had a snack at 9 am and planned to eat with friends at noon but the meal didn't actually happen until 12:45, I could more easily tell myself that I was doing the best I could, and I would still have my next snack at 3 pm and my dinner at 6 pm, or as close to 6 as I could make it, so that I didn't have to think about it too much. This pattern was a true lifesaver for me and really cut down on my binge eating remarkably.

Continuum of Planning

There are a number of different approaches to regular eating, on a continuum from unplanned to highly planned. I am an early riser, so the 6-9-12-3-6-9 o'clock plan was easiest for me. Another possibility would be to start with the idea of eating 3 meals every day at socially acceptable times, and then filling in snacks as needed to prevent going more than 4 hours at a stretch without a meal or snack, one might arrive at: breakfast at 8 am, lunch at noon, snack at 3 pm, snack at 5 pm, dinner at 7 pm, snack at 10 pm. Whatever the pattern, then question then becomes, how planned out should those meals and snacks be?

Everyone has different eating patterns, but it is not normal to be "always" or "never" hungry. Personally, I am a morning person. I wake up early and have more energy early in the day. My brain starts shutting down in the early evening. My hunger pattern mirrors my energy pattern. I wake up hungry most days. If I am not hungry right at the time I get up, within 20 minutes or so, I get hungry. Fasting for blood draws at the doctor's office at 8:30 a.m. is nothing short of torture for me. Unless I am fasting, which I only do under duress once or twice a year, then I eat what at one time was called "a good breakfast" with some kind of protein and some kind of carbohydrate. I have different things for breakfast depending on my mood, but I might have eggs and toast or peanut butter toast or yogurt and cereal. I often have fruit also, usually an apple or a banana because I love them both. I especially love frozen bananas and they are a great thing to have at breakfast because I am almost always home for breakfast and I keep my freezer well stocked with frozen bananas from the ones we buy that others in the family have not eaten (they keep in the freezer for much longer than they do on the kitchen counter). Nothing earth shattering or complicated, but always something filling for me for breakfast. I eat breakfast at or before 6 a.m. most mornings. Not surprisingly, around 9 am I am ready for a snack. I have experimented with five similarly-sized meals per day vs. three meals and two to three snacks and I go back and forth but mostly I find that three meals and two to three snacks works better for me. It is easier to share in social meals at lunch and dinner if I am hungrier for a big meal, and it is awkward to pack and eat larger mid-morning and mid-afternoon snacks consistently. I do not do well on three meals a day, which I have certainly tried, because I get too hungry in between meals. But to say that I am on a three meal and two to three snack per day food plan would not be accurate. I am on a "mindfully eat what I want when I am hungry" food plan, taking into account that I want to feel and be reasonably healthy and I also want to participate in social food opportunities and rituals (and I want the freedom to participate in some social food opportunities and rituals without actually eating, if I don't feel like eating at that moment). For my mid-morning snack, I have found that I want something sustaining. I might have a big blob of peanut butter and an apple or cheese and crackers. For lunch, I try to have some vegetables and protein and usually some carbohydrate and sometimes a sweet, but most often not. In the mid-afternoon is when I am most likely to want and to have a sweet, often with a cup of coffee or tea. True to form, I am an early dinner eater whenever I can and prefer to eat by 6 pm if at all possible. If not, then I have another snack before dinner if I get hungry. In the evening before bed, I have a snack probably about three quarters of the time. Or maybe less. Or maybe more. Basically, if and when I am hungry before bed, I have a snack. If I am not hungry before bed, I do not have a snack. The same could be said for my other snacks, but it is very infrequent that I would not be hungry for my mid-morning snack. Sometimes if I have a big lunch then I am not hungry for an afternoon snack, but that is not very frequent either.

A huge consideration for someone in recovery from an eating disorder is how much to plan and how much to be spontaneous, both around food as well as around other things in life, but for now how about we just focus on food, okay? I think it is important for each person to experiment and find out what works for her. In the beginning of my recovery, I was more structured and planful and I saw it as my goal to become less structured and planful. But as I loosened my grip on planning out every little detail, it quickly felt chaotic to me. I love the concept of taking a leap of faith and sometimes that is a strategy that really works. It takes faith to trust that eating three meals and three snacks per day is truly a good idea. But for me, it was folly to move directly from that to "I'll just wait until I'm hungry and see what I want at that time." What happened when I tried to take such a major leap was that I got very anxious and either due to my anxiety or due to my extreme hunger because I wasn't that great at knowing when I should eat, I ended up bingeing. And then I thought "this will never work" so I went back to my structure. I wish I had been able to trust a more gradual approach, staying at each of these levels for a week or so before determining if I should move on, move back, or stay right where I was. From most to least structured, here is where I have been on the level-of-planning continuum. Right now I would say I am at an 4. I do not plan to move from where I am, although life being what it is, and in my desire to be responsive to my own needs, I am open to changing if it would help me to stay in touch with my own body.

1.Completely pre-planned. Pre-determine exact contents of meals and snacks in advance. Write down food plan before consuming. Eat at scheduled/planned times or "eating windows" (lunch between 11:30 am and 1 pm, for example).

2.Pre-planned times; last minute planning of food. Eat at scheduled/planned times or "eating windows" (lunch between 11:30 am and 1 pm, for example) but leave the content of the meals open and flexible. Right before each meal or snack, determine what is going to be consumed and then eat all of it – nothing more or less.

3.Pre-planned times; mostly unplanned contents. Eat at scheduled/planned times or "eating windows" (lunch between 11:30 am and 1 pm, for example) but leave the content of the meals open and flexible. Right before each meal or snack, determine what is going to be ordered/put on plate and eating according to hunger and satiety cues; getting more food if not yet satisfied, stopping when satisfied, whether or not that means leaving food over. Planning contents for family meals and packed lunches, but also being flexible about what is consumed depending on appetite and food opportunities.

4.Habitual but flexible times; mostly unplanned contents. Eat at "normal" and "regular" times, adjusting as desired for a variety of reasons, prioritizing personal hunger and satiety but also taking social norms into consideration. Being flexible. Right before each meal or snack, determine what is going to be ordered/put on plate and eating according to hunger and satiety cues; getting more food if not yet satisfied, stopping when satisfied, whether or not that means leaving food over. Planning contents for family meals and packed lunches, but also being flexible about what is consumed.

5.Completely unplanned. Eating entirely according to hunger and satiety. Waiting for hunger, seeing what appeals, locating food after hunger arises. Eating to satiety.

I want to address my experience of my eating feeling chaotic because this is an area that can be tricky as anxiety is a real experience that is hard to know how to master. I am not sure that I would have even labeled my experience as one of anxiety. I just knew that I wanted to avoid it. Possibly seeing it as more concrete can help. "The desire to avoid or reduce feelings of anxiety motivates the use of safety behaviors and avoidance strategies, behaviors/strategies that may decrease anxiety in the short-term, but also may help to maintain the anxiety since the individuals are not able to learn that the threat is non-existent or manageable…various disordered eating behaviors can function as safety behaviors and avoidance strategies. For example, dietary restriction can foster a sense of control and a sense of safety, in particular from a fear of weight gain, while binge eating can provide an escape/avoidance of aversive self-awareness and negative affect by temporarily "anaesthetizing" negative emotional states" (Bardone-Cone, Brownstone, Higgins, Fitzsimmons-Craft & Harney, 2013, p. 953). Rather than asking myself "what am I afraid of?" I find it much more helpful to be able to say to myself, "oh, that's anxiety" without feeling pressured to figure out exactly where it is coming from.

In my 2012 article in *Critical Dietetics,* I wrote about how I employed Ellyn Satter's (2008) recommendations regarding following a regular eating schedule (three meals or three meals and for me, two to three snacks) and then leaving the decision about what and how much to eat at those regular meals and snacks up to my mind and body's intuition. Satter calls this permission and discipline – permission for each person to eat what and how much she wants, and discipline to follow plan, prepare, and eat meals and snacks and regular, expected times. This is quite a traditional American way of eating. When I was growing up, in my house and in the house of most of my friends, breakfast and dinner were served at set times, and at school, lunch was served at a set time too. There was an afternoon snack and for most of us, and for some families, probably a bedtime snack too. The contents of breakfast, lunch, and dinner, as well as contents of the snacks, varied widely from family to family and day to day, but one could definitely rely on meals at predictable times. When we "didn't call during dinner" that was a define time, between 5:30 pm and 7 pm. Now families have much different schedules. Adults work later, children have more after school and early evening activities, and some very loving families are not able to sit down to shared meals. Satter is a big proponent of family meals and although I don't disagree with her reasoning, I often find it difficult to gather my family for daily shared meals. I feel like we do the best we can despite our crazy schedules.

Journaling

People who plan out their food often also journal what they ate and how they felt before, during and/or after eating. This is a common recommendation for someone starting in eating disorder recovery, as it can help to identify patterns and triggers for problematic eating. If a person isn't eating very much during the day and then binge eating at night, it is fairly easy to see via a journal that the nighttime overeating was at least partly caused by the daytime undereating. Eating more regularly can really help to cut down on binge eating and to help a person feel more sane around food.

But not all journaling is a record of food eaten. There are many different kinds of journaling to try out. There are "dear diary" entries, pouring one's feelings onto the page. There is the "write it out to figure it out" approach that can be great for getting clarity on whatever is going emotionally. Then there is a themed or topic journal, dedicated to just one topic, such as for career decisions. Some people in recovery write down everything they eat, and some also add a record of their feelings, and/or what happened just before and just after eating. Food journaling can aid with accountability and it can also help with honesty and clarity about what is going on and is particularly helpful in identifying patterns.

I particularly enjoy using a journal to work out my feelings, to figure out what is going on with me. I think of it as "discovery writing." When I am upset or struggling with an issue, I start writing and often not too far into my process, I have an "aha" about my issue that is really helpful to me.

Another approach that I have enjoyed is writing to prompts. I have done this with a coach where she gave me one writing prompt a day for 30 days, and I wrote on those topics. I have seen books for sale that are paper journals with built in prompts. Here are a set of possible questions for anyone who might want to journal to daily recovery prompts for a month:

1. What's going well?
2. How am I feeling connected to my body?
3. What are my goals for my eating?

4.   What concrete action can I take today to get one step closer to meeting my goals?

5.   What do I want to accept?

6.   How can I be kinder to myself?

7.   How can I arrange for more quiet time today?

8.   How do I know that my hunger has been satisfied?

9.   What wondrous things has my body accomplished?

10.   How can I feel more connected to my body?

11.   What do I want to let go of?

12.   What do I want to stick with?

13.   What is my mindset about recovery?

14.   How am I taking good care of myself?

15.   How can I take better care of myself?

16.   What one thing could I do to feel better in my body today?

17.   What motivates me?

18.   What am I committed to?

19.   Who do I admire and why?

20.   What would I say to my 10-year old self?

21.   What do I want to be able to say to myself 10 years from now?

22.   How can I inhabit my body more fully today?

23.   How can I integrate contemplation into my life?

24.   When do I zone out (not thinking about anything in particular)?

25.   When I am "in the zone" (highly focused)?

26.   Who supports me emotionally?

27.   What additional support do I want to seek out?

28.   With what am I satisfied?

29.   How can I find more satisfaction today?

30.   Who can I help?

Surrender

Surrender as a concept is given a bad rap in our society. I have found it a great relief to surrender to what is, to admit or acknowledge what it is that I need to do, to stop fighting the inevitable. Specifically with regard to regular eating, it took a lot of surrender on my part to eat a snack I was not particularly hungry for, to pack my lunch, and then sometimes to set aside my packed lunch in favor of an a social meal at a restaurant. I'm not saying that everyone should do these things, but I had made a commitment to eat every two to four hours and in order to stick with that commitment that I believed to be a good thing for me, it took some surrendering of my ego to stick with it. Over time, I re-evaluated and shifted away from this commitment to one that felt more attuned to my own body's needs, but I am very grateful to both have made this commitment and to have stuck with it even when I experienced some internal resistance (I notice that most of the resistance that I experience is internal – other people and external events stand in my way much less than I think they will).

Whenever I am fighting with myself about something, surrender is the most delicious feeling. It's not that I have to surrender to a particular person or action, but more that I surrender to what is, to the present moment. I get so caught up in my head, particularly in future possibilities. And surrender gets me back into the moment, into reality, into what is and what is going on at the moment and what I need to do next. Surrender is an admission that I am not in control of the universe but that by playing my part and showing up and doing the best I can, I can feel good about my part and enjoy whatever the situation is.

Possibly what I would name "surrender," in part because it feels so difficult for me, others would name a more straightforward process of "acceptance." I do not want to get hung up on the terminology. Call it surrender or acceptance of merely living in reality – it's all good. As long as we are acknowledging what is true and not trying to wish it away or to neglect it out of existence. Some things actually do respond well to being neglected. Years ago, I had a series of old Volvo station wagons. Relative frequently they would develop odd problems like weird noises or difficulty starting. I found that if I ignored the issue for a couple of days, nine times out of ten, it would go away. The tenth time, it would not go away, and that's why I am an AAA member. I could call a tow truck and have my Volvo towed to the nearest garage or dealer to address the issue. With emotions, sometimes it is effective to ignore my own or others' emotions, because they are brief and will pass quickly. But in general, ignoring things is not an effective strategy. I may want them to go away, but they will not, no matter how long I ignore them. Chances are, they will get worse over time. Better for me to surrender to reality and accept things as they are even if I don't approve of them, and do whatever needs to be done to remedy the situation. In addition to the experience of surrender as an "accept things as they are" experience, I also see the "accept what I need to do" awareness as an experience of surrender. Once I get to the place where I know what I need to do, I don't always want to do it. Surrender helps me do what I know I need to do, even when I don't always feel motivated to do it. Surrender is definitely my friend. I feel better about life when I am operating from a surrendered rather than an offensive or even a defensive posture. There are times, of course, when fighting is appropriate, but when they don't work, surrender feels fantastic.

CHAPTER 2
Make sure to eat to satisfaction

Eating enough is really important. Eat to Satisfaction.

I think a lot of people who are in recovery from eating disorders are basically living the diet lifestyle. I have dipped in an out of this because of how much I love structure and rules. Unfortunately for me, structure and rules (or "guidelines") around food lead very quickly to a diet, or as marketers are wont to say, a "lifestyle," which basically means a diet for life (e.g. a paleo lifestyle, a Weight Watchers lifestyle, etc.) Don't get me wrong, I see the allure and benefits of such approaches, and have fallen into the temptation of external structure and rules more times than I would like to admit. The problem is that I don't seem to be able to completely stick with whichever diet or lifestyle I've chosen in the long term. Or maybe that's a good thing. I never would have ended up where I am (which is a really good place to be) if I hadn't repeatedly fallen into the diet trap and fought my way out of it, time and time again. Either I binged my way out of it, or I started slowly adding in exceptions until I was at the point where I really was no longer following whatever the named approach is to which I most recently committed. It is definitely true that this apparent "problem" of mine is actually really good news, because it has helped me learn (after many, many trials) that diets are part of the problem, not part of the solution to eating disorders.

Building on a solid basis of regular eating, the next thing to tackle is eating to satisfaction. Eating regularly cut down on my bingeing dramatically for me. Eating to satisfaction within the context of regular eating completely eliminated my binges. Apparently most of my binges were related to restrictive eating. And yet I can only recognize that in hindsight. Yes, I was counting every calorie (or ounce, or point, or carb, depending on which food plan or diet I was following) but I could not connect the dots between "not enough" and "way too much" until I started eating "enough" and the "way too much" receded enough into the background that I could deal with it as a thought or an urge rather than a foregone conclusion.

My "how not to binge" prescription focuses mostly on feeling satisfied by the food I eat. Working backward from that means I have to let myself eat enough - not too much and not too little, although it's not an exact science and there is plenty of wiggle room in there – and I have to let myself get hungry. If I don't get hungry, I can't really be satisfied. That doesn't mean that I have to be growling in my stomach every time I eat, far from it. I prefer to be hungry enough that it gets my attention when I'm doing something else. I don't do well with the "gosh, am I hungry?" "No, how about now, then?" constant monitoring of my hunger. If I'm hungry, I'll notice. That's the perfect time to eat. The fact that I hate to wait to eat and also the fact that I tend to get hungry for lunch at 10:30 in the morning both work against this "plan" for eating, but I really do feel best when I'm eating in accordance with my own God-given signals of hunger and fullness. In order to support my daily food intake, planning on eating three meals and two to three snacks per day is very helpful in keeping eating in the back of my mind instead of smack dab in the forefront of my brain. I know I'm going to get regular meals and snacks so I don't have to stress over it. I want to think about eating occasionally, but I really don't want to think about it all the time. I've had too many years of that. There are other things I need to and want to think about, I don't need to be fantasizing about food all day long.

Variety of Internal Signals

One thing that I have learned from Ayurveda, which is an ancient Indian healing system, is the notion of paying attention for the "enough" signal via a small burp or internal hiccup as one of my body's clearest and, in my experience shockingly surprising, indications that it's time to stop eating. When I first heard about this, I thought, as many others apparently do "uh…I don't actually burp very often" and the advice that I got was to pay closer attention while eating. At the very next meal, I thought wow, yes, there it is. The process is this: I begin a meal or snack when I am hungry (for me, now that I am no longer binge eating, my hunger rolls around pretty predictably every few hours, so it's not like I'm putting off meals or snacks for long). Ayurveda recommends not to eat until one experiences an "unflavored" burp. In other words, the burp right before a meal or snack should no longer have the flavor of the previous meal or snack. I don't tend to use the "unflavored" burp strategy because when I am hungry, I know it, and I don't have to debate whether or not it's a good time to eat. But for others, this might be useful information, so I include it here. I am a speedy eater, and I don't have to slow down too much to use the "first burp" strategy, but it does help if I take sips of a non-carbonated beverage between bites of food. (Ayurveda cautions against cold or carbonated beverages and recommends room temperature beverages). Then I continue eating until my first burp. I don't burp after two bites, but I usually burp after eating something like a sandwich and a piece of fruit. The next action is to stop eating immediately upon experiencing the first burp. If I have eaten my sandwich and am half way through my fruit, if I burp, then I stop eating my fruit and either throw it away or save it for later. I was surprised how easy and satisfying this is. That first burp comes right at the point when my body truly has had enough. I am not still hungry, and not uncomfortably full. The first burp comes right at the "just right" amount of food and drink have been consumed. Then I repeat this process for every meal or snack. It's amazing. As someone who tends to think I'm eating too much even when I'm really not, one thing I noticed about the first burp is that it doesn't come after two or four bites of food (unless I'm drinking soda, in which case all bets are off because of how gassy soda is). Rather, the first burp comes at the appropriate time. Once I started to trust in my burps, that my body was sending a true signal of satiety, I could relax a bit and also notice that there are other enough signals that come at about the same time as the burp – a tightness or fullness in my stomach, underneath my ribcage, even a fullness-type feeling in my throat. These signals were all there before I started trusting them, but I wasn't giving them enough attention so I didn't realize how reliable they are.

Comfort

Comfort can be a worthy goal around eating. A hungry state is not a comfortable state. Eating to satiate hunger is eating to a point of comfort. Like so many things in life, the key is moderation, and specifically in the case of eating, responsive moderation. The sweet spot of comfort between too hungry and too full is the Goldilocks approach to finding the right food in the right amount at the right time for each individual person. Goldilocks did not find oatmeal that was "just right" or a chair that was "just right" or a bed that was "just right" on the first try. She ate oatmeal that was too hot and too cold, and sat in wrong-sized chairs and uncomfortable beds before she landed upon her own personal "just right." Goldilocks had limited choices, but the rest of us have many more and that can be highly frustrating. Still, it is only through experimentation that "just right" can be found for each person in each situation. After some time experimenting, it will become easier to predict how much and what type of food at what time will be satisfying. I remember the first time as a young adult that I went to a social event with a friend and her young child. Lunch was made available and my friend suggested to her young child that one half of a sandwich would be plenty for him. She was right. He was small and a light eater. No need to take both halves of the sandwich if he was unlikely to consume even one half. He was happy with his half sandwich and ate most but not all of it. His mom knew from experience about how much food would satisfy him. Without intervention, he would have taken both halves and put them on his plate. But given the fact that he did not even finish the first half, my suspicion is that he would have left the second half untouched, so it was a good move to suggest only one half. But if he had quickly eaten the first half and asked for the second half, I am quite sure that his mother would have agreed that he could eat another half sandwich. Her recommendation was based on her knowledge of his appetite, not a desire to limit his intake. In the same way, we can get to know our bodies and discover what is generally satisfying to us. And we can make choices according to this knowledge, always with the understanding that we do not have to eat everything that we had planned, and we can always get more or something else if needed to satisfy our hunger.

Attuned eating

Another thing that can be very supportive of the process of feeling satisfied is to show some wisdom about what foods will satisfy each particular hunger. I've followed every possible food plan that exists including eating vegan, paleo, low carb, low fat, low sugar, Mediterranean, lacto-ovo vegetarian, three meals, six small meals, food pyramid, and so forth. What I have found for myself is that protein is quite satisfying, vegetables and fruits are great, grains are an important part of my daily food intake (they help with satisfaction as well as digestive regularity), and then sometimes I want sweets. I almost never want something salty (people seem to be either "salty" or "sweet" with regard to their preferred indulgences, and I think this is yet another thing to surrender to and accept about our bodies). When I want sweets, sometimes I want just a taste of dark chocolate and sometimes I want half a dozen frosted cookies from the corner store. I have certainly been known to indulge in both and now, finally, I know that it's important to honor both desires. I do not, however, act on the frosted cookie desire immediately. If it's a fleeting impulse, I would rather not act on it because there are likely to be repercussions – possibly a migraine, a fast-beating heart, the desire for more sweets – but I have also found that if the desire comes back a couple times and seems to be really emanating from my body and not solely from my mind, then getting whatever I want and giving myself permission to eat it in satisfying amounts and just eating it and being done with it is well worth the peace of mind and the best part is that if I really want it, then eating it is usually satisfying. If I want a half dozen cookies, I will buy a half dozen cookies. And if it takes all six of them to satisfy my hunger, then so be it. But if I give myself full permission to eat them, sit down with the cookies and a cup of coffee, alternate bites of cookie with sips of coffee, then when I get that "first burp" of satisfaction, I stop. I might eat one or two or three or even four cookies. Fine. I trust my body -- apparently I needed a bunch of cookies. Or, apparently I only needed one, but my spirit needed to know that I would get myself six and allow myself to eat as much as it took to be satisfied. This is quite different from filing the information in my brain "I love cookies" and taking every opportunity to stuff myself with cookies, because then they are not likely to be satisfying. If I do not really want them in the moment, then it's best to pass on them. The fact that I wanted them yesterday or last week or 20 years ago is not going to make them satisfying today. The awareness here is that the more I am in the present regarding my hunger and satisfaction, the more likely I am to be able to choose foods that help me feel satisfied. And as much as I would love to be a food purist (vegan, paleo etc.) or a certain weight, I would rather be satisfied. If I am satisfied, then I have energy to deal with the rest of my life. I do want to add about "staying in the present" that for me that's not a whim-based urge, not an "oh I want it, so I'll have it" sort of head- or desire-driven thrill seeking way of living, but more of a wise, "yes, I really want this" in the same way that sometimes I just know that my body needs some extra rest, or I really need to apologize for something I did or said, or snuggling up with a good book is just what I need to feel nurtured.

In *Diet Survivor's Handbook* Judith Matz and Ellen Frankel (2006) refer to what I'm describing as staying in the present and choosing foods that will satisfy particular hungers as "finding matches." They call eating this way "attuned eating" and describe it in these three steps: "First, learn to recognize when you are physically hungry. This requires tuning into your stomach and noticing how it feels. Next, identify what your body craves in response to your physical hunger. In order to match your hunger with the food that will satisfy you, have a variety of foods available and withhold judgments about what you are supposed to eat. Finally, pay attention to fullness in order to know how much to eat. Tune into the body's physical cues: if you began with a signal of hunger, you will be able to identify a feeling of satisfaction when you have eaten enough" (p. 49). I find that this process is much less cognitive than I expected it to be. Yes, I have to tune in, but the desires for certain foods are known in a different place in my body than the formulas to calculate the area of my living room carpet are stored. Often I know before I check. The checking is more like putting the desire in words. I know I want something. What is it? Oh, yes, a steak salad. That would really hit the spot.

Food Choices

I suffer from migraines and one summer when I heard about eating paleo, I experimented with eliminating grains and buying local, organic etc. The first thing that happened was that my migraines vanished. The second thing that happened is that I felt really great and thought (and told everyone) that I was sold on paleo eating and would heretofore be eschewing grains and eating meats, vegetables and healthy fats, along with some fruits. I lasted a number of months before I can't exactly remember what or when or why but I started eating grains again. I know that we went on vacation in December (so I lasted quite a few number of months, because I think I started in July) to Europe and I ate wheat and other grains and didn't suffer any migraines. This didn't make a lot of sense to me, but I also thought, ok, I guess I can eat grains. By March I was having almost daily migraines again. And I was back to trying to adjust my diet to eliminate the migraines, but also unwilling to go back to the discipline of eating paleo. It just didn't feel sustainable to me. So I cut down on added sugar and saturated fats and that seemed to help quite a bit. And it felt more sustainable. Not that I love having migraines, but I only have a certain amount of energy and I'm not convinced that eating paleo is really living a recovery lifestyle, mainly because of all the food restrictions I was living with. I just didn't have the desire to replicate the enthusiasm that I felt in the summer, especially in dreary March. I haven't gone back to paleo and I don't intend to. I do, however, try to eat and live in ways that reduce my migraines and I am mostly successful with that.

There is really no way around it. What I eat affects how I feel. If I want to feel completely crappy, then processed, sugary, and fatty foods are what's on the menu. I have actually tried that, in an attempt to "eat normally." I thought, okay fine, what do "normal" people eat? After a few days of pre-packaged or inexpensive restaurant foods, I felt awful: tired, hungry, and tearful. So that's not going to work for me. Not that I can never have pizza or a sausage biscuit, just that as regular fare it doesn't work, mainly because it's not satisfying. What's satisfying to me? Protein, vegetables, healthy fats, and high fiber carbohydrates, mainly, which is that same thing that all those dietary recommendations say. How is it that they can be so right? I'm glad that I've tested out the recommendations and found them to be true for me as well as the entire rest of the world apparently.

To be fair, there is great overlap between attuned eating, intuitive eating, and mindful eating. As described by scholars, intuitive eating also "involves awareness of how the body responds to certain foods; people who eat intuitively typically choose foods that help their bodies function well and view taste as only one factor involved in food choice" (Avalos & Tylka, 2006, p. 486). As there are other components of intuitive eating, as will be described later, it is appropriate to conclude that intuitive eating includes attuned eating but also goes beyond it.

Anti-deprivation eating

And then there is this thing called "anti-deprivation eating" (Hirschmann & Munter, 1988/2008) which goes like this: if everyone else is eating something that I don't particularly want or need but that I normally love and am likely to want the minute the social event is over with, it might be smarter for me to have some with everyone than to say "oh, no thanks" now and to eat (or even to want to eat) vats or boxes of it later. The anti-deprivation eating strategy has definitely worked for me in the past, and I have found it to be most effective in social situations. There is another situation in which I know myself well enough to not try anti-deprivation eating. When I am unexpectedly alone with lots of some kind of highly attractive food – a cake that has already been cut or platters of cookies - then is not a good time to just have a few bites. I don't want a few bites. I want enough to make me sick. In that case, what has worked for me is an alternative self-care plan. Something as simple scheduling or getting a massage, going for a walk in the sunshine, anything that's intentionally "for my soul" can help me get out the funk that propels me to desire half a sheet cake or four dozen cookies. Sometimes "just a bite" relieves my curiosity about a food but other times it is not curiosity that I'm dealing with, it's a desire to annihilate desire, to drown myself in sugar, and in that case a bite or two or three or even five is highly unlikely to satisfy.

CHAPTER 3
Truly believe that
full recovery is possible

Learn about what full recovery from an eating disorder really is, and that it is truly possible.

Full Recovery – Research Studies

Remember the research studies I described in the Introduction? These were two research studies that I conducted (along with colleagues Dr. Bengu Ergruner-Tekinalp and Ashley Fee) with women participants who had, at some point in their lives, struggled with an eating disorder. Some participants in both Study 1 and Study 2 were not sure that full recovery was even a possibility, but others saw themselves as recovered and embraced the concept. None of them had a definition of full recovery that matched with those described by other researchers below. Study participants defined full recovery this way:

Alice was doubtful when she said, "*I understand what I have and what I am doing with therapy,*" but "*I still have some doubt about whether I'll ever be able to get better.*" Similarly, Maria worried, "*Of course I doubt whether I will recover. I don't know where to go or what to do.*" Alice predicted, "*There's always going to be some kind of preoccupation with food.*" Natalie was making progress, but still wasn't sure about full recovery. "*I've been working...on maintaining a healthy lifestyle...I've been thinking differently around food- a need for sustenance... I realized that eating disorders aren't just for skinny people...but...I don't think you can ever really do it [recover]...you always have the danger of slipping back into it.*"

Ella felt recovered but was still sometimes bothered by thoughts and urges. "*It bothers me that this still bothers me, that there are lingering feelings that produce anxiety...I am choosing to do this, even if it's a bit uncomfortable in the short term. I know it's healing in the long term*" Cathy was recovered, and owned it. She traced her progress through to full recovery this way: "*I felt heavier than*

34

I should be and uncomfortable with my body…[but]…I don't think about it as much as I used to…I feel good about myself. I don't have those negative feelings anymore… Once I started telling some of my really close friends, they just really helped me through it… I have a healthier relationship with food and my self-image…Yes I consider myself to be recovered… All these events go together to help me who I want to be- healthy and happy and a good person" Alex was also living in full recovery, *"I went to therapy in college when I had trouble concentrating… I will keep figuring myself out…I struggled with a very long time…I have moments where I wish maybe I was skinner or I get frustrated… but I don't have an unhealthy relationship with food now."*

Natalie did not see herself as recovered, but she acknowledged her progress. *"No, I am not recovered. I still struggle with it every day. But my consciousness has shifted to always being consumed with how I look and what I eat and how I eat. Now I'm more focused on "is this a healthy thing to do or is this destructive."* She was resigned about the challenges of recovery, *"I don't think you can every really do it…you always have the danger of slipping back into it…you teach yourself new habits…I don't know, but you have to learn to ignore it and overcome it."* Similarly, Cathy continued to struggle sometimes, and therefore hesitated to claim full recovery. In response to the question, "What would you constitute as full recovery in terms of an eating disorder?" Cathy responded, *"I'm not sure. I feel as close to recovery as I ever could be. I'm not sure I could ever get to the point where I never think about it. I have a healthier relationship with food and my self-image."* In response to the same question, Alice also had mixed emotions, *"It's a tough question. There's always going to be some kind of preoccupation with food; thinking about what I'm eating. Psychologically I'm content."*

Maria saw full recovery as *"Stop eating that crazy way. At least to stop that feeling. It's not something you want to do, it's something you feel."* But the doubt that full recovery was even possible was almost ever present for the research participants. Alex stated unequivocally that she was recovered, yet she added, *"I don't know if I'll ever be at the fully recovered place. My mom is in*

35

her 60s and still obsesses. I don't know if I'll ever be okay with the way I look. But I am close. But I just don't know if it will ever be possible for me."

Participants' persistence is inspiring, at the same time as their doubt in full recovery is heartbreaking. Possibly this is because their conception of full recovery seems to include the notion that they would have no intrusive thoughts and no urges to engage in eating disorder behaviors. They have accepted that this might not be possible, and therefore think that full recovery is not possible for them. But maybe full recovery includes some occasional thoughts and urges. Maybe it's okay not to be perfect. If they were willing and able to claim full recovery, how might this change their conceptions of themselves and of their recovery journeys? Clearly we don't know the answers to these questions, but they also apply to every person in recovery from an eating disorder. How would claiming full recovery change things?

Full Recovery is Possible

When I was first exposed to author Geneen Roth in 1993 (the first book I read was her 1993 *Breaking Free from Compulsive Eating*, which was updated and re-released in 2004 as *Breaking Free from Emotional Eating*), I was more than seven years into recovery from eating disorders. Up until that time, I had been strongly involved in 12 step programs. My belief at the time was that I would always be "in recovery" and I was not aware of the concept of full recovery. Although Roth did not use the term full recovery, it was from her work that I started to think that maybe I could really get better. I developed the desire to be fully recovered. It's been a long time coming, and I think a major roadblock in my path has been my own perfectionist definition of full recovery. I wanted to get back to my pre-eating disorder days, in particular I wanted to never be plagued with the desire to binge or restrict again. Setting my sights so high basically set me up for failure. What I wish I had done was turn to the literature on eating disorder recovery to learn how it is defined. What a relief it was to learn that I did not have to be perfect in order to be fully recovered (in fact, seeing as perfectionism is part of the problem, it is almost a requirement that I let go of perfectionism in order to be fully recovered) and that, if

I were to be psychologically tested, the expectation was only that my worries and concerns around food, eating and body weight fall back into normal ranges along with eating behaviors (weight in full recovery can be above average, but not below a starvation weight), not that I never experience the urge to binge again.

It is possible to reach full recovery (Bardone-Cone, Harney, Maldonado, Lawson, Robinson, Smith & Tosh, 2010). These scholars "set a high bar for recovery" (p. 198) such that 20 fully recovered participants in their study (1) did not have a current eating disorder, (2) had a BMI of at least 18.5, (3) had not binged, purged or fasted in the prior three months, (4) scored within one standard deviation of age-matched non-eating disorder peers on each of the four subscales of the Eating Disorder Examination Questionnaire (EDE-Q) -- restraint, eating concern, weight concern and shape concern (see Appendix A). Not only were their fully recovered participants abstinent from eating disorder behaviors, their thoughts and attitudes about food and eating were indistinguishable from people of the same age who had never experienced an eating disorder. And they found twenty women to participate in their study who fell into this category from a list of 273 possible candidates who had received treatment at the University of Missouri Pediatric and Specialty Clinic over the period of 10 years. Some of these former clients could not even be located. To say that 20 of those who agreed to participate were fully recovered tells me that it is completely possible to fully recover. These scholars concluded that "The current findings provide evidence that full recovery from an eating disorder is possible, including the attainment of normal attitudes toward food and the body" (p. 200), and, "The finding that full recovery exists is important information for practitioners and eating disorder patients and their families so that they have a sense of what recovery can look like" (p. 201).

Two long-term follow up studies in very different cultures indicate that approximately 40% of people in treatment for eating disorders will reach full recovery and stay there in the long term. Five years after treatment, 40% of 71 Finnish women reached full recovery, defined as physical, behavioral and psychological recovery (Isomaa & Isomaa, 2014). Following 233 Japanese women who had received hospital treatment for an eating disorder, almost half of them reached full recovery: 42% reached full recovery, whereas 51% did not reach full recovery (25% were partially recovered and 26% were still active) and 7% had died (Nakai, Nin, Noma, Hamagaki, Takagi, & Wonderlich, 2014). The stakes are high. Death is possible. Not only is full recovery possible and worth it, the alternatives could be catastrophic.

Defining Full Recovery

Full and partial recovery have been defined (Bardone-Cone, Schaefer, Maldonado, Fitzsimmons, Harney, Lawson, Robinson, Tosh & Smith, 2010) to include physical, behavioral and emotional dimensions. For full recovery, a person must meet these requirements: physical -- BMI 18.5 or above; behavioral -- no bingeing, purging or fasting in the past three months; and psychological -- within a healthy range on all four sub-scales of the EDE-Q (see Appendix A) including restraint, eating concern, weight concern and shape concern. If a person meets the physical and behavioral but not the psychological components of full recovery, then they are classified as being in partial recovery. A person in partial recovery scores out of the normal range on the EDE-Q one or more of the EDE-Q subscales. That is a pretty tall order. Someone in full recovery is really in a different place mentally than someone in partial recovery. But, the definition of full recovery is not "like I used to be before my eating disorder," or "completely without urges to binge" or "never worried about my weight." It's actually pretty normal to be worried about weight or shape or calories, it's just not normal to be worried about weight or shape or calories every single day, or, frankly every other day. One shorthand way that Bardone-Cone and colleagues summarized someone in partial recovery is that they are "still thinking a great deal about food" and "her thoughts may still revolve around food, weight, and shape because thinness may still be very important to her" whereas someone who is fully recovered is "no longer thinking as much about or placing as much importance on eating and the body" and "viewing food more as fuel and less as something that aids in managing negative affect" (Fitzsimmons-Craft, Keatts, & Bardone-Cone, 2013, p. 1042).

How eating disorder experts classify a person in recovery may be very different from how the same people classify themselves. When individuals who researchers determined were either partially or fully recovered were asked about their own perceptions of where they were in recovery, "there was no difference in their overall subjective sense of recovery" (Bardone-Cone, 2012, p. 248) regardless of whether researchers had classified them as partially or fully recovered. Participants were asked to place themselves in a stage of change regarding their eating disorder and also regarding giving up dieting. It may have been confusing to participants in this study that the later stages of change are named "maintenance" and "recovery," because the whole endeavor is also named recovery and maintenance has a different meaning in the weight loss world. So, it is perhaps unsurprising that even though participants had been classified as either partially or fully recovered, they did not consistently place themselves at the stage of change that matched their level of assessed progress. Even to the untrained observer, "partially recovered" is not a good match with "maintenance" nor is "fully recovered" a good match with "recovery."

One way of looking at the difference between full recovery ("recovered") and partial recovery ("recovering") is to analyze the way people talk about their experiences. One woman who described herself as recovered told her story to a researcher in such a way that "the reframing is complete, depicting a break from a former relatively incapacitated self and a transformation to a self more capable of handling life's contingencies" (Shohet, 2007, p. 346). Other participants who saw themselves as recovering told their stories to the same researcher in a way that "past, present, and imagined future selves are narrated as continuous and conflicted versions of an ambivalent person who is sometimes cast as an agent of her life, while other times remaining an experiencing patient" (Shohet, 2007, p. 346). It is no doubt too simple to advise a person to reframe her language, to tell her story in a different way if she wants a different life outcome. And yet we have all probably experienced a change in attitude as a result of describing our experiences in a more (or less) positive light. If I say "Yay, I get to go to a movie!" I might feel more positive than if I say "Ugh, I have to go to a movie." This is an area where cause and effect become so intertwined that although I might think that my language reflects my thinking, very likely my thinking is affected by my language and if so, then I will do whatever I can to state things in a way that gives me more of a chance to live my full recovery story instead of a "nope, never getting there" version. On the other hand, I am also familiar with feeling that I had to defend my "recovered" image such that I was tempted to lie about the number of cookies I consumed after waking up from a Sunday afternoon nap. Simply declaring myself "recovered" does not always pan out in terms of behavior. I think the problem with telling a story like "I'm better now, I'm never going back" is that it discourages ongoing authenticity. What if I'm feeling like I'm not so great, like my eating is pretty messy, like I want to eat even more of something that I've already eaten too much of? Am I free to admit to that at the same time as "I'm better now, I'm never going back"? If so, great. But my experience is that absolutes do not serve us well. And yet, I still support the notion of full recovery. My full recovery did not come all in one fell swoop, however. Rather, it almost crept up on me. I let go of eating disorder thinking and behaviors in drips and drabs (no matter how many absolute declarations I made) and I continue to adopt more healthy thinking and behaviors as I grow and mature. Does that make me still recovering? No, that makes me still living, still growing, still learning. At some point, I crossed the line between partial and full recovery even though I don't know exactly when that was.

People who have had eating disorders really struggle with the terms "recovered" and "recovering." "The term recovery to me is tricky because I consistently think of recovery as a process, not something that I necessarily fully achieve but something that I'm continuing to maintain. It's kind of like an action: I'm living my recovery every day, rather than I've reached this one moment saying ok I'm better. Because I feel [that] denies you the space to say that it's hard. To say that it's actually difficult sometimes. To say that sometimes I eat too much pizza and I feel that thing in my chest and I could go and throw up but I don't. Perhaps it would be in those moments I feel that I'm recovered, when I don't do it. That I choose not to, that I make the choice not to. Because it's ok. So in a psychiatric medical model I might not necessarily fully be recovered, because I still think about it, but I don't do it anymore. (Maya)" (Lamarre & Rice, 2016 p. 145). The authors of this study ask: "Can assembling objective criteria for and articulating a privileged version of eating disorder recovery alienate and/or overwhelm some people in recovery?" (p. 137) and go on to say that, "Building on the qualitative literature around eating disorder recovery, we situate the embodied experience of eating disorder recovery within a sociocultural context rife with moralizing imperatives around food, health, and bodies" (p. 137). They call recovery an "illusive construct." But others who have recovered assessed themselves the same way as the researchers did (Isomaa & Isomaa, 2014), at the same time as they also extended that definition of recovery. "In the open-ended answer the participants defined what constituted recovery in terms of living a life not dominated by anxiety over food, eating, and exercise. This included normal bodily functions and also feeling good enough about oneself. Many participants also mentioned not necessarily being free from ED cognitions, but being able to cope with them" (p. 570).

Clearly, recovery from an eating disorder goes well beyond being at a physically healthful weight, but how recovery is defined is frustratingly different, even among professionals and researchers (Noordenbos, 2011). A European team defined partial remission as a one-month stretch of time during which a person experienced one or fewer binges or purges per week and was at a BMI of 17.5 or higher; full remission as a three-month stretch of time during which a person experienced no binge or purge episodes and was at a BMI of 19 or higher and then re-named full remission as "recovery" after 12 months had elapsed (Kordy, Kramer, Palmer, Papezova, Pellet, Richard & Treasure, 2002). By this method, a person is deemed "recovered" after 12 months at a non-starvation weight and without eating disorder behaviors. After monitoring clients for two and half years, they found that approximately one third of patients had reached full remission recovery, another third had reached partial remission, and one third of their participants were still actively eating disordered. Among those who reached partial remission during the two and half years, about half of them relapsed. The one third with the most positive outcomes still may have suffered mentally and emotionally, but at least they were at or above a non-starvation weight and were not engaging in eating disorder behaviors. Possibly the relatively high relapse rates in this study are reflective of the possibility that not everyone exhibiting no symptoms had achieved psychological recovery, and therefore, by others' definitions, were not truly fully recovered.

Self-concept

Self-concept is related to recovery from an eating disorder. After categorizing their participants, researchers found that three of the subdomains of self-concept – self-esteem, self-directedness, and the imposter phenomenon – were similar between healthy controls and the fully recovered group (good news!) and also similar between the active disorder eating group and the partially recovered eating disorder group (eek!), although self-efficacy was higher among the partially recovered group than among the actively eating disordered group (Bardone-Cone, Schaefer, Maldonado, Fitzsimmons, Harney, Lawson, Robinson, Tosh & Smith 2010). Researchers suggested that "those facets of self-concept that tap into individual experiences of worth (self-esteem), ability to affect change (self-efficacy), purposefulness toward goals (self-directedness), and the feeling of disjunction between one's interior and exterior self may represent specific areas of self-concept pertinent to achieving and maintaining recovery" (Bardone-Cone et al., 2010, p. 838).

Bardone-Cone and colleagues (2010) acknowledged that "it could also be that some unmeasured factor, such as social support or decreases in comorbid psychopathology, contributes to both improved self-concept and recovery" (p. 841). I wonder if this unmeasured factor is body acceptance. I think body acceptance may be driving the construct of psychological recovery, as measured by the EDE-Q. Body acceptance by itself would change EDE-Q scores dramatically. Most of the questions on the EDE-Q are indirectly about body dissatisfaction and trying change one's shape or weight (19 of the 28 items), the rest focus eating disorder behaviors (4 of the 28 items) or feelings (5 of the 28 items). There is nothing about poor self-concept that is limited to people with eating disorders – many people without eating disorders suffer from poor self-concept. But lack of body acceptance, now there is something that is specific to those with eating disorders, along with those in recovery from eating disorders.

Body Acceptance

Body acceptance is one of the major issues that separates people who are "recovering" from people who are "recovered." Possibly it is even the number one major issue. Of course, body acceptance is not a binary construct, but more of a continuum along which each person can shift on a daily, occasional, or seasonal basis.

I have come to believe that one of the roots of my eating disorder was in the mistaken assumption that there was something wrong with my body, specifically regarding my weight. My remedy was to restrict my food intake and then I quickly started to think that there was something wrong with my hunger signals. I declared war against my body. No way would I trust my body. This was war that my mind was going to win. I thought that if my weight was okay, within the range that is acceptable in society's eyes and therefore in my own, then I would be okay. But my body did not become trustworthy when my weight became okay, because the whole game/story was predicated on the assumption that "there is something wrong with my body" and it took me a surprisingly long time to question that.

Part of acceptance for me is acknowledging that I am not special. I frankly do not like that one single bit. When I was struggling with my eating disorder, I felt different but not special in a good way. Then when I began recovery, I felt different and special in a weird, socially unacceptable way. That morphed over time into special in a high needs sort of way. Now, I am realizing that although I need to take care of myself just like every other human being, I do not actually have higher needs than the average person. I have different needs, possibly, but not higher needs. I am not special. Or, I am not more special than anyone else. That can be a

43

hard pill to swallow. I want to be special. I want special meals, I want special treatment. My desire to be special no doubt contributed to my staying stuck in partial recovery for longer than might have been ideal. If I were willing to recognize my shared humanity more, able to see that everybody struggles with something and that although our specific struggles may differ, the concept is shared, it might have been easier for me to let go of my eating disorder identity and my inner sense that I am different from others. I thought for a long time that in order to stay in recovery, I need to eat differently and care for myself differently than others. It is just not true. Like all other human beings, I need food, and if I want to feel great in my body, I need nutritious food. If I had to survive on rice and beans I would survive. If I eat junk, I am going to feel like junk. But that is not just me – that is everyone. We are a resilient species and I am not so different from anyone else.

CHAPTER 4
Practice body acceptance
and body appreciation

Each person only gets one body – we might as well accept the one we have been given. And everybody's body does some pretty amazing things! Take time to appreciate all the things the body does.

Body image

After reviewing body image studies, researchers concluded, "the literature suggests that an increased focus on body image might help patient (sic) reach full recovery from their ED" (Fogelkvist, Parlling, Kjellin & Gustafsson, 2016, p. 3). They were not encouraging even more focus on one's body for someone in recovery, rather, they were suggesting that improved body image would likely have a positive effect on a person's eating disorder recovery.

The clinical definition of both bulimia and anorexia have long contained the criteria: Self-evaluation is unduly influenced by body shape and weight (American Psychiatric Association, 1994, 2013). To my ear, this rings very true. But it is also pretty vague and all-encompassing. It is easy to agree: Yes, undue influence of body shape and weight on self-evaluation is part of an eating disorder, but what to do about that and how to remedy it, that is not always so clear. My experience is that it is important to focus on cessation of eating disorder behaviors before tackling this rather enormous culturally-influenced challenge. But when a person is ready, then this is the next challenge. I think it is clearer to describe the problem as "body dissatisfaction" and the solution as "body acceptance."

Defining our Terms

Body acceptance goes like this: I'm not perfect, but this is the only body I'm likely to be issued, so you know what? Perfection is overrated and impossible to achieve anyway. I think I'll be grateful for the one body I have, to care for it as best

I can and to live in it as much as long as possible. The documentary movie Embrace is a great resource for any and all adults who want to explore this issue (warning if you are watching around children – some nudity). The movie is available on Netflix and is narrated by creator Taryn Brumfitt who goes on a quest to find out why so many people hate their bodies and what we can do about it. She uncovers many whys and confirms her suspicion that many people, regardless of age or appearance, hate their bodies. But she also interacts with many courageous people who accept their bodies, who question, as one interviewee articulates: "Your body is the only one that you have; why are you complaining about such a beautiful body?" In the movie, Taryn says, "This body of mine, it's not an ornament, it's a vehicle, so I want to fuel it well and I want to move it and be healthy, but I want to do it on my own terms."

Defining body dissatisfaction is a challenge. One way to do this is to say that one's body dissatisfaction is the difference between one's ideal body and one's actual body (Mayo & George, 2014). But isn't that a bit too simple? For me it is way more complicated and nuanced than that. First, I am not totally clear on my ideal body. I know I will never have long legs or blonde hair and I have never aspired to those characteristics. I will also never have a flat lower belly. I can clearly remember looking at my profile in the ballet mirrors in seventh grade and trying to wish away the lower-abdominal pooch I saw. I was restricting my food and underweight at the time, yet my lower belly was already showing its signature bump. Over time, I have come to accept that my body is the way that it is, and as I have done that, my ideal body image has changed to a sustainable best version of myself. However, I find peace not when I reach my ideal, but when I don't focus so much on my body's appearance, but instead on how I feel inside my body, how responsive I am to my body's signals, and also on how my body functions in so many miraculous ways. For instance, breathing is a miracle, as is the healing of even such minor things as scratches and bruises. Mostly I feel best about my body when I am comfortable with what I am wearing, how I am moving, and I am doing the best I can to meet my needs for hunger and sleep. I dislike being too hot or too cold and I try to avoid either extreme, but sometimes they are unavoidable and I feel okay knowing that I've done the best I can in each situation to try to take care of myself even if I'm shaking from the cold or sweat is dripping down my back from the heat.

Another definition of body dissatisfaction is "body-centric negative affect," (Harney & Bardone-Cone, 2014, p. 441), highlighting the similarities to other manifestations of negative affect, such as depression. I may not always feel comfortable in my body, and I may feel self-conscious at times, but I am amazed at what women and teenage girls will say about their bodies. Such negativity would be considered bullying if it were directed at another person! When I belonged to the YMCA, sometimes I was changing in the locker room when the high school girls came in before or after their physical education swimming class. Some of them would wear tight little suits and look in the mirror and say loudly "blech," with a tone that might be reserved for mold on fruit or a big mess that one did not want to deal with. I was not shocked, unfortunately, but it did make me really sad. I didn't know these girls and they probably would not have appreciated me saying anything, so I didn't, but now I wish I had in fact said something. I wish I had said something like: "All bodies are beautiful," or "Love and cherish that body – it's likely to be the only one you'll ever be given," although even if I had said something, I'm not sure I could have conveyed my desire for them to think completely differently about their bodies with one short comment.

Stice and Shaw (2002) define body dissatisfaction as "negative subjective evaluation of one's physical body, such as figure, weight, stomach and hips" (p. 985) and are careful to distinguish it both from body image distortion, a symptom of anorexia, and from over-emphasis placed on weight and shape in determining self-worth, a symptom of both anorexia and bulimia. It may seem obvious but I think an important point here is that body image dissatisfaction can be a part of any human being's experience, regardless of age, gender, size, or any other way that we try to categorize bodies. I think many peoples' lived experience is that they feel dissatisfied with their bodies and think that they will become satisfied if they change their bodies in some way. This is the lie of diets. The lie whispers in our ears: "follow me and you will feel better about yourself." To identify the tempting lie is to recognize the fallacy. A fallacy is a mistaken belief based on an unsound argument, and it's one that is easy to fall for in this case. But as anyone who has struggled with an eating disorder may have personally experienced, there is no one right weight at which body dissatisfaction becomes resolved. Body acceptance is much less weight-related than we tend to think. It's not like losing 5 pounds is going to make us accept our bodies more. Five, 50, or 100 pounds up or down and we can still accept our bodies or be dissatisfied with them. There is nothing less worthy about a large body and nothing more worthy about a small body. All bodies can be accepted, or rejected.

It is important to note that when 47 participants who were in treatment for eating disorders wrote about body image, they approached the concept of body image from a great variety of perspectives, including self-evaluation of their bodies, whether their bodily self-perceptions were realistic, relationship between body and self, and the effect of body image on self-esteem (Fogelvist, Parlling, Kjellin & Gustafsson, 2016). But despite their diversity of perspectives, they all reported wanting positive body image experiences, including less negative self-judgment, less focus on change and more on self-acceptance so that they could stop avoiding things that they desired to do and instead to experience life. So maybe it's less important how people define the problem as long as they all embrace the solution. Like those corny posters that say Live, Love, Laugh, isn't that a pretty close version of what we all want? We want to quit trying to change ourselves and experience the life that we've been given.

There are four components of body appreciation according to Augustus-Horvath and Tylka (2011): "having favorable opinions of the body despite body size and perceived imperfections, being aware of an attentive to the body's needs, engaging in healthy behaviors to take care of the body, and protecting the body by rejecting unrealistic media body ideals" (p. 110)

Body Dissatisfaction

It is known that body dissatisfaction is a risk factor for eating disorders. "Multivariate etiological models of EDs, extensive reviews and meta-analytic data have established body dissatisfaction as the most consistent and robust causal risk factor for all forms of EDs in both genders" (Dakanalis, Favagrossa, Clerici, Prunas, Colmegna, Zanetti, & Riva, 2015, p. 87). So possibly it is not such a big leap to make the connection between body acceptance and full recovery. It is important to note that not everyone who is dissatisfied with their bodies develops an eating disorder. Just because body dissatisfaction is a risk factor for an eating disorder does not automatically mean that it body acceptance is necessary for full recovery, but it does seem to warrant investigation. "Self-esteem, perfectionism, body checking, long-term interpersonal difficulties (i.e., attachment insecurities), and emotional dysregulation, interact with each other and with body dissatisfaction to predict onset and/or persistence of eating disorder symptomatology" (Dakanalis, Favagrossa, Clerici, Prunas, Colmegna, Zanetti, & Riva, 2015, p. 88).

People who are highly anxious are particularly vulnerable. "Our results generally suggest that low levels of anxiety are associated with low levels of disordered eating (i.e., EAT-26 scores, dietary restraint, binge eating), regardless of one's level of appearance contingent self-worth or frequency of appearance conversations with friends. However, for those with high levels of anxiety, elevated levels of appearance contingent self-worth (and, in the case of binge eating, frequent appearance conversations with friends) are associated with the highest levels of disordered eating" (Bardone-Cone, Brownstone, Higgins, Fitzsimmons-Craft & Harney, 2013, p. 961).

Interestingly, people in treatment for eating disorders who experience a decrease in body dissatisfaction were more likely to drop out of treatment later on (Stein, Wing, Lewis, & Raghunation, 2011), which researchers suggested may have been due to decreased motivation to continue treatment. If a person is feeling better, they may not see the need to continue with months of follow up data collection. That makes it hard on the researchers, but it is good news for those of us who want to know that a decrease in body dissatisfaction can have a positive effect on our overall sense of wellbeing.

Body Acceptance

When women accept their bodies, they are more likely to eat normally and healthfully (referred to below as intuitive eating). In a summary of one study's findings, researchers stated: "For all age groups, an increase in perceived social support was associated with higher levels of body acceptance by others. When women perceived that others accepted their body, they were more resistant to adopt an observer's perspective of their body and felt more appreciative toward their body. Resistance to adopt an observer's perspective of the body was uniquely associated with body appreciation and intuitive eating; women were more likely to appreciate their bodies and eat according to their hunger and satiety cues when they did not focus on how their body appeared to others. Body appreciation was uniquely and positively related to intuitive eating" (Augustus-Horvath & Tylka, 2011, p. 121). In another study, scholars posited the direct relationship between body acceptance and intuitive eating by stating, "In our acceptance model, we assert that general and body acceptance would contribute to women's emphasis on how their bodies function and feel internally rather than their outer appearance. Body acceptance by others may also contribute to women's appreciation of their bodies. Furthermore, an emphasis on body function would likely contribute to women's positive feelings toward their bodies (i.e., body appreciation) and engagement in positive behaviors (e.g., intuitive eating) to take care of their bodies' internal needs to keep them functioning well. Also, women who appreciate their bodies may be likely to eat intuitively to further nurture and respect their bodies" (Avalos & Tylka, 2006, p. 487). Avalos and Tylka (2006) presented two studies to support their acceptance model. Their first study involved 181 college women, and their second involved 416 college women. Positive relationships were particularly high showing that and emphasis on how one's body functions and feels (rather than on their appearance) predicted women's body appreciation, which in turn predicted their intuitive eating. This research is important because it demonstrates empirically the importance of body acceptance to intuitive eating, which is a placeholder for normal (non-disordered) eating. The college women participating in these studies did not necessarily ever suffer from eating disorders, but that makes it all the more powerful – focusing on what one's body can do and how it feels as well as appreciating one's body is important for everyone, not only for people recovering from eating disorders.

Could it be that body acceptance is what separates people who categorized themselves as "recovered" from those who felt more like they were "recovering"? It seems that Stice and Shaw (2002) asked the same question when they wrote, "Although numerous studies have tested whether body dissatisfaction is a risk factor for the subsequent development of eating pathology, far fewer studies have tested whether body dissatisfaction plays a role in the maintenance of eating disorder symptoms. The distinction between risk and maintenance factors is important, because the former are germane to the design of prevention programs, but the latter are relevant to the design of treatment interventions. Thus, a clear understanding of the maintenance factors for bulimic pathology is needed to design the optimally effective treatment programs" (p. 988) and one page later they stated, "preliminary findings provide support for the assertion that body dissatisfaction may play an important role in the maintenance of bulimic pathology" (p. 989).

Among 15 men who had overcome eating disorders, some "experienced themselves as recovered because they placed less emphasis on body shape and physical performance and were not hiding behind others. Instead, they had the courage to express themselves in social situations and felt like a completely different person" (Bjork, Wallin & Pettersen, 2012, p. 463). At the same time, others were more in the "recovering" category and employed "conscious choice to avoid relapse through using specific strategies. One might argue the need for such strategies is an indication that recovery status is fragile and not fully achieved because these former patients are not relaxed in relation to food or physical training. These males, however, did not worry that much about relapsing. They found it pointless to let their behavior trigger thoughts that could risk their recovery status." (p. 467). Maybe the debate is whether recovery is a state or a trait – put another way, how enduring is eating disorder recovery? The "recovering" men seemed to think of recovery as a state, whereas those who experienced themselves as "recovered" may see it as trait. Either way, they protected it with certain strategies. But is body acceptance as strategy? An outcome of recovery? A cause of recovering? Or maybe body acceptance is the one thing that separates "recovering" from "recovered"?

As quoted on the Monte Nido Eating Disorder treatment center website from a book written by its founder Carolyn Costin titled *100 Questions and Answers about Eating Disorders:* "Being recovered to me is when the person can accept his or her natural body size and shape and no longer has a self-destructive or unnatural relationship with food or exercise." (www.montenido.com/why-monte-nido/recovered-vs-recovering/) Aha. Maybe the difference between "recovering" and "recovered" really is body acceptance. Now body acceptance is not easy, that is for sure, but it is something that is completely possible, and something that is within the control of all of us. When I first Hirschman and Munter's (1995) book titled *When Women Stop Hating Their Bodies: Freeing Yourself from Food and Weight Obsession,* I found the title of that book provocative, but I missed the main point, which now I see as a missing puzzle piece of full eating disorder recovery: Body Acceptance. The first half of Hirschmann and Munter's (1995) book is about body acceptance, and the second half is about what they call demand feeding for adults, which is another non-diet approach that falls squarely in the body-led eating category.

In a study where "clinical" recovery was the label used to describe "partial" recovery, Researchers noted: "There was an interesting interaction effect between clinical recovery status and psychological eating disorder symptoms. There was an overall decrease in psychological eating disorder symptoms, but among those who had not recovered an increase in drive for thinness and poor interoceptive awareness was found. Drive for thinness is a core feature of eating disorders and poor interoceptive awareness has been linked to both maintenance of dietary restraint and self-objectification. Thus, an increase in drive for thinness in combination with poor interoceptive awareness might indicate risk for a chronic course of illness" (Isomaa & Isomaa, 2014, p. 571).

Another venue where acceptance is addressed as a recovery topic is the Alcoholic's Anonymous' basic text, fondly referred to by members of 12-step groups as the Big Book. A well-quoted passage in 12 step rooms reads: "And acceptance is the answer to all my problems today. When I am disturbed, it is because I find some person, place, thing, situation – some fact of my life – unacceptable to me, and I can find no serenity until I accept that person, place, thing, or situation as being exactly the way it is supposed to be at this moment. Nothing, absolutely nothing, happens in God's world by mistake. Until I could accept my alcoholism, I could not stay sober; unless I accept my life completely on life's terms, I cannot be happy. I need to concentrate not so much on what needs to be changed in the world as on what needs to be changed in me and my attitudes" (p. 417, Alcoholics Anonymous, 2001). I have found this to be so incredibly true and helpful in many areas of my life.

It makes total sense that body acceptance must precede full recovery if one agrees that body dissatisfaction preceded the eating disorder. Early investigations into the role of body acceptance as critical to recovery from an eating disorder make it clear that this is not a new issue. In 1990, Brouwers wrote, "Many clients do not make progress in recovering from bulimia until their feelings about their appearance are dealt with… Additionally, relapse tends to occur after a negative body image experience such as a real or perceived criticism of their body" (p. 144). Brouwers did not suggest that body image dissatisfaction was the sole cause or cure of eating disorders, but rather that "Feelings about body image must be identified and discussed as being a major contributing part of the bulimia. Most important, the counselor must believe and must communicate to the client that feelings toward body image can change" (p. 144). This is such a breath of fresh air 30 years later. How did we complicate this so royally? While I do not want to succumb to the temptation of overly simplified solutions to complex problems, there really is no reason to unnecessarily complicate relative straightforward issues. So here is my challenge: where does body acceptance fit into eating disorder recovery?

Maybe it is too much to say "I love my body" or "I love my...fill in body part" but, it may be possible to take a less judgmental stance and say "this is my body," or "these are my legs," etc. If judgment is a problem, then it extends to both positive and negative judgments. Rather than transforming negative into positive judgment, how about letting go of judgement all together? Judgment can be replaced for appreciation of what our bodies can do, and awareness of how our bodies feel.

Here are some great affirmations:

My body is not an object to be judged

My body does amazing things

My body operates very effectively independent of my conscious mind

My body communicates clearly with me when it needs attention

My body is fearfully and wonderfully made

My body has done a lot of incredible things in the last 24 hours

It may be tempting once a degree of body acceptance has been achieved to take a picture of oneself and post it to a social media site. This can feel natural in contemporary society, but my advice, based on the research, is to proceed with caution. "Recently, assessment of one's body image through online body display has become popular due to the emergence of social networking sites. Online body display refers to an individual exposing his or her body in an online public space where it can be freely accessed. Existing research on online body display has shown that social networking site users are likely to share images of one's self to attract mates or to express dominance...users are also likely to share images of one's self for self-promotion purposes, including projecting positive self-image" (Ridgway & Clayton, 2016, p. 3). We are not talking inappropriately revealing images here, we are talking pictures of one's face or fully clothed body. And while these pictures may seem innocuous, they immediately make the person who has posted the picture vulnerable to insensitive comments, or worse. I would not necessarily recommend avoiding social media or posting of selfies entirely, but it is important to acknowledge the psychological and sociological complexity behind the seemingly innocuous posting of a selfie.

Appearance-Contingent Self-Worth

In a study comparing people in treatment from eating disorders who were still struggling vs. people who had been in treatment but had not binged, purged or fasted for the past three months or more vs. healthy controls, the people in the middle "recovered" group showed great improvement, but still vestiges of the eating disorder with regard to (1) higher weight concern, (2) higher stress (3) increased vigilance regarding social-rank (4) more fear of negative judgments from others, and (5) more submissive behaviors (Cardi, Matteo, Gilbert & Teasure, 2014). The good news is that even after a minimum of three months without eating disorder behaviors, the "recovered" group showed about the same low levels of self-evaluation, internal shame, and social comparison as the healthy controls. Some aspects of the eating disorder no doubt take more time to heal, but it is important to know which ones, and to be able to put some conscious effort into those aspects of the disorder that tend to hang on so that full recovery may be achieved. Although researchers did not make the case for this implication, it could be that ongoing higher weight concern is what is driving the other behaviors, and that if weight concern could be diminished among the "recovered" group, then so would the other social-rank concerns.

Another social comparison study (Badone-Cone, Brownstone, Higgins, Fitzsimmons-Craft & Harney, 2013) identified the triple-headed monster of (1) high anxiety, (2) high appearance-contingent self-worth, and (3) frequent appearance conversations, which when combined, predicted the highest levels of binge eating among a community sample of college women.

Theoretical Models

I am not the only person who has realized that, hey, body dissatisfaction seems to be a driver here. Stice and Shaw (2002) identified that for eating disorders "one prominent risk and maintenance factor that is emerging from the recent research is body dissatisfaction" (p. 985). They synthesized research findings and explain the theoretical relationships among higher than desired body mass, perceived pressure to be thin, thin-ideal internalization, body dissatisfaction, dieting, negative affect with lots of arrows pointing back and forth but eventually leading to eating pathology.

As it turns out the "body dissatisfaction leads to eating disorders" is called the "sociocultural" model. But there are other models too. A summary of the theoretical models is below, as presented in a review by Byrtek-Matera and Czepczor (2017):

Sociocultural theory: Internalization of the thin ideal leads to body dissatisfaction, which leads to eating disorders;

Dual Pathway theory: Body dissatisfaction plus dieting and negative affect (e.g. anxiety and depression) leads to eating disorders;

Reward Center theory: Once a person develops a restrictive eating disorder, increased dopamine activity in the brain maintains the habits;

Multidimesional theory: Individual, family, and cultural factors contribute to body dissatisfaction and thin-ideal internalization, which, when combined with dieting, leads to eating disorders;

Transdiagnostic theory (aka the Cognitive-Behavioral model): Dysfunctional thinking (around self-esteem, perfectionism, mood intolerance and regarding relationships with others people) leads to eating disorders;

Transtheoretical theory: All of the above. There are many contributors to the major players of thin-ideal internalization and body dissatisfaction that lead to excessive weight and food preoccupation which interact with compensatory eating behaviors and eating disorders.

Even in the transtheoretical model, which is the most complex and even overwhelming approach to thinking about eating disorders, body dissatisfaction is smack dab in the middle of it all. I know it is seems overly simplistic and even old fashioned to say "body dissatisfaction leads to eating disorders" but I really to think that body dissatisfaction is the lever or the opportunity for change for anyone who finds themselves caught in the complex web of causes and effects. There is a lot going on in an eating disorder, no doubt, and it would be folly to suggest that there is only one cause. But there is a way to focus one's efforts and I still think that those efforts are best spent on body acceptance, because without body dissatisfaction, the whole house of cards of an eating disorder starts to fall in on itself.

I really love the thoughtful approach that Stice and Shaw (2002) took when they wrote, "Another interesting possible explanation for the mixed support from prospective studies is that negative affect may only result in eating pathology for a subset of individuals. That is, perhaps most participants develop eating pathology via a pathway involving body dissatisfaction and dieting, but a smaller subset develop eating pathology via an affect regulation route" (p. 988). How refreshing!

Although one might infer that I am a supporter of the sociocultural model, I think all of them are worth investigating, at the same time as I think that body dissatisfaction is the one factor that can make the difference between partial and full recovery. Maybe it's the last thing to go in an eating disorder, marking the line between partial and full recovery?

There seems to be no controversy about the conclusion that body image disturbance and eating disorders go hand in hand. What researchers are struggling with is that nature of those disturbances (Are they part of the cause of eating disorders? Are they a symptom of eating disorders? How long into recovery do they persist)? There is some evidence that a decrease in body dissatisfaction is more indicative of recovery from depression whereas decreases in the undue influence of shape and weight concern on self-evaluation is more a sign of recovery from bulimia (Cogley & Keel, 2003). However, more recent research controlling for negative affect (which includes anxiety and depression), has found that body dissatisfaction has an independent role (Fitzsimmons-Craft, Bardone-Cone, Wonderlich, Crosby, Engel & Bulik, 2015).

Eshkevari, Rieger, Longo, Haggard and Treasure (2014) studied body image disturbance in people recovered from eating disorders and concluded that it may be a "trait." "Recovered" participants in the study were between 18.5 and 25 BMI, prior history of an eating disorder with no behaviors (bingeing, purging, or fasting during the previous 12 months), and free of depression, anxiety and anti-depression or anti-anxiety medication for the previous 3 months. One year into recovery though, the participants were not fully recovered psychologically. "Given the significantly higher drive for thinness and bulimia scores in the sample recruited to comprise the "recovered" group, it appears this group rather consists of individuals that have achieved behavioral recovery (see inclusion criteria) rather than full psychological recovery. Thus, from here onwards the REC group is considered to be a "recovering" group and relabeled as such" (p. 405). This labeling reflects a continuum concept of psychological recovery from eating disorders, from ill (undesirable scores), recovering (better scores) to recovered (scores comparable to healthy controls). Researchers concluded that the results suggest that "eating disorders involve a trait vulnerability associated with heightened sensitivity to visual information (i.e., visual capture) about the body. Reduced somatosensory information processing could also explain the result" (p. 406) and "a pre-existing vulnerability may be exacerbated during the period of acute illness. The findings suggest that a heightened sensitivity to visual information could constitute this proposed preexisting vulnerability. Dominance of visual information over information from other bodily senses could be a trait feature of individuals with eating disorders that becomes further exacerbated during the acute stages of illness" (p. 406-7). …. I wonder if body image disturbance is a "state," but one that persists longer into recovery than others…I hate the idea of being doomed to a lifelong "trait" when it seems that it is within my control to change it.

Researchers argue that social comparisons around one's body, eating, exercise is the mechanism by which the cultural thin ideal translates to personal body dissatisfaction (Fitzsimmons-Craft, Bardone-Cone, Wonderlich, Crosby, Engel & Bulik, 2015). Among 235 college women, those who made more frequent comparisons between their own body and others and who more frequently thought about how they looked also had higher levels of body dissatisfaction. These women provided personal data online multiple times per day and it was found that the body, eating and exercise comparisons truly did cause (precede) their body dissatisfaction, which was experienced after high levels of comparison.

The same researchers suggest strategies that fit well with a scientific outlook on life and may be very helpful to some people in recovery. For instance: "Behavioral interventions emerging from these findings could take the form of behavioral experiments. For example, clients could be guided in being more scientific when choosing someone to whom to compare themselves (e.g., every fifth person encountered versus every very thin person), comparing to non-appearance-related aspects of others for one day, and employing behavioral control strategies (e.g., not using social networking sites) so as to reduce the frequency of comparisons in general for one day; all of these behavioral experiments could be used to help individuals become aware of the different thoughts and emotions they may experience if they were to change their comparison behavior" (Fitzsimmons-Craft, Bardone-Cone, Wonderlich, Crosby, Engel & Bulik, 2015, p. 267).

Demographic Differences

It may be that the sociocultural model does not apply to all racial and ethnic groups. Gilbert, Crump, Madhere and Shultz (2009) examined the sociocultural model among 146 Black women of a variety of ethnicities (African American, African, and Afro-Caribbean) and found internalization of the thin ideal was only operative for the African American and not for the African or Afro-Caribbean women. Others have tested a variety of models and concluded that although there are other factors in play, including negative affect, there is a definite link between body dissatisfaction and overeating (Strien, Engels, Leeuwe & Snoek, 2005). Whether the pathway is through thin ideal internalization or negative affect or other factors that may vary by ethnicity, there seems to be no debate about the fact that there is a definite link between body dissatisfaction and eating disorders.

A study of 450 Brazilian 14-16 year olds found some interesting gender differences regarding teens' body perceptions, which varied by both gender and affluence (Uchoa, Lustosa, Rocha, Deana, Alves, & Aranha, 2017). Less affluent girls (who attended public school) were least dissatisfied with their bodies, followed by more affluent (private school) boys, less affluent (public school) boys, and the more affluent (private school) girls were the most dissatisfied with their bodies. Add to this body dissatisfaction of affluent girls, the fact that the affluent girls also had the lowest BMI and smallest waist measurements of any of the four subgroups. Interestingly, the more affluent (private school) girls also reported less involvement in physical education than any of the other subgroups. In this study, lower BMI and smaller waist measurement not only did not lead to greater body acceptance, it actually led to the highest level of body dissatisfaction. But it is possible from the results that some of these girls' body dissatisfaction could have stemmed from less physical activity. It is also noteworthy that among this large sample of Brazilian teenagers, almost all of them were within the normal weight BMI category, with low percentages of teens in the underweight and overweight categories but almost no participants in the obese category. Any attempt to argue that more or less affluent boys or girls were dissatisfied with their bodies as a result of obesity do not fit the data in this study.

In a cross-cultural study of 544 adults diagnosed with anorexia from the People's Republic of China, Spain, and the United Kingdom, it was found that there were many significant differences between the groups, most notably on the drive for thinness and body dissatisfaction subscales of the Eating Disorder Inventory (Aguera, Brewin, Chen, Granero, Kang, Fernandez-Aranda, & Arcelus, 2017). Average drive for thinness was lowest among the Chinese participants (7.94), slightly higher but not statistically significantly different among the Spanish participants (8.89), and remarkably and statistically significantly higher among the British participants (13.26). On the body dissatisfaction subscale, this time the British participants scored the lowest (3.67), the Chinese participants were slightly higher but not statistically significantly different (4.07) and the Spanish participants scored highest and statistically significantly different (10.71). So the 117 Brits experienced significantly higher drive for thinness than the 72 Chinese or the 355 Spaniards, but the Spaniards were the ones who experienced significantly higher body dissatisfaction than the Brits or the Chines participants. It doesn't seem to make sense. The authors discuss the difference between Western (United Kingdom and Spain) vs. Eastern (People's Republic of China) and Collectivist (Spain and People's Republic of China) vs. Individualistic (United Kingdom) societies and concluded that the Western vs. Eastern split is a more appropriate way to analyze differences than the Collectivist vs. Individualist split, but the results in the drive for thinness and body dissatisfaction scales do not support either split. One country is significantly higher than the other two on each of these measures, but it is the United Kingdom on drive for thinness (Western and Individualistic) and Spain on body dissatisfaction (Western and Collectivistic). The only logical conclusion here is that the Chinese participants, the only Eastern group in the study, was somehow protected from both drive for thinness and body dissatisfaction. But this was not a community sample. Participants were all adults who had been diagnosed with anorexia. So possibly one could tentative conclude that drive for thinness could be linked to anorexia in the United Kingdom, body dissatisfaction could be linked to anorexia in Spain, and something entirely different must be linked to anorexia in China. Clearly further cross-cultural research is warranted. Also clearly, one cannot make blanket statements about such constructs as drive for thinness and body dissatisfaction and their link to anorexia or other eating disorders, as there is wide variation among cultures with regard to these constructs.

Body acceptance is a challenge for men as well as for women. Among 551 Italian men, it was found that the drive for muscularity and bulimic behaviors were exacerbated by emotional dysregulation, body checking, insecure-anxious attachment and perfectionism at the same time as they were tempered by higher levels of self-esteem (Dakanalis, Favagrossa, Clerici, Prunas, Colmegna, Zanetti, & Riva, 2015).

For women, there is some freedom to experience body changes during and after pregnancy. "Participants also scored higher on body satisfaction…the reason may also be that at this stage taking care of the child is more important to mothers, so they have less pre-occupations about their body" (Zaman & Jami, 2016, p. 624).

Studying 100 Pakistani women in the 2-year lactation phase after the birth of a baby, "as appearance evaluation increases (i.e. the individual evaluates himself/herself as positive), disordered eating behavior decreases; and with an increase in overweight preoccupation and investment in appearance, disordered eating behavior also increases" (p. 617, Zaman & Jami, 2016). Interestingly they also found that overweight preoccupation rather than appearance orientation or appearance evaluations was the one strong predictor of disordered eating behaviors among women in the lactation phase. "Overweight preoccupation is the domain of body dissatisfaction that effects disordered eating behavior the most significantly than any other domain" (p. 619, Zaman & Jami, 2016).

The Norwegian Mother and Child Cohort study yielded 19 eating disorder studies published between 2007 and 2014 that were reviewed by Watson, et al. (2014). Findings included information about the mothers "concern about weight gain, desire to lose weight, and believing that one had put too much weight on during pregnancy were also significantly higher among those reporting a recent or lifetime history of eating disorders" (p. 55). Findings also included information about their children, "infant growth rate was significantly lower among infants of MoBa women with all types of eating disorders compared with referent women, although the effects were modest. The findings may ostensibly be related to breastfeeding difficulties and breast milk quality and quantity, which may be affected by maternal dietary restriction in the context of gestational weight gain, hormonal factors, and self-consciousness about nursing in public" (p. 57). And "eating disorders in pregnancy predicted greater maternal ratings of difficult infant temperament at six months of age" (p. 57) and "significantly greater problems in offspring of mothers with bulimia and binge eating disorder" (p. 57) regarding toddler eating problems. In conclusion, the large group of researchers (there were

15 authors on the journal article!) had mostly a pessimistic view of pregnancy on both mothers and babies for mothers with eating disorders, save for those with bulimia, who might experience a window of remission during pregnancy.

During midlife, both men and women tend to gain weight and fat, lose hair, and develop wrinkles, none of which match most ideal standards of attractiveness. A study of men and women during midlife, defined by researchers as ages 30-70, (McGuinness & Taylor, 2016) revealed significant differences between the men and women, with women reporting more body image dissatisfaction. Women at higher weights reported increasing levels of body image dissatisfaction, whereas men's level of satisfaction did not vary by weight. "The sample was characterized by a reasonable degree of dissatisfaction and disordered eating, with 28-41% of the women and 8-17% of the men scoring above normative data on these measures" (p. 9). That is up to almost half of women in a community sample! These are not teenagers and these are not people who ever had diagnosed eating disorders – these are parents and grandparents, friends and neighbors – suffering from body dissatisfaction and disordered eating!

With all this focus on demographic and cultural differences in the experience of eating disorders, it is important to remember that there is a strong genetic component driving the development of eating disorders. "the introduction of Western ideals of thinness may serve to release a biological propensity toward eating disorders possibly by increasing behaviors, such as dieting, that may trigger the spiral of disordered eating" (Bandyopadhyay, 2017, p. 15). In his plea to consider the genetic contribution to eating disorders, this Indian scholar continues, "It is noteworthy that eating disorder symptoms themselves also appear to be moderately heritable. Twin studies of binge eating, self-induced vomiting and dietary restrain suggest these behaviors are roughly 46 to 72 percent heritable. Likewise, pathological attitudes such as body dissatisfaction, eating and weight concerns, and weight preoccupation, revealed heritability of roughly 32 to 72 percent" (p. 16). From my point of view, this genetic vs. cultural debate focuses on the causes of eating disorders and is therefore interesting but not very useful. What

I find useful is how it is that these issues can be addressed and ameliorated once they have been established. Possibly body dissatisfaction is inherited, or not. Either way, I've got it. How do I get rid of it?

There have been a plethora of body image interventions conducted and reported in research journals. Eleven of these interventions conducted with women in midlife were reviewed by Lewis-Smith, Diedrichs, Rumsey, and Harcourt (2016) and 7 of the 11 interventions were found to have a positive impact on the body image of women between the ages of 35 and 55. Researchers argued that even in a non-clincial sample, it was important to study body image interventions due to the strong link between body dissatisfaction and disordered eating, unequivocally stating, "Body dissatisfaction is the most potent and replicated modifiable risk factor for eating pathology among girls and women and therefore constitutes an important target for intervention efforts" (p. 5). They added that, "Evidence to date indicates that body dissatisfaction and disordered eating are prevalent among women in midlife, and it is therefore important to develop and disseminate effective, evidence-based interventions to ameliorate these concerns" (p. 7). Among the successful interventions that they identified, 4 of them employed physical activity interventions (dance, walking, or yoga) and 3 of them employed therapeutic approaches (Cognitive Behavior Therapy, Acceptance and Commitment Therapy, or mindfulness), with the therapeutic approaches that targeted appearance and body image showing the most sustained body image improvements. The most effective interventions took 8-16 hours of participants' time and employed professional facilitators who had been trained in Cognitive Behavior Therapy or Acceptance and Commitment Therapy. The three successful intervention programs included:

1. "Set your body free," a Cognitive Behavior Therapy intervention. "An example session included the following content: recognizing negative self-talk e.g., aging effects on body images and strategies for stopping it (e.g., visualization, developing alternative balance thoughts); self-care

activity scheduling; and exploring the relationship between body image and movement using movement scheduling" (p. 14).

2. "ACT as a Workshop Intervention for Body Dissatisfaction," an Acceptance and Commitment Therapy intervention. "Participants were encouraged to identify their struggle with body image and to become aware of ineffective self-help strategies used to alter their body or change their self-perception. Mindfulness was taught as a method by which to enhance acceptance of previously avoided thoughts and feelings. Clarification of values encouraged individuals to shift focus to other things that mattered in life" (p. 14).

3. Another CBT body dissatisfaction intervention using the book *What do you see when you Look in the Mirror? Helping Yourself to a Positive Body Image,* "which aims to clarify distorted cognitions and alter habitual behaviors that trigger body dissatisfaction using practical exercises" such as "encouraging readers to challenge their self-defeating "body talk," to overcome self-consciousness and distance themselves from appearance-preoccupied rituals, and to develop a positive relationship with their bodies through self-acceptance" (p. 14).

It is not known the extent to which these interventions are culture- or gender-bound, but it is clear from some of the research reported above that men and women from different cultures experience their bodies differently as part of their cultural upbringing and experiences. Therefore, it is always a risk to generalize one person's experience onto another person. Still, there are many similarities among people with eating disorders regarding body issues. The issues are there, but the manifestations change. It would be a boring world if we were all the same!

Dissociation

A generic definition of dissociation is: the state of being disconnected, either accidentally or on purpose. It can be a chemical thing, for instance, molecules can be purposely dissociated from each other. It can also be a psychiatric thing, whereby normally related mental processes become separated from each other. The American Psychiatric Association (2013) names these mental processes as: consciousness, memory, identity, emotion, perception, body representation, motor control, and behavior. These processes are normally integrated, but during a dissociative experience, the normal integration becomes disrupted and/or discontinuous. Of course, dissociation can be a very serious thing, but it can also be part of normal experience. Normal dissociative experiences may be described as daydreaming, or blanking out when somebody else is talking. These normal dissociative experiences can provide healthy relief from our sometimes oppressively boring circumstances. A subset of dissociative symptoms includes somatic, or body, dissociation, and these are the symptoms that have been linked to eating disorders (Fuller-Tyszkiewicz & Mussap, 2008). "Dissociation undermines normal integration of appearance-relevant information and might, in turn, contribute to body image vulnerability...in a society that reinforces unrealistic standards of thinness, this vulnerability could manifest as internalization of the thin ideal, elevated body comparison attitudes and behaviors, and/or body dissatisfaction" (p. 447).

In my article on relapse (Gillespie, 2016), I stated that for me, binge eating was a dissociative experience. Maybe (hopefully!) it did not reach clinical levels but there is a certain turning off of the brain and becoming completely involved in the eating that frankly provided some relief from my incessantly demanding thoughts. I learned through taking a class on contemplative Christian prayer that I could dissociate in a safe, possibly even a productive, way that it was almost shocking. I learned a process called Centering Prayer, which is a meditative form of prayer. There are many other kinds of contemplative practices which involve the same basic process of disengaging with the thinking brain and instead focusing on the breath or a word or an image. 20 minutes of Centering Prayer may involve a heck of a lot of thoughts from my almost-always active brain, but there are definitely moments, sometimes even minutes, when I am blissfully open and thought-free. Even when I feel like I have re-written my to-do list about 200 times in 20 minutes,

I still get something out of it: somehow it seems to dampen that drive that I used to have to binge in order to shut my brain off – I had a perfectly acceptable way to shut my brain off earlier in the day (by centering early in the morning) and don't need to do it again. Read more later about contemplative practices in the chapter entitled Get in the Zone. Here my purpose is to make the clear link between dissociation and contemplation.

Fuller-Tyszkiewicz and Mussap (2008) explored the relationship between binge eating and somatic (body) dissociation symptoms in depth by studying 151 female university students. They found that body dissatisfaction uniquely mediated the relationship between binge eating and dissociation. Their model showed this: Somatoform dissociative experiences significantly predicted three things: (1) body dissatisfaction (2) impulsive urgency, and (3) body comparison practice, but of those three, only body dissatisfaction significantly predicted the number of binge-eating symptoms among participants. In other words, bodily dissociation indirectly predicted binge eating through the pathway of body dissatisfaction – but not through either the pathway of impulsive urgency to binge or the pathway of body comparison practices. The authors concluded, "Dissociation is relevant to uncontrolled eating because it serves to undermine normal processes of self-awareness" (p. 456).

CHAPTER 5
Practice body-Led Eating

Let the body take the lead with regarding eating. Trust and respond to its signals of hunger and satisfaction.

"Body-led eating" is a generic term, encompassing intuitive eating, mindful eating, Health at Every Size®, and any other approach that relies on internal cues from the body to make food and eating choices. Other generic terms, to use as alternatives for the term "body-led eating," are "non-dieting" and "eating by internal cues." In a review of 20 different studies of interventions promoting eating by internal cues, including Health at Every Size ®, intuitive eating, and mindful eating programs, it was found that encouraging eating by internal cues "seems to achieve positive physical and psychological effects" (Schaefer & Magnuson, 2014, p. 757). It is worth noting that in this review, five studies were excluded because they were conducted with eating disorder populations. No doubt results could be different for people in eating disorder recovery as opposed to the general population, which is why they were excluded. Still, there were both mental and physical health benefits to the participants. "Although weight remains a highly regarded clinical indicator of health, it is important to note that intuitive eating programs often take a more health-centered approach. The focus is on overall well-being and improving physical and mental health – weight loss may or may not occur. Essentially, studies demonstrated that weight loss is not necessary for improving systolic blood pressure, diastolic blood pressure, total cholesterol level, HDL cholesterol level, LDL cholesterol level, triglyceride level, and cardiorespiratory fitness (e.g., oxygen consumption during exercise)" (p. 757).

Intuitive Eating

The term "intuitive eating" is often used generically to refer to non-diet approaches that employ one's own instinctive wisdom regarding food and eating as opposed to following someone's else's prescriptive rules or guidelines around food and eating. At other times, the term "intuitive eating" is used specifically to refer to the approach outlined in the book by the same title (Tribole & Resch, 2012). This makes use of the term a bit confusing, but as it is popularized and well known, it is one that describes well an approach that offers a flexible, responsive, personalized way of eating.

Defining intuitive eating

Intuitive eating has been defined by scholars "as a strong connection with, understanding of, and eating in response to, internal physiological hunger and satiety cues coupled with a low preoccupation with food," (Avalos & Tylka, 2006, p. 486).

One might say that intuitive eating is the opposite of rigid control around food. It is more responsive and more personalized. Anyone who has binged her way off a strict diet is familiar with the perils of rigid control around food. This is one of the strongest reasons that so many people can wholeheartedly say and believe with conviction that diets don't work.

Interestingly, Tylka, Calogero and Danelsdottir (2015) found that intuitive eating is not only different from rigid control around food, but it is also different from flexible control around food. Intuitive eating relies on internal self-regulation cues for eating, whereas flexible control relies on external self-regulation cues, such as calories or portion size or personal body weight. Flexibly dietary control is fairly popular in contemporary American culture. But it still has the restrictive mentality behind it, because it is based on following external rather than internal cues. A person recommending flexible dietary control may say sometime like "I have a sweet treat after dinner every other night so that I do not feel deprived," which is quite a bit different than "Am I still hungry? What would make my body most happy right now?"

"Flexible control is generally considered a balanced approach to eating – operationalized by behaviors such as taking smaller than desired servings of food to control weight, being conscious of foods eaten, taking weight into account when making food choices, and engaging in compensation (i.e., intentionally eating less and/or healthier alternatives at the next meal) if too much is eaten or less healthy options are chosen at the previous meal" (Tylka, Calogero & Danelsdottir, 2015, p. 167). In fact, researchers found that flexible dietary control and intuitive eating are actually inversely related. Not exactly intuitive, is it? Flexible control, as it turns out, is closely related to rigid control and everybody pretty much agrees that rigid control around food never ends well. Researchers concluded that "our findings therefore call into question the clarity and utility of flexible control…it is not clear what adaptive flexible control *is* in the absence of rigid control, as both constructs are intertwined within 11 of the 12 flexible control items…we discourage professionals and health organizations from advocating that community adults adopt flexible control strategies to promote health and well-being" (p. 173). Although researchers did not write to an audience of people in recovery, if that had been the case, no doubt they would have recommended that people in recovery not adopt flexible control as a strategy for health and well-being either, as it is so tied to the construct of rigid control that it is asking for trouble. So, in the end, letting go of rigid control also means letting go of flexible control, as scary as that sounds to a lot of people in recovery, myself very much included.

Characteristics of intuitive eaters

According to Augustus-Horvath and Tylka (2011, p. 110) people who eat intuitively are:

1. not preoccupied with food and dieting;

2. often choose foods that help their bodies function well and are pleasing to their palate;

3. permit themselves to eat foods they desire when they are hungry;

4. do not ignore their hunger cues or classify food into acceptable and unacceptable categories;

5. rely on their hunger cues to determine when and how much to eat; and

6. respect their satiety cues by ceasing to eat when they are no longer hungry or are comfortably full.

Intuitive eaters have been found to be both happier and leaner than non-intuitive eaters. The four factors important components of intuitive eating are: (1) Eating for physical rather than emotional reasons, (2) Unconditional permission to eat, (3) Reliance on hunger and satiety cues, and (4) Body-food choice congruence (Tylka & Kroon Van Diest, 2013).

Popular book

The term "intuitive eating" is complicated by the fact that although it is a four-part or six-part construct for research purposes, but in the book entitled *Intuitive Eating* (Tribole & Resch, 2012), there are 10 principles involved, which are:

1. Reject the diet mentality

2. Honor your hunger

3. Make peace with food

4. Challenge the food police

5. Respect your fullness

6. Discover the satisfaction factor

7. Honor your feelings without using food

8. Respect your body

9. Exercise—Feel the difference

10. Honor your health (gentle nutrition)

This list is comprehensive, but it can also be a bit overwhelming. It can be hard to know how to prioritize. When I first read the book, I did not get much beyond the first chapter. Rejecting the diet mentality is something that took me a long, long time. I had a hard time moving on to the next principle, when I felt that I had not yet accomplished the first one.

Rejecting the diet mentality

To support the statement that "diets don't work," I find it helpful to turn to research. "Independent comprehensive reviews of behavioral weight-loss interventions all reach the same conclusions: In the short term, some weight loss is possible on *any* diet program, but nearly every dieter regains the weight they lost within three to five years, and as many of two-thirds of dieters regain *more* weight than they initially lost" (Logel, Stinson & Brochu, 2015, p. 681). It's one thing for people to say that diets don't work and quite another for research to demonstrate it (at least in my book). The extremely rare folks who are maintaining individual weight loss from dieting are generally putting a huge amount of energy and attention into their efforts. Even more damning is this: "Not only does evidence that weight loss directly improves health appear to be weak, but evidence that weight-loss efforts can be harmful appears to be stronger, and includes correlational but also experimental evidence. Dieting requires sustained acts of willpower which can eventually break down, resulting in overeating and a lack of self-regulatory capacity needed for other tasks. The stress of dieting increases the stress hormone cortisol, potentially compromising dieters' immune functioning. Dieting also predicts elevated rates of depression and negative self-image, and in adolescents, predicts future weight gain and binge eating. And it appears that the more often people attempt weight loss, the more their health is at risk – frequency of dieting predicts decreased markers of immune functioning among higher-weight, currently-healthy women" (Logel, Stinson & Brochu, 2015, p. 681). I find these sorts of reports of research to be much more convincing than any vignette about a person who gave up dieting and is now healthier and happier. Data-based research supports letting go of the diet mentality for people of all weights. "Since dieting has been associated with the onset and maintenance of eating disorders, and the cessation of dieting is a crucial step in the treatment of eating disorders, encouraging higher-weight patients to enter a weight-suppressed state by dieting is likely physically harmful and hence violates professional codes of ethics" (Tylka, Annuziato, Burgard, Danielsdottir, Shuman, Davis & Calogero, 2014, p. 4) for health care providers.

I have a seemingly automatic response to want to get away with something when I am given new and unsupervised freedom, and I know I am not alone in this. All of a sudden, I'm 10 years old again, climbing up on the counter to reach the cookies that were supposedly stored higher than I could reach. When I first read "let go of the diet mentality" some part of me heard, "food frenzy!!" but upon reading further into it, I realized that "food frenzy" is still part of the diet mentality – it's the part that says "I can't be trusted." Just because I have an urge to rebel, though, does not mean I have act out the temptation of rebellion.

I think the major complicating factor around my difficulty of rejecting diet mentality is that it is not as simple as rejecting diets themselves. Objectively, I can agree that diets themselves are counter-productive and even harmful. But I need a constant infusion of such research articles as are referenced above in order to remind me and re-convince me that really and truly, diets don't work. More later about keeping the focus off weight, which for me is what is behind the conclusion that "diets don't work."

Another challenge to rejecting the diet mentality is the friends I made in diet groups. The social component to being a member of a group of people who are all following the same diet or food plan is a big deal. It's hard to reject diets but not to reject dieters. I got to know and trust people in these groups. I have relied on their stories to keep me going in hard times, and they were alternately inspirational and supportive to me. Whether it was my experience in 12 step food-plan based groups (which are basically groups of people following the same diet) or my experience in Weight Watchers, there was such a strong social support element that it was no easy thing to extricate myself. As the main element keeping these groups together is the diet/food plan, if I rejected their diet, then for all intents and purposes, I rejected the people as well. I didn't want to lose them as friends, but I had to take that risk. In order to be true to myself, I had to risk that they also might reject me. Once I wasn't following their diet or food plan anymore, I wasn't one of them. It turns out that all we shared was the diet or food plan, but that didn't make it easier to say goodbye. I was leaving them – it was my own choice and it was a good thing for me to do – but it was still sad and hard for me.

The process of letting go of the social support found in diet/food plan groups would not have been so hard if there were vibrant social groups of people in eating disorder recovery, but those groups have been hard for me to find. Most face-to-face eating disorder recovery groups are for people early in recovery and often quite pricey because they are facilitated by counselors. There are a lot of facilitated recovery groups, but I have found that groups with a paid leader are not the same as a group of friends – once the class is over, it's really hard for the members of the group to self-organize and stay together as a group. There are some online groups and that is very good news to those of us who like to feel affiliated with others on the same path. In particular, intuitiveeating.org offers a community component that is vibrant and encouraging. There are plenty of people to follow on Twitter also who are body positive and recovery oriented. For me, it is important to identify both with my own individualized path as well to see myself as part of a group of people who are on a similar path. See more on this later in the book under "Tech Support."

Relationship to eating disorder recovery

One of the best parts about intuitive eating is its positivity. It is something that a person can do, practice, and/or embrace rather that something that a person must avoid, abstain from, or reduce. In my many years of working with young children and their teachers in the field of early childhood education, I have seen first-hand the many benefits of positivity. If children are told "don't hit," they do not necessarily know what it is that they should actually do, only what they shouldn't do. But if they are told to please "use soft touches," they are much more likely to be able to implement their teachers' or parents' wishes. Similarly, being instructed to use their "walking feet" instead of "don't run" and the statement "inside voices" instead of "don't yell" are so helpful and are now commonplace in most preschool settings. So why would the rest of us be any different? We also want to know what to do, not just what not to do. Intuitive eating tells us what to do. In fact, intuitive eating is NOT the exact opposite of eating disorders in the same way that "use a quiet voice" is the exact opposite of "don't yell." Research has shown that the only part of intuitive eating that is the exact opposite of eating disorders is limited to the "unconditional permission to eat" feature (Tylka & Wilcox, 2006). The other components of intuitive eating go above and beyond eating disorder recovery.

The number of components of intuitive eating keeps shifting, but the basic concept is always the same. "Three central but interrelated components of intuitive eating have been identified: (a) unconditional permission to eat when hungry and what food is desired, (b) eating for physical rather than emotional reasons, and (c) reliance on internal hunger and satiety cues to determine when and how much to eat" (Tylka & Wilcox, 2006, p. 474). While each one of these components are important, the first one, unconditional permission to eat when hungry and to eating what food is desired, is the only one that is the direct opposite of eating disorders. Researchers conducted two separate studies and assessed a total of 737 college women to determine the links between these characteristics, eating disorder symptoms, and overall wellbeing (measured by assessing positive affect, self-esteem, proactive coping, optimism, hardiness, unconditional self-regard, and social problem solving). They found that the second two items added value to wellbeing above and beyond eating disorder recovery – in other words, eating for physical rather than emotional reasons and reliance on hunger and satiety cues to determine when and how much to eat lead to extra bonuses in wellbeing that are not accounted for by lack of eating disorder symptoms. If one is struggling with eating disorder symptoms, it seems that priority focus should be given to unconditional permission to eat.

Given that only one component of intuitive eating, unconditional permission to eat, is the most directly opposite intuitive eating skill from an eating disorder, then if our loved ones are tempted to call to us across the room and give us the unhelpful command, "don't engage in eating disorder behaviors!" they could safely reframe their directive to the more positive and helpful statement, "give yourself unconditional permission to eat when you are hungry and whatever food you desire!" "Individuals who give themselves unconditional permission to eat do not try to ignore their hunger signals nor do they classify food into acceptable and nonacceptable categories and try to avoid food in the latter category. They are aware of how their body responds to certain foods; thus, they typically choose foods that help their bodies function well and view taste as only one component of food choice. Researchers have found that people who give themselves unconditional permission to eat do not overindulge in food or engage in binge eating, whereas people who place conditions on when, how much, and what foods they can eat (i.e., by restricting timing, amount, and type of food eating according to some external standard) often overindulge in food when they perceive that their dietary rules have been broken and therefore become preoccupied with food" (Tylka & Wilcox, 2006, p. 474-475). Sounds pretty straightforward, doesn't it? I know, simple but not easy. Despite the challenge (or perhaps because of it), focusing on practicing these skills is a good use of anyone's time.

I think it is important to note that if one focuses on unconditional permission to eat, then the generic terms "body-led" eating, "non-dieting," or "eating according to internal cues," as they are typically understood, may be confusing. The other two aspects of intuitive eating, eating for physical rather than emotional reasons and reliance on internal hunger and satiety cues to determine when and how much to eat (Tylka & Wilcox, 2006), seem to be more popular ways of describing any of these approaches to eating. Almost never, outside eating disorder recovery professional circles, is the statement, "give yourself unconditional permission to eat" not qualified with "but…" The whole point here is that there are no "buts." Just unconditional permission to eat. Okay, that can be really, really scary. Because we are dealing with people (myself very much included) who learned through many repeated experiences that our bodies are not trustworthy. If we give ourselves unconditional permission to eat, we fear we will start eating at breakfast and never be able to leave the house because we will still be eating hours later. That is the fear. And, with me anyway, the minute the fear arises, the safety or maintaining behaviors arise to keep the anxiety in check and boom I am back to engaging in some form of keeping myself emotionally safe around food, such as counting calories or limiting myself to eating at certain times. Whatever my safety or maintaining strategy, it's not unconditional permission to eat. Argh. This is why it's so easy for me to see that the unconditional permission to eat aspect of intuitive eating is so clearly directly opposite to eating disorder thinking. If I really allow myself unconditional permission to eat, then I am really not living in my eating disorder. If I am binge eating because I think that I won't ever get a chance to eat this food again because I am going to start a new food plan tomorrow, then I am not giving myself unconditional permission to eat. Unconditional permission to eat has to extend over time. I have unconditional permission to eat when I am hungry – now, later today, tomorrow, next week and even next month. I have unconditional permission to eat what I am hungry for – now, later today, tomorrow, next week and even next month. No "buts." Unconditional means without condition, without any conditions. It has not been easy for me to wrap my brain around, but it is extremely powerful.

Keep in mind that the book by Tribole and Resch (2012) was not originally written for people in recovery from eating disorders, but more for people with more normative food struggles. It can be a helpful resource, but also it may need to be adjusted a bit for each group of people who use it. Intuitive eating has been tested empirically by researchers with 120 women in recovery from eating disorders (Richards, Crowton, Berrett, Smith, & Passmore, 2017). Participants were in treatment for anorexia, bulimia, and eating disorders not otherwise specified. They started out in treatment with prescribed meal plans, and were expected to eat everything on their plates. After they were successful with this stage of treatment, they were moved to a little bit more freedom where they got to choose the items they put on their plates, but they were still expected to eat all of the items they had chosen. Lastly, participants were allowed to choose what and how much to eat. This last stage – the intuitive eating stage -- was still part of residential treatment. "Only after a period of time wherein patients were able to demonstrate ability to plate and eat appropriately, accurately assess hunger-fullness, and resist eating disorder urges were they advanced to intuitive eating. Once they received approval to begin intuitive eating, patients were allowed to choose menu items in accordance with intuitive eating principles and choose what portion of a meal or snack to complete. Throughout this process, patients were closely monitored to assess integration of intuitive eating principles" (p. 101-102). Clearly the process was executed with care and with the best interest of patients' well-being in mind. I think it is fantastic that intuitive eating was introduced in an experiential and supervised way. It seems that many people who transition to intuitive eating from a more structured food plan are not prepared to make the transition slowly or even with much support. Certainly, that was my experience the first time I attempted to go off a food plan and to attempt body-led eating. I jumped in with both feet but unfortunately without any support. Then when I hit a bump in the road after a few weeks, I didn't know what to do. I thought it was too much for me, so I gave up. Richards, Crowton, Berrett, Smith, and Passmore's (2017) study shows that people in recovery from eating disorders can be successful with intuitive eating when they are provided with support. "Our study also provided evidence that improvements in patients' ability to eat intuitively is associated with other important indicators of healing and recovery, including reductions in eating disorder symptoms, depression, anxiety, and social conflict and improvements in body image and spiritual well-being. These findings are consistent with, and add to, previous experimental studies that have shown intuitive eating interventions help reduce disordered eating behaviors and attitudes such as binge eating and chronic dieting" (p. 108). So, make sure to get some support. It can really help.

Mindful Eating

According to the non-profit organization, The Center for Mindful Eating, "Mindful eating is allowing yourself to become aware of the positive and nurturing opportunities that are available through food selection and preparation by respecting your own inner wisdom. By using all your senses in choosing to eat food that is both satisfying to you and nourishing to your body, acknowledging your responses to food (likes, dislikes, or neutral) without judgment, and becoming aware of physical hunger and satiety cues to guide your decisions to begin and end eating you can change your relationship to food" (thecenterformindfuleating.org retrieved 5/25/17). What mindful eating offers that intuitive, attuned or other non-diet approaches don't include is a grounding in the spiritual practice of mindfulness, which The Center for Mindful Eating summarizes as "paying attention, non-judgmentally, in the present moment" (thecenterformindfuleating.org retrieved 5/25/17).

Mindful eating might be less daunting for people who are recovering from an eating disorder than intuitive eating. While the two approaches are very similar and include much overlap, intuitive eating emphasizes freedom, whereas mindful eating emphasizes awareness of inner wisdom. Intuitive eating proponents would certainly never argue against depending on one's inner wisdom, but at the beginning, it is often suggested that the new intuitive eater experiment with eating with an abandon that can feel terrifying to someone in eating disorder recovery. It's that whole unconditional permission to eat thing that can be terrifying. The pauses and present moment awareness of physical sensation associated with mindful eating, while also possibly a bit intimidating, do not tend to bring on the same level of anxiety that "eat what you want when you are hungry for it" might. Often when people begin an intuitive eating approach, they are told that they are likely to initially gain weight initially and then re-stabilize later. Using mindful eating, there is not likely to be an initial experience of weight gain, because it is a more tentative approach. It's less of an emotional risk, really. There is no "out of control" initial period that is so commonly discussed with intuitive eating. It is up to each person, obviously. I offer both here as options to consider. In the end, I think that people who see themselves as intuitive eaters and people who see themselves as mindful eaters are engaging in very similar practices, but the path to get there might feel different.

Using all five senses to experience food

Mindful eating does not involve rules, but it offers ways of being around food. Sometimes it feels manageable to me and sometimes it feels like an unattainable ideal that offers a vision of how I might eat and approach both my eating and my life. I can be more or less mindful but I am never completely mindless unless I'm in a coma. There are different flavors of mindful eating, different experts who have put their spin on it and packaged it in various ways.

One important point that I think gets lost in mindful eating and even in the terminology "mindful eating" is that for me, primary attention during mindful eating is on the body, and secondary attention is on the food. That does not mean not to focus on food, but it means that signals from the body are the ones to privilege. The two interact, of course. Food tastes better when we are hungry, and the first few bites of any food taste better than the next few bites. But when we focusing on taste, that is a bodily experience, not something inherent in the food. It's the interaction between what we are eating and the body, but the focus is on the body.

An easy way to put mindful eating into practice is to become aware of all five senses during the eating experience. To review from elementary school, the five senses are: sight, touch/feel, smell, taste and sound. They can be experienced in any order, but generally the sight, touch, smell, taste and sound order are ones that can be employed in eating. Say, for example, I am eating an apple mindfully.

Sight: It is so red, but it has flecks of yellow also, and even brown.

Touch: When I hold it in my hand, it is firm and a bit cold.

Smell: I cut a slice, it is very hard and crisp. I couldn't smell it very well until I cut into it, but now I smell the sweetness.

Taste: It is firm in my mouth. Biting into it releases the sweetness. This apple tastes very rich. There are a number of flavors here. It tastes like fall. The skin has a different flavor from the flesh.

Sound: Cutting the apple made a squishy noise. It crunches in my mouth, more than it did against the knife. Biting into a piece is satisfyingly loud.

Most mindful eating suggests focusing on the experience of the food in the body, not merely on the food, and paying attention to one's own senses is a good way to start that process.

Mindful Eating Review Articles

Mindful eating intervention studies have blossomed, if not exploded, in the past decade, such that multiple review articles and meta analyses are now available of mindful eating interventions. One review of 21 mindfulness-based interventions aimed at individuals with problematic eating behaviors that might lead to obesity (binge and emotional eating) found very promising results overall, with 86% of the studies reviewed reporting improvements in targeted problematic eating behaviors (O'Reilly, Cook, Spruijt-Metz & Black, 2014). Successful interventions reviewed included mindful eating components, not merely generalized mindfulness or meditation training. Specifically, 11 of the 12 studies that targeted binge eating were found to be successful. These hard-to-treat behaviors can be exacerbated by restrictive approaches to moderating eating but were positively and effectively addressed through mindful eating practices. Another review of 11 mindful eating intervention studies (Pannowitz, 2015) found that although many studies were described as pilots or novel interventions, they had comparable to or more impressive results than comparative interventions. Another review of 8 mindful eating intervention studies among those recovering from eating disorders (Wanden-Berghe, Sanz-Vallero & Wanden-Berghe, 2011) found promising results, even with small sample sizes. Finally, a review of 19 studies examining mindful eating interventions among people struggling with binge eating (Godfrey, Gallo & Afari, 2015) concluded that "overall, mindfulness-based interventions were associated with effects on binge eating of large or medium-large magnitude and can be considered effective" (p. 358). These four review articles demonstrate that mindful eating interventions show promise in adding value beyond what other non-mindful eating interventions might be able to provide.

Binge Prevention

One specific way that I have found mindful eating to be helpful is when I had an urge to binge, I gave myself permission to eat some of the food that I have been wanting to binge on. When I used to binge, my go-to foods were often sweet bakery items – cookies, donuts, etc. for the most part. If the idea of eating a dozen or two donuts occurs to me as something I might like to do, I have some inner work to do (What's going on? Am I hungry? Do I need to give myself a break?) but in addition, there is the direct experience with the food that will happen sooner or later. I have been known to go to a donut shop, order my favorite (Bavarian Cream) and some coffee, sit at one of the tables, and enjoy the donut mindfully – truly tasting all of it. This approach to donuts is very different from what I would do if I were bingeing. Binge eating donuts does not occur for me when I'm truly paying attention. I may eat a bit more that my body needs, but if I am truly aware, then I don't have that awful out of control feeling that I had when I used to binge eat.

Zoning out

When I do the inner work around a desire to binge, often what I find is that I want to zone out. Life seems a little too challenging and I feel that I deserve a break. Sometimes I am truly hungry and the break I need is from a semi-restrictive cycle that I have fallen into. I need more treats or more something else. But other times it is not so much food related as it is related to mental or emotional overload. Mindful eating comes to my rescue here because mindful eating is all about not zoning out around food but is also highly consistent with other forms of mindfulness, such as mindful meditation, which contain a zoning out component that meets my zoning out needs perfectly. As I wrote in my article on relapse, "zoning out during eating has turned what could have been deliciously indulgent experiences into destructive eating binges. When I engage in contemplative prayer or meditation, I do not seem to need to use food for that purpose" (Gillespie, 2016, p. 14).

A new language

Sometimes I feel like I am learning a foreign language when I try to listen to the signals that my body is sending me. It reminds me of trying to communicate with someone who speaks a different language than I do. I remember when I was in Italy for the first time, I asked an Italian speaker directions from the train station to the youth hostel. He used his hands enough that I could get the gist of what he was saying, but none of his words were comprehensible to my brain. I made it to the youth hostel unscathed based on what seemed like incomprehensible directions. Listening to my body can sometimes feel just as confusing. But as it turns out, the details are less important than the basic idea of the communication. I am quite familiar with the hunger scales that many people use to rate their hunger but I don't find putting a number to my hunger to be very useful. Aren't I trying to get away from quantifying my experiences? My body has many subtleties, but with regard to hunger, the messages fall into some basic categories:

1. Moderate hunger: This is when I feel a bit empty in my stomach, and the thought occurs to me, "When's lunch?" or "I could eat." This is a great time for a snack if a meal isn't planned in the next hour. If a meal is coming up soon, I can wait, but if I wait too long, I'll get to strong hunger and I prefer to eat before I get there. I used to try to wait for strong hunger because it was clear, but I've noticed that eating at moderate hunger feels more normal, nurturing, and effective for me. It allows me to eat consistently moderately and to satisfaction without needing to eat too fast and without feeling too desperate.

2. Strong hunger: This is when my stomach is growling or sometimes I feel a bit headachy or shaky if I've been involved in physical activity and haven't had much to eat. It is really important to get something to eat at this point. Really, I've waited too long and need to think about how to prevent this situation in the future.

3. Craving: Sometimes I really want a particular food even though I am not necessarily experiencing the routine rise and fall of my normal hunger patterns. I used to fear these times and feel out of control and

fight them and generally make myself miserable. What I've found is that the easiest, most natural response to craving is just to have a moderate amount of whatever I'm craving and to be done with it. I have come to think of craving as a form of hunger and not to judge it negatively. It comes and goes and isn't as big of a deal as I used to think it was.

Really there isn't much else. I make an effort to eat a reasonably wide variety of foods and food types. Sometimes a sandwich sounds good so I'll have that and sometimes it doesn't, so I'll see what sounds good. The more I overanalyze the signals from my body, the more miserable I make myself. If I think about other body signals I get, they are very similar. For instance, when my body needs rest, I have some basic signals that I don't have to stress over, but that I do want to heed:

1. Tired. It's the end of the day and I'm tired. This is a good time to turn out the light and go to sleep.

2. Bone tired. Extra rest is needed. I've waited to long for sleep. Either I haven't been getting enough sleep or I've overexerted myself or I'm fighting off some illness. Whatever the cause, I need to take a nap if at all possible, or go to bed early or sleep late. My body needs rest.

3. Sleepy. Sometimes this coincides with tired, but other times I am bored or feeling a little lazy and, depending on my schedule, it might be a great time for a nap or for going to bed early or for sleeping late. It's more like craving. It's a signal coming from my body that isn't the normal routine tired feeling, but who doesn't love Saturday afternoon naps or extra sleep on vacation or nodding off in the car while someone else is driving?

I can give myself permission to take naps on weekends when I feel like it, trusting that there is nothing terribly wrong with that just like there is nothing terribly wrong with eating food that I'm craving. It's not always convenient or possible, but as much as I can, I try to let my body rest as much as it needs to in the same way I let my body get as much nourishment as it needs.

CHAPTER 6
Stop thinking so much about
food, eating, body or weight

Health at Every Size ®

American health culture is highly weight-focused. Getting and keeping the focus off of weight is a revolutionary suggestion, and it is also supported by research. I am emboldened not so much by personal testimony as by this kind of report: "Attempts to suppress weight are associated with poorer outcomes in treating patients with bulimia: those who have bulimia who try to maintain a weight-suppressed state are likely to binge eat, gain weight, and drop out of psychotherapeutic treatment" (Tylka, Annuziato, Burgard, Danielsdottir, Shuman, Davis & Calogero, 2014, p. 4).

In her groundbreaking and influential book, *Health at Every Size* (2008), Linda Bacon cogently argues in favor of a weight-neutral approach to health, convincingly pointing out that it is a better use of our resources to encourage each person to engage in healthful behaviors that assist them to feel their best, regardless of the impact of those behaviors on their weight. Similarly, social psychologists argue in favor of a well-being orientation rather than a weight loss orientation in helping people to feel their best (Logel, Stinson & Brochu, 2015). They acknowledge that while higher body weights do predict health problems over time, the cause of these health problems may not be the actual weight, but other factors linked to higher body weights, including lower socio-economic status, physical activity and fitness, and social determinant of health including rejection, stress, and lack of social support. They cite research indicating that higher body weights not only may not be the cause of health problems, but also they may contribute to higher weight individuals' ability to recover from various illnesses including pneumonia and heart disease. They present solid evidence "that most of the population's variance in body weight is determined by individual differences in genetic heritage, not individual differences in behavior," (p. 681), pointing out that this genetic impact even extends to individuals' susceptibility to environmental influences, which explains why some people get very muscular if they start an exercise routine, whereas others do not. This is both bad news for people who would like their bodies to change and a great relief to those of us who want to quit trying to change the bodies we have but instead to appreciate our bodies as they are.

Please note that the term Health at Every Size® and HAES® are now registered trademarks of the Association for Size Diversity and Health, which, according to their website http://sizediversityandhealth.org involves these basic principles:

1. "Weight Inclusivity: Accept and respect the inherent diversity of body shapes and sizes and reject the idealizing or pathologizing of specific weights.

2. "Health Enhancement: Support health policies that improve and equalize access to information and services, and personal practices that improve human wellbeing, including attention to individual physical, economic, social, spiritual, emotional, and other needs.

3. "Respectful Care: Acknowledge our biases, and work to end weight discrimination, weight stigma, and weight bias. Provide information and services from an understanding that socio-economic status, race, gender, sexual orientation, age, and other identities impact weight stigma, and support environments that address these inequalities.

4. "Eating for Well-being: Promote flexible, individualized eating based on hunger, satiety, nutritional needs, and pleasure, rather than any externally regulated eating plan focused on weight control.

5. "Life-Enhancing Movement: Support physical activities that allow people of all sizes, abilities, and interests to engage in enjoyable movement, to the degree that they choose."

I find the HAES® model, as described by both the Association for Size Diversity and Health and the 2014 article by Tylka and colleagues to be very helpful. HAES® does not aggravate my rebelliousness. When I first encountered the recommendation to "ditch diets" I had not fully understood, yet alone embraced, the complexities involved in diet culture, or the diet paradigm. What Health at Every Size® does for me is that it provides a theoretical or philosophical framework in which to place the strategy of intuitive eating. Intuitive eating is a process that demands a complete mindset or paradigm shift in thinking, and for me, Health at Every Size® provides the convincing arguments and data to support that shift. Mindful eating could also be placed in the same framework, although mindful eating also comes with its own Buddhist philosophical framework, which is highly comprehensive and full of ancient wisdom that is still relevant to many in modern times. It is a very powerful option for those who wish to pursue it.

HAES® offers an alternative to focusing on weight. "Under this paradigm, weight is not a focal point for medical treatment or intervention. Weight is not viewed as a behavior, but eating nutritious food when hungry, ceasing to eat when full, and engaging in pleasurable (and thus more sustainable) exercise *are* self-care behaviors that can be made more accessible for people" (Tylka, Annuziato, Burgard, Danielsdottir, Shuman, Davis & Calogero, 2014, p. 6). They propose the model that appears below:

Health at Every Size: A model using a weight-inclusive approach

(Tylka, Annuziato, Burgard, Danielsdottir, Shuman, Davis & Calogero, 2014, p. 7):

"Definition: A model to support the health of people across the weight spectrum that challenges the current cultural oppression of higher-weight people. Specifically, the model seeks to end (1) stigmatizing of health problems (healthism) and (2) weight-based discrimination, bias, iatrogenic practices within health care and other health-related industries, as well as other areas of life. The model acknowledges that weight is not a behavior or personal choice and that normal

human bodies come in a wide range of weights and seeks alternatives to the
overwhelmingly futile and harmful practice of pursuing weight loss.

"Principles

(1)   Do no harm

(2)   Create practices and environments that are sustainable

(3)   Keep a process focus rather than end-goals, day-to-day
quality of life

(4)   Incorporate evidence in designing interventions where there
is evidence

(5)   Include all bodies and lived experiences, a norm of diversity

(6)   Increase access, opportunity, freedom, and social justice

(7)   Given that health is multidimensional, maintain a holistic
focus

(8)   Trust that people (and bodies!) move toward greater health
given access and opportunity.

"Applied to policy: Provide environments that give access to all the things
that support the well-being of human bodies of all sizes. Examples: Respect for all
ages, abilities and sizes. Living wages to provide time for self-care. Nourishing,
affordable, and accessible food. An end to weight discrimination in schools,
insurance, workplaces, housing and so forth. Regulation of weight loss advertising.
Support for communities and social networks. Community involvement in making
policy. Medical research and education in health needs of higher-weight people.
Redress of structural racism and inequality.

"Within health care: Provide interventions that give benefit to people at any
size, without discrimination or bias. Examples: Medical education on "best
practice" for providing health care to higher-weight people. Assist patients in
developing long-term health practices rather than pursing weight loss. End BMI-
based treatment decisions. Require >5 years of maintenance/outcomes for all
participants in weight-change interventions and all benefits for the majority before

use. Base practice on the lived experiences of patients: listen and learn. Defend the therapeutic relationship.

"In personal life: Provide yourself with the features of life you find sustainable, within the context of your life, that support your well-being. Examples: Reconnect with your body's cues to make decisions about what you need now. Find playful and/or purposeful motives for moving that are not tied to weight loss goals. When hurt, direct your anger to the person who hurt you rather than blaming your body. Look for direct ways to improve life and health that do not require a thinner body. Find others who are opting out of weight cycling and developing sustainable practices. Know that your worth is not based on health."

HAES® is clearly an approach that can be used at a public policy and health practitioner level, but it also has very personal implications. I particularly resonate with the "in personal life" section. This involves shifting the focus on weight as the target outcome for my eating, exercise and sleep behaviors to a broader focus on health and wellbeing. I find this both liberating and possibly not surprisingly, a bit anxiety producing. It does not necessarily mean never weighing oneself or never knowing one's weight, but it definitely means not perseverating on weight, not allowing it to be the focus, not judging one weight as better than another weight. In other words, it's a weight neutral approach. I have heard people say, "why do I need the scale? I have jeans," but really, isn't that still a weight/shape focus, just using a different external form of measurement? If I am to rely on internal signals, then how I feel in my body, how I have been sleeping, how much energy I have – those should be my indicators, not the scale or my jeans.

Keeping the Focus off Weight

Many HAES® interventions have been researched. One such study was of a HAES® intervention conducted in Sao Paulo, Brazil among women between the ages of 25 and 50 with BMIs over 30. Weight was not the focus of the intervention. "Rather than focusing on the body weight and what to do about it, participants were encouraged to reflect whether they had struggled with body and eating issues throughout their lives and whether the diet experiences intensified these aspects.

More specifically, they were stimulated to gain new perspectives and to develop skills of their own that would enable them to change their eating behaviors (if and when necessary), their level of physical activity, and patterns of thinking and acting that might have been preventing them to change" (Ulian, et al., 2015, p. 8). Even though the 14 participants who were followed for one year did in fact lose a modest but statistically significant amount of weight and body fat, researchers concluded that "weight loss was not mandatory for them to develop a better perception and attitude toward their bodies. It is likely if they kept their previous weight-centered way of thinking they would feel disappointed and would possibly abandon the intervention for not meeting their goals" and one participant reported (in her own words), "*happiness is not the weight loss, it is about feeling good. So if my 'feeling good' today is coming to college, doing my things, it may be part of my happiness*" (Ulian, et al., 2015, p. 8).

Too much focus on weight and shape is actually a symptom of an eating disorder. Researchers have suggested that one of the criteria of recovery should be a reduction of the reliance of weight and shape in one's evaluation of oneself (Cogley and Keel, 2003). A strong argument in favor of this criteria is that the difference between remission (or partial recovery) and (full) recovery is that a person in (full) recovery is less likely to relapse. And if a person holds on to an undue influence of shape and weight in her self-evaluation, then she is at higher risk for relapse back into her eating disorder. In other words, changing behaviors is not enough, in order to be in sustainable recovery, thoughts (cognitions) must also change.

Behaviors and Thoughts that need to change in recovery (DSM 5)

Behaviors that need to change in recovery	Thoughts that need to change in recovery
No more restricting/starving	No more undue influence of body weight on self-evaluation
No more binge eating (including no more eating much more rapidly than	No more undue influence of body shape on self-evaluation

normal, eating until uncomfortably full, eating large amounts of food when not physically hungry, eating alone because of feeling embarrassed by how much one is eating, feeling disgusted with oneself, or depressed or very guilty afterward).	
No more purging (including no more self-induced vomiting, misuse of laxatives, diuretics or other medications, fasting, or excessive exercise)	No more disturbance in the way one's body weight or shape is experienced
No more persistent behavior that interferes with weight gain among people who are significantly low weight	Recognition of the seriousness of low body weight
No more night eating	No more intense fear of gaining weight
No more eating of non-nutritive foods	No more intense fear of becoming fat
No more regurgitation (re-chewing, re-swallowing or spitting out) of food	No more sense of lack of control during binge eating (no more feeling that one cannot stop eating or control how much one is eating)

To measure "undue influence" it might be helpful to use the Eating Disorders Examination Questionnaire (EDE-Q) found in the Appendix. Cogley and Keel (2003) used an average score of 3 or lower to demonstrate acceptable/normal influence and an average score of 4 or higher to signify undue influence on the weight concern and shape concern subscales of the EDE-Q, where an average of 4 indicates moderate dissatisfaction with some associated distress or concentration impairment on more than half of the days (16 to 22 days out of the last 28 or moderate importance – definitely one of the main aspects of self-evaluation). Note that community norms are lower (1.6 for weight concern and 2.1 for shape concern according to Mond, Hay, Rogers & Owen, 2006).

The hardest things to change according to 40 women who had recovered from bulimia were: body image, a desire to be thinner, and fear of getting fat (Rorty, Yager, & Rossotto, 1993). Non-diet programs, which focus on health and/or body positivity have been developed in order to help people make progress in the area of body image, which in turn also impacts their eating disorder symptoms. "Efficacy studies of non-dieting interventions have demonstrated improvements in eating behaviors and attitudes, including decreases in dietary restraint, disinhibition, overall eating disorder risk, and binge eating and greater awareness of hunger and satiety cues" (Bloom, Shelton, Bengough & Brennan, 2013, p. 2).

As an example of one non-dieting approach, the Australian No More Diets program covers food and eating, body image, and movement for two hours each week for seven weeks, followed by a final summary and reflection session (Bloom, Shelton, Bengough & Brennan, 2013, Table 1, p. 4). The seven food and eating topics covered were: why diets do not work, regular eating pattern, hunger scale, hungry eating vs. non-hungry eating, how to reduce non-hungry eating, eating with awareness, and fine-tuning nutritional knowledge. The seven body image topics covered were: looking at spine and identifying basic spinal movements to music, exploration of pros and cons of body acceptance and body dissatisfaction, introduction of concept of overvaluation of shape and weight, introduction of concepts of extreme and or unhelpful cognitions regarding body image, coping with extreme and or unhelpful cognitions regarding body image, review of concepts and effects of overvaluation of shape and weight, avoidance and body checking, and linking movement with community options (guest instructor to demonstrate available exercise programs). These body image topics are what is often not emphasized in any cursory approach that starts with "dump the diet" and proceeds immediately to body-led eating. Taking the time to address body image is important. Avoidance of body checking is a great example. Without questioning this behavior, is it going to stop on its own? Unlikely.

Focusing on weight does not bode well for people recovering from eating disorders. Researchers (McFarlane, Olmsted & Trottier, 2008) found that among the 41% of participants who relapsed over a twelve-month period, four factors predicted relapse: severity of pretreatment caloric restriction, slower response to treatment, more remaining symptoms at discharge from treatment, and, the one factor that might be possible to change after treatment: higher weight-related self-evaluation. Researchers wrote: "Weight-related self-esteem was the only measure of psychopathology that predicted relapse. This suggests that it may be beneficial to focus on and challenge weight-related self-evaluation during intensive treatment and relapse prevention interventions. One novel way of approaching this self-schema may be to take a mindfulness approach by teaching individuals to observe these thoughts, label them as eating disordered or unhelpful thoughts, and to not engage these beliefs about weight and shape. This active awareness strategy can be taught with mindfulness skills. Mindfulness-based cognitive therapy has been successful in preventing relapse in depression, and may also prove to be a helpful intervention to prevent relapse in eating disorders. Although a harm-reduction approach or partial symptom control may not be optimal for behavioral symptoms, learning to detach from cognitions related to weight-related self-esteem may be an effective and feasible step toward relapse prevention" (p. 592). Researchers also found that weight concerns after pregnancy were positively correlated with disordered eating behavior and with body dissatisfaction.

There seems to be strong evidence that focusing on weight is not a good idea for anyone who wants to achieve full recovery from an eating disorder. Yet to focus on health can also be problematic, not necessarily related to the eating disorder, but who says that we always have to be healthy? Is a healthy person better than an unhealthy person? What if a person has cancer? Does that make them bad? We would probably all agree, that no, a person with cancer is not a bad person just by virtue of the fact that they have cancer. But what about that focus on health?

Cancer isn't particularly healthy is it? From a HAES® point of view, the goal for each individual is to be as holistically healthy as possible under the circumstances – that includes mental, physical, and emotional health. It's all a balance. In order to attain and maintain optimal mental health, what needs to happen? Is mental health being sacrificed to physical health? Is that truly healthy, in the broadest sense of the term? Those are the kinds of questions that must be considered. It's not wrong to focus on physical health, but we also need to be careful not to privilege physical health or longevity over other possible positive areas of focus for our lives (relationships, kindness, industriousness, creativity, etc.).

Not everyone who has a higher BMI is suffering from an eating disorder, but compared to community norms, 17 people who had BMIs over 25 and signed up for the Australian No More Diets program showed more evidence of eating disorders. "These findings are consistent with previous research that has indicated that although obese individuals do not exhibit a greater level of psychopathology than the normal population, treatment-seeking individuals are more likely to exhibit a greater level of psychological disturbance and disordered eating patterns (Bloom, Shelton, Bengough & Brennan, 2013, p. 5). At the end of a 7-week positive body image, non-dieting program, they showed improvements in a wide variety of areas including body shape preoccupation, shape concern, eating attitudes, weight concern, eating competence, stress, and overall health. They did not show improvements in dietary restraint, emotional eating, uncontrolled eating, or eating concern, which may require longer or more targeted attention.

To weigh or not to weigh?

To weigh or not to weigh? That is the question. There are very conflicting messages out there, even within the eating disorder recovery community, and so I think each person needs to work this out for herself. Clearly, weighing multiple times per day is not a good idea. Weighing once per week is often recommended for people recovering from eating disorders, as a so-called "normal" behavior. There is some debate about whether this should be done by another person or not, and whether the recovering individual should be aware of her weight or not.

Weighing once a month is another option for those who want a relatively consistent but infrequent reality check. A third alternative is "at the doctor's office only," which can be a great relief because it's not "not weighing" but, depending on how often a person goes to the doctor, it could be only once or twice a year. Finally, there is the "never know your weight again" approach.

Research studies

Georgia was struggling with bulimia. She was working at distancing herself from the relationships involved in maintaining the eating disorder, including her relationship with her bathroom scale, as she so eloquently wrote:

Dear Scale,

This is letter serves as the last communication I will ever have with you again. You are the most deceptive thing in this world. You tell me that everything will be all right, that I will be happy and all my problems will dissolve if your numbers go down. But you never kept your promise. You have made me feel miserable so many times, I could not even begin to count. You tell me that I am fat and ugly, every time I stand on you. Yet, you act like you are my friend and guess what, I believed you. But not anymore, I have gotten wiser in this last couple months and now I can see through your lies and at the real you. You will never make me happy. If your number goes up, you make me depressed and if your number goes down, you only make me want to achieve a lower number...Leave me alone, for once and for all. I will bury you, because I will not let you control anybody's life. I will stop your lies forever. Just be quiet and lay where nobody can hear you anymore.

Your victim,

(Georgia)

Francesca was further along in recovery when she decided with her partner to try to conceive a child. *"This changed everything!!! I knew that I could not have a child and continue on this path of self-destruction. I decided then that if I was going to have children I was going to have to change my ways. I stopped weighing myself and started to slowly eat more."*

Alex did not like being weighed, even by others. *"The weekly weigh-ins made it worse. I was happy if I lost or didn't gain. I was recently pregnant and I had to get weighed and I didn't like getting weighed – I didn't gain a lot of weight during the pregnancy and it reminded me of getting weighed before."*

Ella reported that she is not sure of her weight *"since I haven't weighed myself in ages"* but she's not completely comfortable with her body either. She wrote, *"I'm often surprised when I look in the mirror – the body I feel I'm in doesn't match what I expect to see on the outside. It's a place where I'm still learning to accept myself as is, right now."*

To weigh or not to weigh? Options in recovery

Option	Frequency
1	Once per week
2	Once per month
4	At the doctor's office only (aka "no self-weighing," but paying attention to the number when weighed)
5	Never (even if weighed at the doctor's office, decline to be told the number)

Although I admire the "never weigh again" approach, after several unsuccessful attempts, I settled on the "at the doctor's office only," or as I prefer to think of it, "no self-weighing." I have not had a scale at home for many years so the only place I could realistically weigh myself was the doctor's office or the gym. I have always paid attention to my weight at the doctor's office, but I don't go to the doctor very often – only once or twice a year. For years, I weighed at the gym only. But it was always an emotional experience and one that I both relied on and wanted to be over. No matter how often I went the gym (this varied by season and other commitments, but was between once and three times per week), I used to weigh every time I went. Then I conducted my own "no weigh" experiment for a little over five weeks (the time that it took me to accumulate 30 days free of self-weighing), and at the end of it, I was committed to continue never weigh myself again.

Regardless of whether a person ends up adopting the "never self-weigh again" or the "never weigh again" approach, I have found it useful to deemphasize weight by considering the implication of never weighing again. These may be considered journal prompts, or for use in discussing with others.

If I never weigh again, then...

1. I will be more connected to my body and less driven by the number on the scale.

2. I will worry about the number on the scale less.

3. I will be forced to think of myself in new ways, and not to define myself by my weight.

4. I will....fill in additional personalized responses here...

Another useful exercise for me is that when I start thinking about weighing myself, I tell myself "it doesn't even matter what I weigh," which of course must be logically followed up with "what matters is..." Use these as journal prompts also, or for discussing with others.

It doesn't even matter what I weigh. What matters is...

1. My connection with my own body.

2. That I am taking good care of myself, or at least trying to.

3. That I am waiting for hunger and eating to satisfaction, or at least trying to.

4. That I am a good person.

5. That....fill in additional personalized responses here...

Cognitive behavior therapy historically has recommended weighing once per week in the therapist's office. The argument is that it is important for clients to know their own weight in order to combat overvaluation of weight. Here is a fascinating excerpt aimed at cognitive behavioral clinicians:

"In session weighing will need to be discussed. Many clients and clinicians are unwilling to engage in this activity, but it is another essential tool of CBT-E for eating disorders. The client must know her weight. As with self-monitoring, the clinician must understand and believe in the usefulness of in-session weighing and discussing weight. The rationale should be clearly given: Knowledge of weight is a necessary part of treatment. It permits examination of the relationship between eating and weight and is needed for addressing associated weight problems (e.g., underweight or significant weight fluctuations) and the overvaluation of weight and shape. Most clients with eating disorders are concerned that their weight will increase drastically if they cease their disordered behavior (e.g., purging and restricting), and regular weighing will ensure that all changes are tracked and can be reviewed and interpreted objectively.

"In-session weighing can be difficult for clients with eating disorders for two reasons. First, many clients with eating disorders weigh themselves at home, often several times a day, and are reluctant to rely on once weekly in-session weighing. However, frequent weighing results in preoccupation with weight and provides misleading information. The likelihood is that clients will interpret any weight fluctuations as signals to diet, either to avoid further weight increases, if weight has gone up, or to maintain weight reductions if weight has gone down. For these reasons, at-home weighing is a key process that maintains dietary restraint and should be discouraged. In contrast, some clients with eating disorders avoid knowing their weight at all, and this provides a second obstacle to in-session weighing. As clients typically overestimate their weight and any weight increases, weight avoidance becomes just as problematic as frequent weighing: There is no feedback to confirm or disconfirm fears of weight gain. Thus, in-session weighing is necessary to address both forms of unhelpful weight-related behavior" (p. 323-324).

Here the solution is to be weighed by someone else once per week. But note that the goal is to reduce overvaluation of weight. So what works best? The goal is clear. Each individual, in concert with her trusted team of advisors, must decide what works best for her at any given point and time.

As much as the non-diet and pro-attuned/intuitive/mindful/health at every size eating folks are in favor of ditching the scale ideally forever and the cognitive behavior therapy folks are in favor of weekly clinical weigh-ins, there have also been studies that support self-weighing as a positive thing. In a meta-analysis of 17 research studies that used self-weighing as a weight management strategy, (Yaguang, Klem, Sereika, Danford, Ewing, & Burke, 2015), found that regular self-weighing helped participants to lose or maintain their weight without the previously documented costs of negative psychological consequences. Researchers went as far as recommending daily self-weighing, which they note had been found to have a negative influence on psychological state and body satisfaction in earlier studies but more recent studies have found not to have such effects. It is hard to reconcile these self-weighing studies with those that reach almost the exact opposite conclusion (Schaefer & Magnuson, 2014). It seems that the question is one of mindset. If the goal is weight loss and weight loss alone, then probably self-monitoring of weight is going to be appropriate. But what if over-focus on weight is part of one's mental health diagnosis? If a person is in recovery from an eating disorder, then is it wise to weigh daily? Conventional wisdom says no, even cognitive behavioral therapy (Fursland, Bryne, Watson, Puma, Allen, & Bryne, 2012) does not encourage self-weighing, but instead recommends in-office weighing once per week. This is where the anti-obesity and the anti-eating disorder recommendations collide and each person has to come to her own conclusions.

For me, reading and learning more about the pitfalls of weight stigmatization from a scholarly in addition to a popular perspective has helped me to see that this is not just about me and a bunch of other diet suckers. This a whole culture, and I have both suffered from as well as participated in this culture. I can identify its harmful nature and refuse to participate. I can do more that refuse to participate, though – I can actively work against a weight focus in my own life and in the lives of those around me. I am pretty sure I will not be perfect at this. It's a personal issue and it's a political issue, and I am still a member of American society and am vulnerable just as others are vulnerable. But I'm ready.

My 30 day "no weigh" experiment journal (which took me 38 days)

After reading all of these research reports on the benefits of becoming more weight-neutral, I was finally convinced to experiment with not weighing myself. I had done this before but it had not "stuck," therefore I gave myself the goal of making it 30 days in a row without weighing myself and a commitment to accomplish that before I re-assessed, to see whether it was something I was willing to incorporate into my life on an ongoing basis. Below are excerpts from my journal.

Day 0. My weight has been shockingly consistent since my now-teenager was six months old. And yet, I still think about my weight way too much and check my weight when I go to the gym. I weighed myself at the gym this morning even though it really was not helpful for me to do so. In fact, it was counter-productive. I wish knowing my weight was more like other health data that I might receive, such as blood pressure or cholesterol, but each number on the scale has a special meaning to me, so even if I am not very surprised by the number on the scale, it affects me emotionally and distracts me from paying respectful and loving attention to the signals my body is sending me regarding what, when, and how much to eat would be best for my body.

I hereby pledge to myself that I will not weigh myself for thirty days.

The longest I know for sure that I have gone without weighing myself in recent years was the month we spent in Europe. I am sure I did not weigh myself for an entire 30 days. Otherwise, I weigh approximately once, sometimes twice a week. And every time I do it, I suspect that it is keeping me from truly being free from every aspect of my eating disorder. Self-weighing is just plain not helping me and I'm ready to let go.

Day 1. It's easy for me to get up and not weigh myself because I haven't been doing that lately (for a number of years). The day that I want to go to the gym at work is going to be the time that I will likely struggle with overcoming the habit of self-weighing. Hopefully by the time that day rolls around (next week?) I will have convinced myself that I really don't want to do it. Or maybe I will be motivated to keep my streak of non-self-weighing days. I do tend to rise to a challenge, so a little personal gold star every day isn't a bad idea. There has to be more benefit to me than merely not weighing. I want to feel more connected to my body, more in tune and able to respond to my body in a nurturing, effective, and loving way.

Today I am noticed that contrary to the way I have been eating lately, with five to six small meals or larger snacks throughout the day, I ate more concentrated meals. I started by eating breakfast as a small meal, but I was still hungry, so I had more, and it ended up being a substantial meal. I wasn't hungry until 5 hours and 15 minutes later, whereupon I had my medium sized lunch but then about a half hour after finishing lunch, I felt like eating a bit more, so I had a bit more and that rounded out a pretty filling meal which tided me over nicely (another 5 hours and 15 minutes!) until dinner. I know every day won't go the same, but it is a heck of a lot easier for me to eat three satisfying meals than to pack and tote snacks. I would love to fall into a three meal a day pattern, although I know my body gets to drive this process, not my mind.

Gold star for starting this challenge today :)

Day 2. My eating was appropriately responsive to my hunger and hunger patterns today. In fact, things went so well that after dinner, I had to fight with myself not to make and eat and entire batch of chocolate chip cookie dough. I was definitely looking for a ticket out, for an excuse to say, "actually, I'm not up to this," or better yet, "this doesn't work," and to find a more weight-focused approach to managing my food, one with an app and measurements and lots of that fun concrete stuff that I both rebel against and at the same time I find them hugely attractive. I was not hungry when I was contemplating the cookie dough thing and there were other pleasant ways for me to spend my time, so I washed the dishes, made a cup of herbal tea, and spent time with the kids and later, reading. I'm glad I'm keeping the journal because it definitely helped me to stay on track. I am doing a project and quitting on Day 2 isn't much of a project. I have a perverse pride that says "Catherine is not a quitter" and that also helped keep me going. No surprise that I've had trouble with this before, it's exhausting at times. But I also know from previous experience that there will be days, weeks even, when I'm feeling fine and weighing myself is not a big temptation. I also know from prior experience that acting out in some way that "gives me permission" to quit is not good for me in any way (as if I don't have permission to weigh myself!? For crying out loud – nobody but me cares about this, I could go and buy a bathroom scale and nobody would care!! This is about me trying to get better, fighting to hold on to the best of myself and not to sink back into maladaptive behaviors around food).

Gold star for not weighing myself!!

Day 3. Not tempted either to weigh myself or to binge. I ate breakfast at a restaurant. I get up so early and am hungry so early that other people's "normal" breakfast time of 8 am is hard for me, so I had something small when I got up at 5 am and then my second breakfast at 8. Not sure if that makes me a Hobbit or not, but I'm pretty sure they ate second breakfasts too! Dinner was a bit delayed due to unexpected traffic on the way home, but that worked out fine. I was definitely hungry when I finally got home. Getting home late also meant that I didn't have much time before Tae Kwon Do, but I didn't need much time, so it was fine.

Gold star for living my life and not being distracted by food or weight.

Day 4. No temptation to weigh myself today, no real opportunity either, which always makes it nice. Two food observations: I had two packets of high fiber oatmeal as a snack and a few hours later when I was hungry again, I kind of wanted two more packets but I also kind of didn't. I couldn't decide. So I waited a bit, about 15 minutes or so, and realized that I really was hungry but that more sweet stuff wouldn't really satisfy me. I had a pouch of tuna which wasn't screaming at me "eat me! I'm so tasty!" but did taste good and really held me over for a number of hours. I don't eat a low protein diet (or a high protein diet, for that matter) but I do sometimes forget how much staying power protein has. I think I might invest in

more protein-heavy snacks like nuts and cheese and protein bars, or maybe buy some packets of oatmeal that are labeled high protein instead of high fiber (when will someone sell high fiber, high protein, low sugar oatmeal instead of forcing me to choose?)

Gold star for taking care of me.

Day 5. I went to a killer two-hour Tae Kwon Do class last night and woke up at 4:15 am hungry, with a headache and no desire to sleep any more. I had a cup of tea and a bowl of cereal and a banana along with two ibuprofen and tried to relax even though I knew I wouldn't go back to sleep. Forty-five minutes later, my headache was gone. Phew. The rest of the day was reasonably uneventful. I did go to the gym with my kids and wasn't at all tempted by the scale there. I think it helped that I was with other people that I knew. I didn't tell them that I wasn't going to weigh myself or ask for their help, it just felt good that there were there and it kept me focused on other things besides the scale.

Gold star for something else to focus on besides my weight.

Day 6. I wish I hadn't bought protein bars when I went grocery shopping. For some reason, one protein bar is never enough for me. Two protein bars "hits the spot" but they leave the weirdest sickly sweet aftertaste in my mouth! As I spent $18.00 on two boxes, for a total of 8 protein bars, I am not going to throw them away, but I will experiment trying to figure out how to incorporate them into a larger snack or meal so that I'm not just eating protein bars, but can eke them out over a larger number of days. They are satisfying in the long run (I don't get hungry for at least 4 hours after eating them) but the mouth feel is really odd.

I had a clothing issue today. I wore a camisole bra instead of my regular underwire and it changed my whole shape and didn't feel good. I had a hard time separating the "not feeling good" from the "changed my whole shape" but I didn't like either of them, so it wasn't hard to decide to change as soon as I had the opportunity. I'm pretty sure I was the only one who noticed, but nonetheless it was a bit shocking to me how uncomfortable it felt to wear something new and how different it seemed to me that I looked (even though possibly nobody else thought I looked different). I have definitely been one of those women who wore the wrong bra size until I figured out how bras are actually sized online and getting good fitting bras really made a difference in how I feel in my clothing. Having clothes, and especially underclothes, that fit to my liking is really, really important, even if it's hard to separate out the "my inner experience of this clothing item" vs. "me looking in the mirror at myself and noting that my entire silhouette appears to have changed."

A gold star for me for showing up and doing the work.

Day 7. I wore a t-shirt and jeans today that I haven't worn for a while. I remember the t-shirt being a bit tight, but I thought the jeans were a bit looser before than they were today. Somehow the part of my body that felt bigger and exposed was my ribcage area. It felt uncomfortable and I felt self-conscious. I hate that. I like feeling good in my clothes and I don't like feeling self-conscious.

I've been reading more about Health at Every Size ® and find it pretty convincing and inspirational. I'm realizing that it's pretty simple – just focus on health and/or wellbeing instead of weight – and also that I love its simplicity. I am such an "easy 17-step process" kind of person, until I realize that I can don't need to live that way, and then I am hugely relieved. I remember when I wrote my story about coming out of eating disorder relapse (Gillespie, 2013), my big aha there was the powerful simplicity of awareness/mindfulness. If I was truly aware/mindful of what/when/how much I was eating, then I wasn't binge eating. Ta da. Combine that with a health/wellbeing focus and I've got a pretty powerful combo!

Cheers to simplicity.

Day 8. I distinctly remember probably 30 years ago (give or take 5 years, whatever), declaring myself "independent from my eating disorder." The idea was fine, but I didn't have any tools. I was totally in diet mentality and didn't realize that was a problem. I was trying to stop binge eating while still restricting. I was doomed to failure and I didn't even know it.

Here's what I wrote at in my journal at 8 am: I am realizing that the concept of a 30-day experiment in not weighing is setting me up for a "reveal" after two months that I'm not sure is a good thing. Maybe I would be better off to plan to never engage in self weighing again, and to have this first month be my pilot-experimental period (?) I'm just worried that I am still too weight focused by planning on a reassessment at the end of this experiment. I think it would be better for me to plan to have that reassessment without weighing myself. It feels better to write it, it's like I can breathe a sigh of relief. The judgment about this experiment and whether or not I am going to continue it is not going to be dependent on my weight. I will have a different set of questions: How do I feel physically? Am I eating well for my body? Am I taking good care of myself? Those are the kinds of questions I want to be able to entertain, not "did my weight change in any way?" because that question kind of defeats the whole purpose, doesn't it? Wow. I feel a lot better now!

How things can change by 8 pm: I was at the gym a couple of hours ago, alone in the room with the scale, and after about 2 seconds of inner struggle, slipped off my shoes and weighed myself. Argh. I'm up a bit from last time I weighed, I think. Not much, but enough to start questioning everything I'm doing. The cascade of thinking and eating did not end in disaster, but it definitely tilted in that direction. I basically thought "f-it," and "I need more structure around my food," which for me means a definite food plan, none of this intuitive eating hooey. I came home and ate a reasonable dinner, a bit more than I intended, but not bad. I was thinking about bingeing, and even went in search of the chocolate chips that last time I checked (last month?) were in the baking cabinet, but someone apparently ate them, and it definitely wasn't me. That gave me enough space to consider what the heck I was doing, so I left the room to start writing in this journal. This would have been Day 8 without weighing, only I actually only made it through 7 days because of my apparent inability to keep a promise to myself. And…now what? I honestly don't know. A big part of me wants the structure and social support of a food plan. Not a weight-loss diet, mind you, but some plan that would do the thinking for me around food, so I could just follow a bunch of rules and not think about it too much. Yet I also know that those kind of regimented plans, while great in the short run, really sets me up for binge eating. The temptation to binge today was really the temptation to go back to my old regimented ways. Because if I binge then I can use it as an excuse to tell myself, "see, I really can't be trusted on my own – I need more structure, more social support, I am not really recovered yet." Another part of me wants to kick that part of me in the teeth. Argh. I want guarantees, I want clarity. I want easy. I also want to be able to weigh myself if I feel like it. If I get to eat pistachio ice cream when I feel like it, then why can't I weigh myself when I feel like it too???

My star today is for not bingeing even though I am doubting and questioning and also for journaling through my issues and finally for being able to handle "I don't know" as an answer to the "what now?" question

Back at Day 1. As I review my journal, I notice that there were some body self-consciousness feelings coming up for me before my self-weighing yesterday. Is that a bigger problem than I make it out to be? A smaller problem? Is self-weighing really that big a deal anyways? Shouldn't I just be happy that I'm not binge eating? Yes, of course, I should be happy that I'm not binge eating – I want to give myself credit for that. At the same time, if I'm going for true full recovery then just not binge eating isn't enough. Argh. Sometimes I feel like I'm pushing myself too hard to be perfectly emotionally recovered and perfection isn't a good thing either, is it? So maybe I should just give myself a break. Whatever. Writing down my food today helped me feel better. It helped relieve my anxiety. Does that mean that I'm shooting myself in the foot by relieving my anxiety in short run and maintaining it in the long run? I honestly don't know. I have to take care of myself, and this feels like taking care of myself emotionally. Planning my food isn't such a bad thing, especially if it helps me to feel less obsessed, right? I do feel like I'm failing HAES® though, and intuitive eating, and mindful eating, and attuned eating. Maybe I'm just not cut out for any of it. Or, maybe I don't have to follow everyone else's recommendations. Maybe I can just do what works for me. But maybe that means that I'm actually shooting myself in the foot. Dear God, please help me find some clarity! At least I won't be able to weigh myself today, as it'll be a full one and I won't have time to go to the gym.

My solution today was to journal/plan/track my food. It helped me feel a bit more sane. Call it a safety behavior, or a maintenance factor, but it helped me get through the day without anxiety.

This is what I planned out right after I got up:

5 am. Up early to my alarm. Tea with soymilk, protein drink, apple.

8:30 am. Work breakfast. Eggs and toast, with butter, fruit cup, coffee.

Lunch. Pre-cooked veggie mix – onion, potato, Brussels sprouts, ½ tablespoon oil -- with cheese melted on top.

Afternoon snack. Cinnamon oatmeal and tea with soymilk.

Quick dinner. Salmon sandwich, mixed veggies.

It was helpful to come home and know that I had pre-decided what I would eat for dinner. I mixed my salmon with mustard and horseradish and put some of the veggies in the mix and had it on dark German bread, which is my favorite. I knew I would like it and I did. In addition to planning to have a quick dinner – I knew I would have only 45 minutes at home tonight before I had to leave again – I loved the feeling of having thought through what I planned to eat.

I get a gold star for perseverance today.

Back at Day 2. I think the whole concept of "never" really set me up for rebellion. The second I told myself that I would never weight myself again, there I was, weighing myself. The "one day at a time" approach that I learned in 12 step programs just makes me mad, because it's a manipulative way of saying never. Not today, and then tomorrow, not today either. Well, of course if I keep doing that day after day, it's the same as never. But I get tense around never. Not today and hopefully not tomorrow, but not never is much more my speed.

I did benefit from planning my food yesterday. In fact, it went so well that I decided to eat basically the same food today as I did yesterday, which went fine until after dinner I decided that I wanted some of my favorite pistachio ice cream. I ended up finishing the pint I had, which was probably less than a cup total, but it wasn't what I had planned and that both made me mad at myself for not sticking to my plan and mad at myself for thinking that planning my food would be a good idea. I feel like I have to learn the same darn lessons over and over again. I generally do well when I eat three meals a day with a mid-morning snack and a mid-afternoon snack and then and evening snack if I am hungry for it. But I have to do it mindfully because if I robotically eat by the clock in pre-determined amounts then I can either eat too much or not enough because I'm not paying attention to my body and that doesn't feel good. I noticed today and yesterday when I was eating what I had planned that I wasn't paying as much attention to my body while I was eating. Argh. Recovery is a lot of work! But I do think it's worth it because I feel more connected to my body. I can't guarantee that I'll never weigh myself again, but I will get back on the "no weigh" bandwagon and eat my meals and snacks within the boundaries of hunger and satiety. That I can do. But I can also complicate it and fall into that trap where I am hustling for my own worthiness. I am worthy no matter what I do or how I eat. Maybe I'll keep it simple and settle for trusting my own hunger.

Gold star for taking care of myself.

Back at Day 3. I can't believe how well today went in terms of my not being bothered by food, eating, my body or weight. I didn't do anything fancy, I just didn't focus much on any of it. I ate meals and snacks, but I didn't plan them out. I waited for my body to signal that it was time to eat, I chose foods I thought would satisfy me and opted for fairly healthful things (we had dinner at Wendy's and I had a chili, which to me is the most satisfying and healthful choice they have), and then I ate until I burped, which in a couple of cases was earlier than I would have expected. I had tomato barley soup as a bedtime snack (the chili was good, but I needed more before bed) and after I ate the soup, I thought maybe I would get some bread to soak up the remains of the soup, but I burped as I was getting the bread, so I put the bread back and called it a day. I let my body signals drive my eating.

"Stop focusing so much on food, eating, my body or weight" seems like pretty good advice for me to follow, but it also feels pretty vague. Did I focus on something else? Well, sure, I went to work and got stuff done and went to Tae Kwon Do class, and although I wasn't spectacularly "present" during my work day, I always find that I have to be very "present" (paying attention) during Tae Kwon Do, because if I don't give it my entire brain, I mess up. Definitely focus is a mental thing. Maybe my not focusing so much on food or body was really not thinking much about it. Maybe "don't focus so much on…" is the same as "don't think so much about …" I would love to get to a place where I say with breezy lightness, "oh, I just don't think about food or my body so much anymore," which is not to say never, but just not as much, not much at all, just enough to take care of myself and to meet my needs to take care of myself. I'm liking it! As I re-read my first paragraph, I did actually focus on my body, but I focused on my body's signals rather than using my planning brain. So really, I shifted my focus from "in my head" to "in my body" and although I definitely used my brain (I do realize that it's all connected), my focus was not so much on my thoughts as it was on my body's signals, but I also didn't anticipate and monitor them much – they are pretty clear and when they signaled, then I acted. Like going to the bathroom, maybe. I don't think about it, but when my body signals, then I respond appropriately.

Gold star for connecting with my hunger and satiety.

Back at Day 4. I tried on clothes today at one of my favorite clothing stores. I remember when, as an adult, I figured out that I take petite sizes. I had been wearing ill-fitting clothes for the better part of my adulthood and when I finally tried on a petite and it seemed made for me, I was amazed. This time, I went directly for the petite department. I also went directly for the 80% off sales, because who doesn't love a bargain? I was really more wanting to try on clothes than I was wanting to buy anything, so I was happy to leave without any purchases. I picked out some real doozies to try on. I'm not surprised they were 80% off. Too sheer, too big, too small, too much extra material in places where it wasn't needed, not enough material in key spots. It was really a comedy of errors. I was so glad to recognize that it was the clothes, not my body. Some of the clothes fit quite well whereas others did not, even though they all had the same sized label on them. Another win for me: how clothes fit depend on the brand, and if they don't fit it's not my fault!

Gold star for keeping my wits about me in the clothing store dressing room.

Back at Day 5. My meals were a bit chaotic today due to my schedule. I count this as a win. I trusted my hunger and had three small meals/large snacks before noon, but then at noon, when I had a chance to eat, I wasn't really hungry, so I waited, but then because I was engaged in other things, it turned out that I didn't get lunch until 2:30. A bit late, but whatever. Then I left the house again at 5 pm, planning on returning at about 8 pm. I packed a dinner for myself to eat during that time, but then completely forgot about it and left it in the refrigerator. Another win. I wasn't overly focused on the food and I actually forgot about it. I remembered though around 6 pm, when I started to get hungry. I decided that I would just wait until I got home and eat the dinner I had planned, but by 6:30 I was really ready for a meal, so I stopped at Wendy's and got my favorite large chili with crackers and that really hit the spot. After I got home, I had some yogurt before bed. I am really loving not focusing so much on my food, eating, body, or weight and although I will endeavor to remember to take my packed food out of the fridge in the future, it's really not that big of a deal if I forget it and I am so relieved to know that. When I was in my 12 step food program, that would have been a huge deal. I would have had to call my sponsor and let her make an alternative plan for me. I'm so glad to let my body be in charge of my eating, not another person.

Gold star for developing flexibility.

Back at Day 6. I had Cheerios for breakfast. That may not sound very impressive, but I used to have Cheerios for breakfast as a child sometimes, and when I first was attempting to eat according to hunger and satisfaction as part of my first foray into full recovery in the 1990's, I have a clear memory of wanting to eat "normally," which at the time I defined as "like I did as a child," which is not a bad definition really, because I did eat in a pretty normal way as a child. The problem with my first attempt is that I was still restricting myself to three meals per day, and although a bowl of Cheerios can really hit the spot, it does not last all that long in my stomach. So a few hours after eating my "normal" breakfast, I was hungry and completely freaked out. I stayed hungry for hours before lunch. I was doing the best I knew how. This morning, I had a small bowl of Cheerios for breakfast with a cup of tea, knowing full well that I would be likely to eat again before lunch. And that's exactly what I did. About three hours after the cereal, I got hungry and had a piece of peanut butter toast and half a frozen banana. That held me over till lunch. What I realize that I'm doing differently now as compared to the '90s is that I am trusting my body's signals more. One bowl of cereal truly is satisfying to me first thing in the morning. It's not like I need to eat a larger (first) breakfast, but I need either a second breakfast or a midmorning snack or whatever one calls it. Most likely as child I had midmorning snacks as well, I just somehow conveniently forgot about that.

Gold star for being willing to learn and for keeping at it until I get it.

Back at Day 7. I realize what a low maintenance eater I am. It's not that I don't cook, it's just that I tend to rely mostly on easy-to-prepare foods. Lately I've been eating a lot of yogurt, cottage cheese, steam-in-the-bag vegetables, apples, frozen bananas, peanut butter sandwiches, tuna and salmon in a pouch, boiled eggs and toast, cereal, etc. Healthy fast foods, I guess. I'm not a big one for going out to eat unless necessary, and even then, I'm the one who goes to Wendy's and orders the chili. I cook chicken and vegetables and so forth but I don't cook beautiful meals or prepare things with care. I'm more of a functional food prep person. I have no desire to make fancy sauces or to combine ingredients for some beautiful effect. I am definitely not a foodie. I have my preferences, and I enjoy healthy, simple food. I have no desire to be fancier than I am.

Gold star for accepting myself for who I am.

Back at Day 8. My eating felt a little chaotic today, but I feel like I'm learning the difference between letting my body dictate times/amounts of food and true chaos. In other words, I think I need to rename or reframe my idea of chaotic eating, which I tend to think is anything other than eating a meal or snack every three hours, and recognize that the pattern I had yesterday was perfectly acceptable because it was responsive to my body's signals of hunger and satisfaction. I had chicken for a snack around 4 pm, and would have liked to have eaten more but that's all I had packed. What I really wanted was a soft serve ice cream (because that goes so well with chicken?!), so I got one after work at 4:30 pm. I had an appointment that went till about 6:30 pm and got home around 7 pm, at which time I wanted something else but not much. I had little bit of yogurt and a piece of bread and a half a frozen banana. The whole snack, snack, snack thing felt uncomfortable to me. But uncomfortable isn't wrong or bad. Why is it so hard for me to get that?

Gold star for letting my body take the lead in my eating and not reacting to my anxiety.

Day 9. I feel like I'm getting the hang of this. I haven't weighed myself in more than a week, but then again I haven't been to the gym since then either. I have been going to Tae Kwon Do classes, so it's not like I haven't been getting any exercise at all, but I'm feeling quite free without the gym at the same time as I'm not sure that I want to avoid it forever. I'm not really avoiding it right now – I'm getting enough physical activity without it. But what about when I want to go? Should I avoid it because the scale is too tempting? Not sure exactly how to deal with this, but I want to note to myself that the past few days have really felt good in terms of taking care of myself without obsessing about it, not thinking much about food other than to make sure that I have reasonably healthful options for myself when I'm likely to get hungry. Yesterday I had a donut and coffee with colleagues in a spontaneous kind of way, and it felt good and right and the way I want to be living my life. I feel recovered is how I feel, and I like it. I'm not sure how much of that is the not weighing part, but my suspicion is that not weighing contributes heavily to my not worrying about food, eating, body or weight. AND I feel good in my body – I'm eating moderately and so-called normally. It's a miracle, really, but one that I've experienced before. It's just always come to an abrupt end before only I could never really figure out why. Could it be as simple as "I weighed myself and that's what went wrong"? Seems unlikely, but it could be "I was thinking too much

about food, eating, body or weight" and that's what went wrong, and if I hadn't weighed myself in the past, then maybe I could have avoided all the too much thinking. Hmmm…not weighing myself today, that's for sure. Not going to the gym any time soon. This is definitely a topic to consider later.

Gold star for eating normally and staying away from the scale.

Day 10. I've been pretty energized by work lately and today I kind of hit a wall. I am realizing that just "suiting up and showing up," as people in my 12-step program used to say, is often more than half the battle. It's not that I don't want to get out of bed or get dressed or go to work, it's just that once I get there, I have plenty to do and worrying about it or trying to figure it out in advance is less effective than I would prefer. It felt like an effort to show up today, but I did it. And I didn't worry about my food, eating, body or weight while I was doing that.

Gold star for showing up.

Day 11. Woke up feeling kind of sick this morning, not quite sure why. Gassy and headachy. I hate that feeling because I don't really want to eat at the same time as I am actually hungry, but food doesn't sound all that good. I partly discovered this by having eggs and toast for breakfast, which is probably the most acid-reflux inducing meal I could have concocted and then I was consumed by a headache. Thank God for modern medicines is all I can say. It didn't take me long to feel better.

Gold star for taking care of myself.

Day 12. I was feeling kind of sorry for myself yesterday. I didn't feel great and it felt like there were too many commitments that I had to fulfill and although I had enough time to meet all my obligations, I didn't have enough time for me, to read novels or take baths or whatever. Not to denigrate time to read novels or take baths, but for the next three weeks, I am basically stuck with a fair number of commitments. What turned around my thinking was that my husband and I visited a friend who is in a nursing home. She was in remarkably good spirits despite her terminal illness. We had a lovely visit. As we left I realized that me complaining about all the busyness in my life is only going to make it worse. I am committed to following through on each of my commitments, so as long as I am not willing to let anything go, I am only making myself miserable by feeling sorry for myself. There is a cost to every decision, and living with the cost of my decisions is something that I would rather do without complaining than with complaining. Yet it took at least two days of feeling completely victimized by my schedule and a visit to a terminally ill friend for me to recognize this! Eek! A bit slow on the uptake, perhaps, but I do get things eventually! I went to bed an hour early last night in hopes to shaking off whatever is affecting me physically. I also found some nasal spray to help with my annoying post nasal drip, which may be viral or may be some kind of low-level allergy symptom. I think both of those things helped a bit. But switching my attitude to one of surrender/acceptance/letting go of the complaining will be what I carry with me today. Accepting that life is busier than I had expected, that I've taken on a bit more than I realized, that I will get some relief in a few weeks, and that there are some things I can do to put breaks in for myself so that I feel better taken care of by me, are all contributing to me feeling like I can handle tomorrow.

Gold star for walking the walk.

Day 13. I went to the gym today for the first time in 12 days and somewhat surprisingly I really did not want to weigh myself. This is different from

experiences I've had in the past, where I wasn't tempted to weigh myself. This time, not only was I not tempted, but I was highly aware of the anguish it caused me last time I weighed myself at the gym and I didn't want to repeat that anguish. I noted the scale but was almost repulsed by it. I know this won't necessarily always be my reaction, but it was a nice one to have so that I didn't have to fight the temptation and then either give in and start back on Day 1, or just fight with myself because I really hate that inner struggle, even when my wiser-self wins.

Gold star for getting some exercise (it felt good) and for embracing scale-repulsion.

Day 14. I saw myself in the mirror at Tae Kwon Do and I was slightly distressed. I hate that how I look doesn't completely match how I experience my body. I also hate that what bra I wear really affects my silhouette. I saw myself in the mirror and thought, oh, I look that way because of the bra that I'm wearing, but then when I got home and got undressed, I wasn't wearing that bra, so then I didn't know what to think. Maybe the point is that the appearance of my silhouette is immaterial. What bra I wear is not important. I am the same person inside no matter what my appearance. But there is still that little shock of recognition, "oh, that's me in the mirror, and that's not how I thought I looked." I remember the same thing happening a few times as a kid when I rode the school bus – I would see my image reflected in the school bus windows and think "is that me?" There was this moment of panic during which time I wasn't quite sure if it was my reflection or someone else's. Then I would realize it was me, and be a little weirded out by it. Somehow I never quite look the same as I feel. Maybe that's normal. Maybe it doesn't matter if it's normal. It's not that big of an issue, but it does come up every once in a while and it makes me uncomfortable and it makes me self-conscious about my body, so in that respect, it is important to me. It's also important to me with regard to me being comfortable not weighing myself. That urge to weigh myself sometimes starts with "my body is not okay" and when I

catch a glimpse of myself in the mirror, I am tempted to think "my body is not okay," when in fact of course my body is just fine and really what is bothering me is that how I experience my own body is not the same as the way it appears in a mirror. It helps me to remember how my dog deals with mirrors – mostly he doesn't recognize a dog in the mirror, certainly he doesn't see himself in there, because when sometimes he does see a dog in the mirror, he starts barking hysterically. At least I'm not as bad as my dog with regard to mirrors!!

Gold star for injecting some humor into my weirdness.

Day 15. I felt so run down late this afternoon before dinner. I had a busy but not very active day and ate well, mostly food that I had packed. Dinner revived me in a way that it doesn't usually do. Maybe I don't usually need such reviving, but I felt so much better after eating a solid dinner that I was amazed. I had imagined myself asleep two hours before normal, but I didn't need that and went to bed at my normal time.

Gold star for remembering that food is truly nourishing.

Day 16. I'm feeling good in my body, good about the amount of food that I'm eating and the clothes that I'm wearing. I could be getting more walking in during the day. I sit a lot during the day, but my activity in the evenings feels right to me. I'm less run down than I was. I feel settled. I am not tempted by the scale like I was either. Things are going well. The scale issue is still there, though. I'm just over half way to my goal of 30 days without weighing myself and I'm starting to second guess whether this is something I want to continue beyond 30 days. I remember when we came back from our European trip and I immediately weighed myself and the freedom I had felt to eat in accordance with my internal signals just evaporated. My eating wasn't perfect during that trip, but it was much more

attuned to my body's signals than it was in the month before the trip. These past couple of weeks have been very attuned. I am eating six times a day most days, snacks or small meals, many of which I've packed at home and brought with me to work or wherever it is that I'm going. Sometimes I've eaten out. I've had sweets in moderation and haven't over-eaten or under-eaten. It's a miracle, really, especially compared to a few years ago when I was holding so tightly to my eating rules. It feels so much more natural. Why would I want to wreck it by weighing myself? I'm still letting go of the notion that what I weigh is truly important. I'm working on that.

Day 17. I've been feeling pretty darned good lately. I suddenly realized today that it feels like a long time since I had an urge to binge. Two weeks isn't really a long time in the grand scheme of things, but in terms of not being plagued with urges to binge or to weigh myself, it's a miraculous eternity. I do know from previous experience that it pays to maintain my beginner's mind. Beginner's mind is a Zen term meaning that even long-time practitioners never really "get it," and nobody graduates, everyone is always learning. For me, a good beginner's mind attitude is something like: every day is a new day in which I need to be present and available. When I start thinking "I've got it," which essentially translates to "I'm done learning," some part of me says, "Whoa, Nelly!" and that urge to prove myself wrong via self-destructive means rears its ugly head and there I am, right back where I thought I had escaped from. Maybe "stay humble" is another way of looking at it. I think this is the profound truth that keeps people wanting to say that they are "in recovery" instead of "recovered." But to me "recovered" is different from "graduated" and also different from "done learning." I have a lifetime of learning ahead of me. Hopefully I will learn something every day from now until the time that I die. That doesn't mean I can't be recovered, though. I can put the eating disorder completely behind me but I still have to eat moderately and reasonably healthfully and move my body and get enough sleep and show up to work and spend time with family and do all the things that I am privileged to do in my life, many of which are things that people who never had an eating disorder also do. Yes, humility is key. I have not beaten my eating disorder into submission, I have shifted my focus away from food, eating, body and weight and am opening up to other things to focus on, at the same time as I am engaging in normal, healthy self-care around the things that I used to over-focus on. Sounds pretty good to me! I almost can't believe I'm here. I've been here before, and have had the huge frustration of backsliding and never quite knowing what hit me. Hopefully my journal will help me to clarify what's going on with me so that I can avoid backsliding or at least be able to identify what's going on and catch it as early as possible.

Gold star for recognizing my need for humility without a humbling experience.

Day 18. It occurs to me today that I have been very present in the here-and-now lately. Not escaping reality, not checking out. No matter how I've been feeling every day, I've been acknowledging it and walking through it, good, bad or ugly. This is a huge accomplishment and I want to acknowledge to myself that I am not running or hiding from anything. I also want to note for later reference that although it is not always an enormous challenge to stay present, it is the challenge, or perhaps more accurately, my challenge. As long as I am staying present and dealing with whatever comes up, I am not avoiding, ignoring or escaping from my reality. And it's not just the "things" or situations in my life, it's also very much my experience of my body. That's what it's hard for me to stay present to. The discomfort I sometimes feel when I see myself in the mirror, staying aware of the changes in my experience of hunger and satiety – that's the stuff that I have a hard time staying present with. I remember when I first tried to come off the food plan that I had been following for over seven years, it felt almost impossibly hard to stay present. I was so used to following the rules of the food plan that I had down pat, but being open to the possibility of being more hungry one day than another felt beyond my abilities. I was able to stay present and aware for a while, but really,

honestly and truly, each time I binged it was an admission of failure as well as permission to quit trying. I was saying to myself "I give up – it's too hard to stay present – I want someone else to do this for me, to tell me what to do." I want to have compassion for myself during that time. I was doing the best I could. And I didn't fully understand the nature of my struggle. Only in hindsight can I see the nature and enormity of the task I had undertaken. I also want to have compassion for my current struggle, which isn't constant or even daily, but sometimes it is still hard to stay present, and I think if I can see my struggle as that, "it's hard to stay present," instead of "it's hard not to binge," that will make it easier to successfully navigate being present as much as possible.

Gold star for being and staying present.

Day 19. I am not feeling the pull to weigh myself. I am also not in the situation where a scale is available to me because of my schedule and possibly the two go hand in hand. On the occasions where I have had access to a scale, I have imagined acrid smoke emanating from it. It stands there like an innocent piece of machinery, but really it has an evil influence on me and I want to remember that there is good reason for me to stay away from it. The next thing for me to tackle is calorie counting. I have not restricted my calories to an unreasonable level lately, but for many years, I have estimated the number of calories that I have eaten each day and there is really no good reason for this. The Ayurvedic system of attending to my burps is really more effective than the calorie system. For the first time the other day in weeks, I purposely continued to eat after I had my first burp, but for the most part, I am stopping eating right at the first burp. I much prefer to be connected to my body vs. calculating in my mind how much I should/could/will eat. Really the calorie counting is pointless. If I eat a meal of a certain calorie count and am still hungry, I always eat more. My calorie counting reminds me of what I learned in Weight Watchers, which was the idea that although each person has a certain target number of points to each every day, nobody is perfect, so even if a

person eats more (even if a person eats 10 times more) than their allotted points for the day, it's best to count each point, record them, and move on. At first blush, that approach seems reasonable. Of course nobody is perfect. And of course we should all be honest about what we are eating or not eating. But calculating the number of points or calories in a binge after the fact doesn't make it not a binge. I prefer the body awareness approach, where I let my body lead my eating. I can use my brain and eat vegetables and so forth but mostly for me my struggle is less about food quality and more about food amounts, about making sure that I don't under-eat, that I eat to satisfaction, and that I honor my satisfaction signal even if comes before the food on my plate is finished, and even if I have to get a bit more to eat before the burp comes. Eating the right amount of food for my body is entirely separate from counting calories. I am going to practice not counting calories but instead listening more attentively to my bodily signals.

Gold star for making progress.

Day 20. Not counting calories was a great success. I felt much freer. I felt like I was working more closely with my body – we were more like a team and less like enemies. In order to avoid being able to calculate calories, I did not use pre-packaged or measured amounts. When I had an English muffin with peanut butter, I stuck the knife in the peanut butter and whatever stuck on the knife went on my English muffin. Maybe it was a tablespoon, maybe more. It was a reasonable amount. It seems ridiculous that this was a big deal for me, but it was. Trusting that it doesn't really matter how much peanut butter I am consuming and not having that be triggering for me is leaps and bounds ahead of where I have been in the past.

Gold star for taking risks.

Day 21. Not counting calories is not hard most of the time, but when I feel a pull toward it, it's like watching a slow-motion horror movie of myself. I think, "eek, I've eaten too much!" and my not-completely-automatic response is to try to calm myself down by adding up the calories that I've consumed. This is not restrictive calorie counting as much as it is anti-anxiety calorie counting. I might as well start counting clouds in the sky or freckles on my hand. It really is pointless. Actually, it isn't pointless. It reduces my anxiety about possibly having eaten too much because as long as I'm not bingeing, whatever I've consumed is within the realm of reasonable. But, as I have learned, reducing my anxiety in the short term only serves to maintain my eating disorder in the long term. What I should be spending time on is critically questioning the "eek, I've eaten too much!" concern. What's that all about? Fear of gaining weight. Yes, but more so I fear that my body isn't trustworthy. I don't particularly want to gain weight but really my fear/concern centers around the (FALSE!) belief that my body isn't trustworthy. I've come by this fear honestly and held it for many years, but it's time for it to go. My body is completely trustworthy. I really do know this to be true. But I forget, and I operate with these knee-jerk reactions that I don't even question. I think "eek!" and forget that I'm supposed to question what's behind the anxiety instead of trying to calm myself down. Phew, this is exhausting. But it's good. I'm moving forward.

Gold star for moving forward.

Day 22. About an hour after breakfast this morning, I had a desire for a little bit of chocolate. I know from vast experience of denying cravings that fighting this desire is likely to backfire. I got a small amount of chocolate and ate it. Three more small amounts of chocolate later, I felt satisfied. This was completely unplanned

and not something I necessarily wanted to happen, but I feel really good about it because first of all, I had chocolate in the house for times like this, second of all I let myself have it when I wanted it and third of all, I let myself have enough to be satisfied. I have to admit that after the second small amount of chocolate, that little voice popped up that says, "Oh, Catherine, look at you go, you can't handle this, you don't know what you are doing, you're going to binge, you are going to need to go back on a strict food plan," and in the past I would have paid attention to that voice and I would have binged and that voice would have ruled the day. But today I told myself, "I can eat chocolate all day long if I want," and "I am going to eat this slowly and really enjoy it," and "I am going to eat chocolate until I'm satisfied," and "no matter how much I eat now, I can have chocolate later today or tomorrow whenever I want it." And it was that voice, the voice of recovery or wisdom or whatever it is that I should name that nurturing and true voice that contributed to me being able to eat a reasonably moderate amount of the food that I was craving and be done with it and go on to be engaged in my day and not distracted by food, eating, my body, or my weight.

Gold star for listening to my voice of recovery/wisdom.

Day 23. I'm just about a week out from finishing my 30-day challenge and I think I have a lot of evidence that I should continue not weighing myself, but I also have a pull to do so. And it's a definitely anxiety-reduction pull. I know from how I feel in my body, how I am sleeping, and how my clothes fit that I weigh basically the same as I did 23 days ago, but there is that part of me that wants to verify this with a scale. At the same time, I know that in the past when I've weighed myself after a significant time of not weighing myself, it's not had a positive effect: The scale serves as a wedge between my mind and my body. I'm working so hard to stay connected and it is an almost automatic disconnect. It doesn't serve me or my goals. Even though I know this, I still doubt or am tempted, or whatever that niggling is in my brain.

If I make the decision to continue to stay away from the scale, I know there will be challenges but I also know I can handle them if I stay convinced of my reasoning. I know from many years of living with myself that it is far easier to "just say no" than it is to say "every once in a while." I've tried weighing myself "every once in a while," that has turned into "multiple times per day" in short order. Argh. I really wish I didn't have to deal with this, but this is who I am and I'm glad I'm not pretending to be someone I'm not.

Gold star for accepting the issues I have and dealing with them head on.

Day 24. Another reason for me to continue to stay away from the scale is that if I don't know my weight, I can't use my weight to define me. Each number on the scale somehow symbolically represents a different me. I've been up and down the scale, although surprisingly steady within a 10-pound range for 15 years or so, and still, even slight differences in my weight are way too meaningful to me. Other numbers that are used to measure my health (cholesterol, fasting glucose levels, blood pressure) are known to me, but they don't define me. Mostly these numbers are in the healthy range (my cholesterol has crept up a bit over the ideal line in the past few years, but my doctor doesn't seem concerned) so that could be a reason why they don't define me. But my weight is in the healthy range too. My attachment to the number on the scale goes way beyond a reassurance that I'm still healthy, if that were even a reliable marker, which I know that it is not. I would definitely notice if I gained or lost 10 pounds. I might not know the exact amount, but most of my clothes wouldn't fit any more. No, I've used my weight as a marker of health/recovery/social acceptability and I've monitored it much too closely. It's time for me to exercise some of the mindfulness that Kristin Neff talks about in her self-compassion work regarding my weight -- not to identify so closely with it, not to let it define me. Defining myself by my weight or by my appearance is not an enduring proposition. If I'm lucky, I'll grow old and my hair will go completely

white and my skin will change and most everything about my appearance will change. I don't know if my weight will change, but if it does, so what? I suppose if I make it to my 90's I might weigh less than I do now as a result of lost muscle mass. Or maybe I'll weigh more. Who cares? If I can live independently and remember who I am and who other people are, I'll be happy. Or maybe I won't be able to live independently – I could still be happy with that. As long as I'm doing the best I can to take care of the body I have at any weight and at every age, then what am I worrying about?

Gold star for thinking things through.

Day 25. I realize that every day for the past few days I've been trying to convince myself that staying away from the scale is important for me to commit to. What I realize is that I haven't yet committed to it. I'm giving myself till the end of my 30 days, but I'm considering my options. Even if I make the commitment, I can always change my mind later, but after I decide, hopefully I won't be dithering so much. What I'm thinking about today is how much full eating disorder recovery is a choice. I could live in partial recovery for the rest of my life if I chose. At least I have the choice! Not everyone is even aware that full recovery is possible. I really do completely believe that it's possible, but I am also quite aware that there are things I have to do (and not do) and attitudes I need to adopt if I am going to stay in full recovery and keep getting father and father away from the behaviors, thoughts, and feelings associated with the disorder. As much as it pains me to admit it, I can't weigh myself and then not focus on it. If I want to take my blood pressure when I pass by the pharmacy section at a big box store, I can probably do that without over-focusing on my blood pressure. I've never used my blood pressure as a badge of honor or as a personal goal in my life. I'm glad that I don't have high blood pressure, but that's about it. If there were a scale at every big box store like there used to be in fancy banks when I was a child, I could avoid them. But if I didn't avoid them, then I would re-activate that obsession each time I

learned about my weight. There used to be scales at malls and when a person passed by them, they would beckon in a woman's voice, "have you checked your weight today?" and I would think, "whatever makes you think I would want to do that wearing these heavy clothes?" but possibly others were tempted. I think today I am recognizing my need to surrender to the reality that if I want to get better and stay better, I need to stay away from the scale. The fact that I have to debate with myself for weeks about it is probably indication enough that it's a bigger issue for me that I want it to be.

Day 26. I had a bit of a meltdown after trying on dresses at home that I bought on a whim. I hardly ever buy anything on a whim but these were on super sale and seemed like such a good deal that I didn't want to pass up on the opportunity. I didn't even bother to try them on in the store, which was either my first or my second error. When I tried them on at home, I made the further mistake of asking for input from my family members. The dress that fit well got mixed reviews from my family; the one that didn't fit so well got better reviews. This put me in tug of war with myself, debating what I should do. I was much more upset by this than I felt like I should have been. In the end, I decided that it would be easier to just return both of them. This really shouldn't have been that big of a deal but it took me a good hour to try to figure out what was going on and why I was so upset. Trying on clothes and getting others' opinions before purchasing an item of clothing is something that I have done before many times and am quite comfortable with. When I am still in the store, I am really looking for an unvarnished opinion to help me decide whether or not to buy an item. When I modeled my purchases at home yesterday, I wasn't really looking for unvarnished opinions, but I got them, and then I wasn't sure what to do with them. I don't generally dress to please others, but I got such positive feedback about the one that didn't fit well and such a lukewarm reception for the one that did fit well, that I started to question myself. Self-doubt is a real bugger. If I had been sure, then I

wouldn't have been bothered so much. Now I am kicking myself for buying anything, even a super sale item, before trying it on and assessing it myself prior to asking anyone else's input. I finally figured out that what upset me was that I hadn't figured out my own opinion first and I was relying too much on my family members' gut reactions. If I had known my own mind first then I would have been in a better position to consider their input. As it was, I was sort of blindsided and then I got upset as a result but I didn't even know what I was upset about.

Gold star for taking the time to figure out what was bothering me.

Day 27. I think I've convinced myself that I want to continue to stay away from the scale. Now I want to consider what will happen if (1) I am strongly tempted to weigh myself or (2) if I actually weigh myself. I know from experience that fighting temptation is a losing battle. But temptation can fade without being fulfilled – in fact, it really can only fade if it is not fulfilled, if the temptation is something like this, something that can't really be satisfied. What I will endeavor to remind myself if I am strongly tempted to weigh myself is that for me, self-weighing is a safety or maintaining behavior and what's likely behind the temptation is some kind of anxiety that if I can address, or even possibly merely acknowledge, then I have a hope of the temptation fading. Regarding (2), if I actually weigh myself, or, I suppose, if I go to the doctor and learn my weight, I will endeavor to not over-identify with my weight the way I have in the past. It's a number, like my cholesterol or my blood pressure. It tells a part of story of my body, but certainly not the entire story. Realistically based on a lifetime of weighing myself too frequently, I know my weight within a five or ten-pound range because my clothes won't fit in the same way if I gain or lose more than ten pounds. I really don't need the scale to alert me to large weight changes. And small weight changes really don't matter and are more likely to cause me grief than to help me. Also, I will spend some time reviewing what happened before I weighed myself (Was something bothering me? What was going on?).

On a slightly different topic, something I need to process, is a feeling of perfectionism that I've been experiencing lately. I've entered into one of my decluttering phases and this is fine for the most part, but I can get really obsessive about it and the feeling of pushing myself to get it all done, to get some decluttering done every day no matter what, really doesn't feel good. I do have a couple of drawers that I'd like to clean out and I have cleaned out a few other areas of the house, but for my sustained mental health, I need to not engage in decluttering every single day. Maybe every other day or once every weekend or something like that. I get so driven that I exhaust myself. I need to take it easy. When I started in 12-step programs I was bowled over by the slogan, "easy does it," and even bought a bumper sticker for my car with the saying on it. In the years leading up to me starting in a 12-step program, I didn't have a single day where I lived the slogan "easy does it." I was amazed and relieved to be given permission (encouragement, even) to do so. Mostly I have incorporated "easy does it" into my life, but at times, the perfectionism or driven-ness or obsession or compulsion or whatever label describes that horrible feeling of need to do more, be more, keep going, etc. overtakes me and it doesn't feel good any more. Today I will practice "easy does it" and not engage in any decluttering, although I do want to get back to it, possibly tomorrow, possibly over the weekend.

Gold star for thinking things through.

Day 28. If I have a personal slogan, sometimes I think it should be "every day a new emotion." Today's emotion is not exactly depression, but something more akin to low level grief. I experience it as a combination of sadness and lack of purpose. It's not front-and-center in my daily interactions, but more at the edges of my consciousness. I think it's directly related to the fact that I seem pretty darn close to resolving this self-weighing thing on the side of "just skip it, Catherine." Ok, I can reason with myself and agree that this is truly the best thing for me to do. But what will I work toward, worry about and identify with instead? There are

plenty of alternative answers in my life – work goals, Tae Kwon Do goals and tests, projects at home including sewing projects and more decluttering. But I don't want to pretend that it isn't a big deal to set aside all the angst that I've had about my weight and to feel a void as a result. It's natural. It's really sad to think that I've devoted so many years to goals around my weight, even as my weight has stayed amazingly constant in the past 15 years of so, and the energy that I've devoted to that could have been directed elsewhere. But now that I am finally letting go of that misdirected energy, there is definitely a letdown, which, for today, I am willing to let be.

Gold star for accepting my many emotions.

Day 29. I've been thinking about the slogan that I wrote for myself yesterday and although it's still true, I'm not sure I want to take it on as a slogan. Instead, I hereby adopt, "it's not always easy, but it's worth it!" That has been so true in my life. Everything that I've done that's been worth it has been hard at times. Nothing seems to come easily all the time. Marriage, kids, career, recovery, becoming a black belt. All of these have involved so much effort and at times some frustration, but all of them have been worth it. I'm glad I've stuck with things when I wanted to quit, because I've wanted to quit all of those endeavors at various points but I didn't and I'm so glad I've stuck with all of them.

Gold star for recognizing that things aren't always easy, but they are definitely worth it.

Day 30. I knew I'd get to Day 30 eventually, but I wasn't expecting to feel as excited as I do right now. I feel like I am about to embark on a new and exciting adventure. I don't feel particularly scared, but I do anticipate that I will encounter the unexpected, and that the unexpected will be part of the adventure itself. How

did I get such a positive attitude? I certainly didn't have this when I started, 38 days ago. Looking back at my journal, I would say that I felt hopeful and determined. Those are perfectly acceptable feelings, but this anticipatory excitement feels a lot better. I think I am so positive because I've had good experiences. It really hasn't been that hard to avoid the scale, but my ability to do so has come from my willingness to work through my feelings on a variety of food- and body-related topics and to not let those topics get to me so that I felt like I needed to weigh myself to get relief from my anxiety about food- or body-related concerns. My plan is to continue to stay away from the scale, except at the doctor's office (which I visit once or twice a year). I think I'll just go with my mantra from yesterday: "It's not easy, but it's worth it!"

Gold star for embracing the excitement!

Conclusion. It's been a little over five weeks. I weighed myself on Day 8 and started over again, so to be exact, it's been 38 days. I've been getting up every day and living my life. It's not particularly hard to not weigh myself, but it does require attention to what's going on with me at an enhance level because I don't have this maintenance/safety behavior to turn to. I am going to continue to stay away from the scale. In case I need reminding of what I journaled about during these past 38 days, here's my summary:

1. I eat more responsively to my body's signals when I stay away from the scale.

2. I don't want my weight (or body shape or eating choices) to define me. Staying away from the scale helps me to not identify with my weight.

3. Weighing myself is a maintaining behavior for my eating disorder. Weighing myself reduces my anxiety in the short run but serves to maintain it in the long run. Only by continuing to stay away from the scale can I walk through the anxiety and fully let go of my eating disorder.

4. Full eating disorder recovery is a choice, and I surrender to the truth that staying away from the scale is part of what I need to do to make the choice to proceed in my recovery.

When I let go of any maintaining behavior, I open myself up new possibilities but I also experience a void. It's not always going to be easy,

CHAPTER 7
Start thinking about other aspects of life besides food, eating, body, and weight

Personality and Self Care

Self-care is not selfish at all. If I do not engage in self-care, I am not much good to myself or anyone around me. I get short with people and frustrated with myself. When I take good care of myself, or even when I merely acknowledge that I am worthy of self-care, I feel better – stronger, more patient, more able to focus. The thing about personality and self-care is that what is self-care for others is practically torture for me, and possibly vice versa. The idea of going to a party to relax is like some kind of unknown foreign language to me. Parties are stressful! Reading a novel? Now that is relaxing to me! I know and trust this about myself. And I know and trust both that I am not alone and that not everybody is exactly like me.

Psychological personality is an entire area of study. Personality can be categorized in many ways, including probably the most well-known way, the Myers-Briggs Type Indicator or MBTI®. A popular understanding of personality extends well beyond enduring individual preferences to learned or adaptive qualities that may change over time. I remember somebody once commenting about a high schooler that she knew had begun to restrict her food, "she'll never develop an eating disorder – she doesn't have the self-discipline." People who have eating disorders may be perceived as having self-discipline, but many do not necessarily experience themselves that way. Or they may identify themselves as self-disciplined in some areas of their lives, but report that around food, they have less self-discipline. It's clearly complicated, and where personality fits into it is also complicated.

There are some personal characteristics that people who have recovered from eating disorders still have, even 10 years later. In a study of 17 people who had been in recovery -- both physical and psychological -- from anorexia for 10 years, demonstrated aspects of "the anorexic personality" including more depression, more anxiety, and more obsessive-compulsiveness than matched controls. (Holtkamp, Muller, Heussen, Remschmidt & Herpertz-Dahlmann, 2005, p. 106). Researchers concluded that "our results support the hypothesis that a higher degree of depressive, anxious, and obsessive-compulsive features may be personality traits in subjects with former adolescent anorexia nervosa" (p. 108). It is not known from this study whether the participants were anxious, depressed, and/or obsessive-compulsive prior to developing anorexia. It's a bit of a chicken and egg situation. Did these characteristics contribute to the development of anorexia? Did they develop as a result of anorexia? We do not know. Also, it is a fair question to ask whether these characteristics are indeed personality traits. Anxiety, depression, and obsessive-compulsiveness are usually seen as diagnoses, not as personality traits. What we do know from this study is that 17 of the original group of 39 people who were treated for anorexia in their teens in an inpatient setting were recovered enough to be included in a study 10 years later. And even though they were physically and psychologically recovered, they tested as psychologically different from age-matched, non-eating disordered controls.

Lest one think that the persistence of traits after recovery are only limited to those diagnosed with anorexia, 11 women who had experienced no physical symptoms of bulimia for one year had similar results, showing elevated levels of body dissatisfaction, drive for thinness, perfectionism, ineffectiveness, social insecurity, depression, anxiety and stress when compared to 15 non-eating disorder age-matched controls (Stein, Kaye, Matsunaga, Orbach, Har-Even, Frank, McConaha & Rao, 2002). The chicken and egg problem persists. Researchers commented, "It is not known whether the persistence of core eating disorder concerns and related personality traits following recovery from bulimia is a premorbid vulnerability for, or as a consequence of, having an eating disorder" (p.

228) although they added that "Perfectionism has been implicated as a risk factor for anorexia and predicts bulimic symptoms in women who perceive themselves as overweight" (p. 228). So it is possible that perfectionism is one of those traits that just comes with eating disorders. But it is also possible that if these researchers were using a complete definition of recovery, including psychological recovery, they would have concluded that after one year, these women had achieved only partial eating disorder recovery and over time might achieve full recovery, including both psychological and physical markers. I find that the most helpful interpretation. Full recovery is not going to happen overnight, and there may be certain aspects of one's personality that seem less likely to completely change, but still, there are perfectionist people out there who do not have eating disorders, and perfectionism can fade or lose its destructive edge somewhat with attention. There has got to be hope. I will never let go of hope.

It seems to be the case that all personality types can develop eating disorders. There is not one particular MBTI® personality type that is any more or less likely to display eating disorders thinking or behaviors (Burger, Hoffeditz, Firmin, Hwag, & Wantz, 2008). Interestingly, researchers argued that the reason there is no correlation between personality type and eating disorders is that personality is enduring and stable, whereas eating disorders are temporary. That's a very positive message! Still, I think it's important to note that personality definitely interacts with eating disorders. Once a person has developed an eating disorder, personality may interact with treatment, as it is still generally very difficult to predict who will respond positively to treatment and who will not. Levallius, Roberts, Clinton and Norring (2016) found that extraversion predicted positive treatment outcome, and in particular the subcomponent of extraversion labeled assertiveness (extraversion can be broken down into the subcomponents of warmth, gregariousness, assertiveness, activity, excitement-seeking and positive emotions). Other traits found to be significantly predictive of recovery: straightforwardness (a subcomponent of agreeableness), trust (another subcomponent of agreeableness), and competence (a subcomponent of conscientiousness) (Levallius, et al, 2016).

I went through a four-day training to become a certified Myers-Brigss ® facilitator. It was during this training and right after it that I developed a profound respect for the contribution of personality to self-care. For instance, I am an introvert even though I did not realize it until I started learning more about personality. My family knew it, mind you, but I did not spend much time or effort considering whether I was an introvert or extravert, although if asked I would have said that I was an extravert who required uncharacteristic amounts of time on her own, in silence if possible.

The powerful part of personality for me is finding the right match for each individual regarding self-care. Similar to the concept that if you really want something salty and crunchy, a sweet piece of fruit is a poor match, if what you really want is non-stimulating down time to reflect and regroup, spending time at a children's birthday party is not a good match. Matching personality type and what people need to recharge during their discretionary time and activities can go a long way toward helping a person in recovery (or any person, really), to feel more whole and more at peace. Because I had not really thought of myself as an introvert, I had also not paid much attention to making sure that I honored my own need for quiet activities like reading, writing, meditating, etc. I had actually been doing these things because I really enjoyed them, but I had not realized how tied they are to my innate personality trait of introversion.

If a person who is recovering from an eating disorder knows her Myers-Briggs (MBTI®) type, then here are some things that might be useful during the transition from partial to full recovery:

Introversion vs. Extraversion

This component of the MBTI® describes where a person gets her energy and what she finds exhausting. "I" (introverts) get energized by going within, being alone, reducing external stimulation. "E" (extraverts) get energized through social interaction, being with others, increasing external stimulation.

If an "I" is in partial eating disorder recovery, wanting to make the final push to full eating disorder recovery, she is going to have to take her energy needs into account. Time alone to reflect and recharge is likely to fill a need. On the other hand, an "E" will want to make sure to seek social interaction, to spend time with others and to meet her needs.

I thought for the longest time that I was an extravert, but it turns out that I am not. I do enjoy people, but I get my energy from being on my own. There have been times in my life when I had very little alone time, and I still find that there are times when alone time is hard to find. But it is a critical part of my recovery. I am not saying that everyone in recovery must spend time alone. I am saying that every introvert must spend time alone if she hopes to maintain a sense of equanimity (calm). I remember one vacation years ago when my children were young. We had a wonderful time but I had almost no time alone. I remember telling a friend that over the course of our week-long vacation, I had one moment when I was sitting outside waiting for others, and I sat admiring the way that sunlight came through the leaves. That moment was fleeting, probably lasting less than two minutes. Is it a wonder that I came home from vacation and had a really hard time emotionally? I was completely emotionally and spiritually exhausted. I had not realized that in order to maintain my charge, or to re-charge, I should have built such contemplative opportunities into each day of my vacation. After learning more about myself as well as learning more about self-care for introverts, I now make a point of alone-time or down-time every day, very much including during vacations. Often it is easier to find these times in the early mornings or late evenings. For me, early mornings work better because I am much more of an early bird than a night owl. But I do other things on vacation, such as bringing novels to read or volunteering to run errands on my own, or taking time to sit or walk on the beach, and so forth. It may only be five minutes, but those times can be so valuable to my sanity. I also find that on return from a vacation, building in contemplative times is incredibly helpful to my smooth re-entry to work and family life. It helps to reduce my sense of being overwhelmed and I don't have to turn to my food or eating as a way to regulate my over-stimulation. Binge eating certainly bought me alone time, but at what cost? Why not skip the binge and just admit that I need time alone without the self-destructiveness of a binge.

Sensing vs. Intuition

The term Intuitive Eating is confusing here because the way the words are used are different. In describing a way of eating, "intuitive" generally means relying on one's own internal signals of hunger and satisfaction to decide what, when and how much to eat instead of relying on external cues or rules such as social conventions or following a prescribed plan of eating. In the MBTI® world, intuition is one way of processing information. An intuitive "N" processes information by starting with the big picture, they "why," whereas a sensing "S" processes information by focusing on the details, or the "how." It's not true that "N" people on Myers-Briggs are going to have an easier time of becoming intuitive eaters than will "S" people. But they will process the whole concept differently. When introduced to any new idea, an "N" will want the theoretical or big picture first before the details; an "S" will want the details and concrete steps first. In the end, they will both come to the same holistic understanding of the concept.

Whenever attempting to learn or wrap one's brain around a new concept, or even to change a habit, is a great time to take one's "S" or "N" preference into account. Everyone can learn, it's just that people learn differently. To make it easier to learn, cater to the learners' preferences.

Thinking vs. Feeling

This personality dichotomy describes a person's priorities when making a decision. A "T" (thinker) is going to be logical and fact-oriented whereas an "F" (feeler) is going to prioritize relationships. All people can be both logical and relationship-oriented, it's just that given the need to make a choice between the two, a "T" will choose facts and an "F" will choose relationships.

It can be very helpful in understanding one's own and others' motivations. One time when my son and I were listing all the reasons why we should continue in the Tae Kwon Do class that we were taking together, my list read: physical exercise, mental exercise, convenient class schedule, close to home, etc. My son's list literally named all the people in our class. Hmm… who is the "T" and who is the "F"? I like the people in our Tae Kwon Do class, but I am more motivated by other, what I consider more logical, reasons. Or possibly that's reflective of his "E" extraversion and my "I" introversion? Either way, it's helpful to know that people operate differently, have different motivations and different ways of understating the world and living in it. The main thing for a person in recovery is to learn more about oneself so as to be able to engage in self-care that's the best match possible with one's personality.

Judging vs. Perceiving

This is a very complex component of the MBTI® but one way that it manifests is how one experiences time. A judging "J" is planful, the type who might say that in order to be on time, a person really should arrive early. A perceiving "P" is more of a "just in time" person. My husband, who is a journalist, calls this "working to deadline." If I ask him to do something that takes five minutes to accomplish by noontime, he will start it at 11:55 am. It's done by noon and he is rightly proud of himself for accomplishing the task on time. He is a clear "P." I, on the other hand, am a clear "J," and if I know at 9 am that I have a task that needs to get accomplished by noon and will take me only five minutes, I will not put it off, not because I am such a great person, but because I cannot stand the feeling of having something hang over my head. It will be all I can think about and it will be less painful to just get it accomplished than to put it off. I am likely to have it completed at 9:05 am. We both got the task done, but we have different relationships with time.

Again, this aspect of the MBTI® is a great tool for self-awareness. A "J" (judger) might tend to feel superior to a "P" (perceiver) and it is easy for a "P" to feel less than, disorganized, and so forth. But both are perfectly normal personality preferences that are unlikely to change. So why not accept ourselves for who we are and try to work with what we've got? This is not really all that different than body acceptance. I have legs. I may not love my legs, but they are the legs I have. I can appreciate them, accept them, and do the best I can with my legs, or I can reject them, feel bad about them, and wish that I had someone else's legs. The same with personality. We are who we are, so we might as well figure out who that is and do the best to appreciate and take care of the people we are. We are much more likely to be happy when we do.

It is important to note that there are many skills, abilities and attitudes that cut across all personality types. For people interested in becoming more self-compassionate, it may be a relief to know that although it may be more natural for certain types, it is possible for everyone to practice self-compassion. Neff (2003) reported that "in terms of personality traits, self-compassion was significantly associated with extroversion, agreeableness, consciousness, and neuroticism (negatively), although self-compassion still predicted unique variance in positive functioning after controlling for personality" (p. 8).

Coping with Stress

One aspect of habits is how a person copes with stress. Like all habits, these are learned behaviors and hard but possible to change. "Coping refers to the thoughts and behaviors that people engage in so as to manage, tolerate, or reduce internal or external demands that are appraised as exceeding an individual's resources and is typically thought of as a factor that mediates the relation between stress and the onset of psychiatric illness" (Fitzsimmons & Bardone-Cone, 2010, p. 689). A person can cope by getting self-centered and emotional or by attempting to avoid the stress. Neither of these approaches are the best for mental health. The most mentally healthy coping approach involves focusing on tasks aimed changing or solving the stressful situation. Interestingly, when non-eating disorder controls were compared to fully recovered, partially recovered and people with active eating disorders, the non-eating disorder controls were most likely to use supposedly mentally unhealthy avoidance-oriented coping strategies. This shows that avoidance is not always a bad thing and/or just because a person does not have an eating disorder does not mean that they are always completely mentally healthy. The non-eating disorder controls were least likely to use emotion-oriented coping strategies. The non-eating disorder controls were just about as likely as the fully recovered participants to use task-oriented coping strategies, and both groups which were more likely to use task-oriented coping strategies than the partially recovered or active eating disorder participants. Researchers concluded that "the partially recovered individuals looked more similar to those with an active eating disorder than to the fully recovered group" (Fitzsimmons & Bardone-Cone, 2010, p. 692).

Self-Compassion

I am trying to be generous with myself, to allow myself some latitude, to recover as fully as I can from perfectionism. I want to give myself permission to be imperfect and pretty darn fine and reasonably healthy and full of self-compassion. At the very least I want to show myself a modicum of self-compassion for wanting what seems hard to describe, what doesn't follow a carefully planned out script, for being complicated and authentic and for making myself cry because I have wants and they don't make sense to me. Even if I don't always make sense even to myself, I still want to try to meet all my needs and as many of my wants as I can without being greedy and unfeeling either toward myself or others. It is much easier for me to have compassion for myself when I see that my struggles are not so different from the struggles of others. It is very lonely to feel "terminally unique," but having a healthy sense of shared humanity makes it easier to be more self-forgiving and more patient with myself.

I love it when academics take up topics that we might otherwise not understand deeply and research them so that we can see them from new angles. This is what Dr. Kristen Neff (2011) has done with self-compassion. In addition to very accessible, readable books, she has authored many research articles. In sum, and very clearly articulated in her books, self-compassion involves three components: self-kindness, common humanity, and mindfulness. I must admit that part of me gets very impatient with this. "Really?" I want to ask, "mindfulness again? Can't I ever get away from mindfulness?" Apparently not. Mindfulness is actually really important, not just something that sounds good and spiritual. It's not just frosting on the cake. Mindfulness is a key ingredient of the cake itself. The components of self-compassion (self-kindness, common humanity, and mindfulness) contain these details: "1) extending kindness and understanding to oneself rather than harsh self-criticism and judgment; 2) seeing one's experiences as part of the larger human experience rather than as separate and isolating; and 3) holding one's painful thoughts and feelings in balanced awareness rather than over-identifying with them," (Neff, 2003, p. 224). This third component is a different way of describing mindfulness than I had read before, although it is perfectly compatible with other descriptions I had read. I have no problem saying that self-kindness is the opposite of self-criticism or self-judgment. Similarly, common humanity seems logically opposite from isolation, but this is the first time I had thought of over-identification with one's own painful thoughts and feelings and the opposite of mindfulness. Self-compassion, according to Neff's (2003) Self-Compassion Scale, is both the increase of the positive aspects of these three elements (self-kindness, common humanity, and mindfulness), as well as the reduction of their negative expressions (self-judgment, isolation, and over-identification). "In many ways, self-compassion can be viewed as a useful emotional regulation strategy, in which painful or distressing feelings are not avoided but are instead held in awareness with kindness, understanding, and a sense of shared humanity. Thus, negative emotions are transformed into a more positive feeling state, allowing for the clearer apprehension of one's immediate situation and the adoption of actions that change oneself and/or the environment in appropriate and effective ways" (p. 225). Wait, hang on, who wouldn't want that? As an emotional regulation strategy, self-compassion becomes something that directly addresses my needs as a person in recovery from an eating disorder. Neff (2003) goes on to confirm this by stating, "Self-compassionate individuals should evidence better mental health outcomes than those who lack self-compassion, such as a lower incidence of anxiety and depression, because their experiences of pain and failure are not amplified and perpetuated through harsh self-condemnation, feelings of isolation, or over-identification with thoughts and emotions (p. 225).

Sleep

Probably most of us are aware that it's a good idea to get enough sleep. But maybe we don't really know why it's a good idea. I find both personal experience and research to be convincing in this matter (and in all matters, frankly). With regard to personal experience, at some point I noticed that if I am not eating enough, I have trouble sleeping through the night. And if I am eating too much, I have trouble getting up in the morning. When I am in an about-right zone of food intake, I can get 6-9 hours of sleep per night and be functional and not fuzzy headed. When I don't eat enough during the day, I do get hunger signals, but if I ignore those hunger signals or try to dampen them with water or coffee or tea (others might rely on soda), then the hunger will rear its persistent head sometime around 2 am, after I've been asleep for a number of hours. Or maybe 4 am, at which point my stomach is growling and I need something to eat. The only time this happened for me in a way that I would consider normal was when I was breastfeeding. When I was waking up to feed and diaper a baby, it made sense to me that I might be hungry in the middle of the night. But at other times, it has been more of an indication that I wasn't doing a great job of listening to my hunger during the day. On the other hand, when I've eaten too much, I get sleepy and want to doze. This is not the I-need-to-catch-up-on-my-sleep-and-today-is-the-only-opportunity extra two hours that I sometimes get on Saturdays, but more a general sense of sleepiness that seems unrelated to actual sleep needs. Before anyone gets too worried about their own sleep cycles, I should also note that I have noticed that when people around me are coughing or complaining about catching the latest virus, I am often not sick, but I am likely to be more tired than usual. And if I let myself sleep at those times, the extra sleep seems to aid my body in fighting off whatever virus is going around at the time. A couple of nights of extra sleep yield shockingly great benefits in helping to fight off and to ultimately avoid whatever everyone else got. For those reasons alone, I love sleep. It helps keep me healthy and it is yet another way for my body to communicate its needs to me.

With regard to research, it is also a good idea to get enough sleep, but the research is not as definitive as I had expected on this matter. Rather, it is what they refer to as "equivocal," which means uncertain or open to interpretation. I learned some very interesting things when I started to investigate the literature, but I am not quite sure what to do with them, and I am definitely disappointed by what I have read in the popular media that comes across as "sleep or die." First, sleep disorders are common among people with active eating disorders. In particular, when 400 women in Korea who had been diagnosed with either bulimia or anorexia were interviewed about their sleep habits, 56.8 percent of the women who binged or purged (regardless of diagnosis) reported sleep disturbances and 34.1 percent of those who did not binge eat or purge reported sleep disturbances (Kim, 2010). One hundred and thirty women in the study suffered from difficulty falling asleep and 71 of them woke up in the middle of the night. Dr. Kim (2010) noted that eating disorder recovery tended to resolve difficulty sleeping, and that improved sleep can be seen as a recovery marker. Second, I learned that the popular notion that insufficient sleep leads to weight gain is not always borne out by research findings. Although high BMI and short sleep (less than 5 hours per night) are correlated at the extremes, it is not clear if obesity causes sleep difficulties or if insufficient sleep causes obesity. Among 9,321 high school students, average nighttime was sleep was only related to weight among those who slept 5 hours a night or less on average (Culnan, Holliday, Daly, Aggarwal, & Kloss, 2013). There was no statistical difference between the short sleepers (less than five hours per night), usual duration sleepers (6-8 hours per night) and longer duration sleepers (9 hours or more per night) among the students who were in the BMI categories of underweight, healthy weight or overweight – there were almost identical percentages of high school students from these weight categories in each of the sleep categories. Among students who were above the 95th percentile in their BMI, 15.25 percent were in the short sleep category, 11.67 percent were in the usual duration category, and 13.23 percent were in the longer duration category. In the longer sleep duration category, the students who had the highest BMIs were more likely to be female and in the shorter duration category, the students who had the highest BMIs were more likely to be Hispanic. It is important to point out that causes and effects are not clear in these correlations. When we know that two things are related, we do not know if one caused the other, or if they were both caused by other factors. Finally, in a study of 125 women in midlife who did not have eating disorders (women with eating disorders were actually excluded from the study), less sleep was predicted by more family stress, and less sleep in turn predicted higher health stress, which then contributed to lower life satisfaction (Darling, Coccia & Senatore, 2012). BMI was not significantly different between women who slept less or more than 7 hours per night. See why I don't know what to do with these results? There does not appear to be a one-size fits all solution to sleep, darn it.

A final study with somewhat surprising (to me) results was one conducted with college students to determine whether or not weight gain in the first semester of college was related to sleep habits (Roane, Seifer, Sharkey, Reen, Bond, Raffray, & Carskadon, 2015). The first finding that I found surprising was that of the 71 females and 61 males in the study, only about half of them gained weight during their first semester of college. For those who gained weight, they only gained an average of 2.5 kilograms (5.5 pounds) and for those who lost weight, they only lost an average of 1.6 kilograms (3.5 pounds), in other words, these students' weight did not change very much during their first semester in college, which really puts the lie to the "freshman 10" or the "freshman 15." The second surprising result was that there were no statistically significant differences between those who gained weight and those who lost weight regarding sleep duration or consistency/variation in the amount of sleep they accrued nightly. I am personally still going to try allow 8 hours a night for sleep whenever I can and hope that I will actually sleep at least 7 of those hours, because I feel better when I get what I think is an adequate amount of sleep. But however much sleep I get or don't get may or may not be related to my weight.

Movement

Contemplative movement is covered in another section. Other kinds of movement can help a person feel better in both the short and long term. Health benefits of physical activity have been established for some time to include prevention and management of cardiovascular disease, diabetes, and osteoporosis. "There is incontrovertible evidence that regular physical activity contributes to the primary and secondary prevention of several chronic diseases and is associated with a reduced risk of premature death" (Warburton, Nicol, & Bredin, 2006, p. 807). Although researchers found that physical fitness was more important than physical activity, both were deemed important to wellbeing. In particular, especially for older people, muscle fitness is very powerful. "Enhanced musculoskeletal fitness is positively associated with functional independence, mobility, glucose homeostasis, bone health, psychological well-being and overall quality of life and is negatively associated with risk of falls, illness and premature death...The evidence provides direct support for the recent recommendation that resistance training and flexibility exercises be performed at least twice a week to maintain functional status, promote lifelong physical activity and enhance overall quality of life" (p. 805).

In addition to physical health benefits of physical activity, there are substantial mental health benefits also. Research supports both purposeful exercise as well as more general physical activity as supportive of both health and happiness (Lathia, Sandstrom, Mascolo, & Rentfrow, 2017). Now that so many people have cell phones with apps that monitor physical activity, researchers were able to track the physical activity and moods of over 10,000 users of their research app. They found that the people who reported being happier were also the people who reported being more physically active. Of course this can be a chicken-and-egg thing – possibly more activity creates happier people, or possibly being a happier person causes one to be more physically active. But researchers also tracked moment-to-moment happiness and physical activity and found that participants were actually happiest during times of physical activity. In researchers' technical language, "physical activity predicted more positive valence on the grid responses, more intense high arousal positive affect, and less intense low arousal negative affect" (p. 9). For people in recovery from eating disorders, it is important to note that constant physical activity and over-exercise do not make a person happier. There is such a thing as too much of a good thing. If a person has engaged in over-exercise in the past, finding a balance of healthful physical activity can be a challenge. In college, I used to run for miles after I engaged in binge eating. And I ran for miles in order to get ready for a binge. I definitely did not have a positive relationship with exercise. Now my exercise routine is more circumscribed by my other daily commitments, but if I go to the gym, I almost always use the stair stepper for 30 minutes. That's literally all I do at the gym. I love the idea of resistance training, I just don't like actually doing it, so I usually don't. I participate in Tae Kwon Do classes 2-4 times per week and that gives me a variety of strength, flexibility and cardio training. Before I started Tae Kwon Do, I got the same positive and varied experiences from yoga (with a little less cardio in the yoga classes that I attended). I also enjoy walking and try to incorporate walks across campus or walks with my dog into each week, although I am not always successful at that. At the very least I try not to sit at my desk all the time, but to get up once an hour and move my legs a bit. The benefits of movement are many, but as with eating, each person must stay in touch with her own body to determine that "just right" amount.

CHAPTER 8
Get in the zone

Find healthy ways to disconnect mentally such as meditation, reading a really good book, or any other activity that is completely mentally absorbing, including physical or creative activities. Do this daily if possible.

The power of thinking about something else is vastly underrated by those of us who feel that we are obsessed and can't not think about whatever it is that our brain is currently stuck on. As is possibly clear from my journal excerpted in the "to weigh or not to weigh" section of this book, sometimes seemingly out of the blue, I am concerned about my body. There is no doubt usually a cause, but I can't always put my finger on it. Generally the cause for me is some kind of anxiety – I am worried about something, possibly related to my own capabilities – and my brilliant eating disorder brain follows its well-worn shortcut to "there is something wrong with my body." This both avoids the anxiety and keeps the eating disorder alive. This whole thinking pattern, however, can be disrupted. One way is to disrupt the chain of thoughts somewhere along the way and get to the place where I am able to calmly say to myself, "worried about your body again, Catherine? Hmmm…what was worrying you before you started down that path?" and I do not want to diminish that kind of thought-stopping. However, I haven't found it to be very effective. It's almost like it's too late by the time I get to that point. I need more prevention and less intervention. Prevention for me involves at least three different kinds of zoning out.

1. The first kind of zoning out is where I let my mind wander. Maybe I am walking or doing some other soothingly repetitive activity such as knitting, swimming, or washing dishes that doesn't require a lot of

brain power or fixed attention, and my brain has the opportunity to wander, to remember things that I hadn't even realized I had forgotten, or to solve a problem that focused attention was not very successful at solving earlier. Some people find that listening to music gives their brain a chance to wander. I only experience brain-wandering with classical music – I get too distracted by other kinds of music.

2. The second kind of zoning out is where my mind is completely absorbed in some activity. For me, things that involve my entire brain (so that I can't actually think about anything else because my brain is so fully engaged) are movies in a theater, or physically demanding activities that require focus and concentration. Sewing can be one of these because I need to really focus on what I'm doing or I'll make a mistake. I don't play team sports, but I have heard others say that basketball, soccer and other team sports require them to concentrate and occupy their entire brains. I love martial arts for this purpose. It takes my whole brain. After an hour-long Tae Kwon Do class, I feel like I've received a "brain re-set." This experience of being intensely focused is called "flow," and is discussed further below.

3. The third kind of zoning out is meditation or contemplative prayer. The point is not to let the mind wander (#1) and also not to be intensely focused (#2), but rather to let go of thoughts and open up to an experience of "silencing of the mind." Depending on the meditative tradition, this might involve focusing on the breath or a word, but the point is never intense focus on breath or a word, but rather to use the breath or a word as an alternative to the normal chatter of one's brain when mental silence is attempted. I am a huge fan of contemplative prayer, but I also recognize its pitfalls and challenges. More about that below also.

Mind wandering

Letting my mind wander is surprisingly restorative to me. I seem to do this best while I'm taking a walk or a bath. It's not meditation; I guess maybe it's more like day dreaming. Sometimes taking 5 or 10 minutes to "do nothing" can be just the mental break I need. Because I, along with millions of other Americans, always have my phone at my fingertips, it's easy to take 5 or 10 minutes relaxing and spend the entire time checking Twitter or Facebook. There is nothing wrong with checking social media, but if I am doing that, I am not letting my mind wander. I think the relatively recent popularity of coloring books for adults is an indication of many people's need to engage in some easy activity that allows the mind to wander. I suppose I could really focus on coloring within the lines, but it is more likely that I would pay little attention to the actual coloring (or walking or bathing) and my mind would be free. If I think of my mind as a computer program, mind wandering time is the update process. Nothing much is going on, so my mind app is free to update. The complete reset is more involved, and is discussed below in the section on flow.

Flow

The concept of "flow" was developed by Csikszentmihalyi (1990) to describe the coveted experience when a person engages in a demanding activity and finds a balance between skill level and task demands such that one feels both in control and free of self-reflective thoughts. It is a blissful feeling of being fully absorbed in an activity. Sometimes people refer to this as being "in the zone." I have never participated on sports team, but I have heard people who play basketball, for instance, describing the game of basketball as something that predictably snaps them into the zone where they are only playing basketball. They are fully involved in the experience of what they are doing and not worrying about how they look or what they need to do an hour later. This sort of activity may be thought of as active contemplation, the second type of zoning out listed above, with less day dreaming and more complete brain involvement. Flow research (Csikszentmihalyi, 1990), tells us that it is during these times that people feel happiest. They are completely immersed in an activity, they lose track of time (in a good way) and they are engaged in something that they love. People who experience flow are happier than people who don't. But it isn't a random thing. Flow can be cultivated. "Happiness, in fact, is a condition that must be prepared for, cultivated, and defended privately by each person. People who learn to control inner experience will be able to determine the quality of their lives, which is as close as any of us can come to being happy" (Csikszentmihalyi, 1990, p. 2). He described flow as optimal experience, "It is what the sailor holding a tight course feels when the wind whips through her hair, when the boat lunges through the waves like a colt – sails, hull, wind, and sea humming a harmony that vibrates in the sailor's veins. It is what a painter feels when the colors on the canvas begin to set up a magnetic tension with each other, and a new *thing*, a living form, takes shape in front of the astonished creator. Or it is the feeling a father has when his child for the first time responds to his smile…The best moments usually occur when a person's body and mind is stretched to its limits in a voluntary effort to accomplish something difficult and worthwhile. Optimal experience is thus something that we *make* happen" (p. 3). When I read these words in the first few pages of the book *Flow: The Psychology of Optimal Experience*, I couldn't help but wonder if some of what I was doing when I restricted my food or binged wasn't an attempt to reach flow. I certainly experienced a lot of the characteristics of flow, but over time I realized that it was hurting me. So how could I find something else that involved my body and mind so fully without hurting myself or someone else in the process?

There are a number of characteristics that combine to create the concept of flow. This is list is meant not to judge a person's experiences and say, "oh, that wasn't flow, it doesn't count!" but instead to help understand the phenomenon and then, of course, to research it (because I'm not the only one who highly values research):

- "Intense and focused concentration on what one is doing in the present moment
  - "Merging of action and awareness

- "Loss of reflective self-consciousness (i.e., loss of awareness of oneself as a social actor)

- "A sense that one can control one's actions, that is, a sense that one can in principle deal with the situation because one knows how to respond to whatever happens next

- "Distortion of temporal experience (typically, a sense that time has passed faster than normal)

- Experience of the activity as intrinsically rewarding, such that often the end goal is just an excuse for the process" (Nakamura & Csikszentmihalyi, 2009, p. 90).

The defining quality of flow is intense concentration, according to Nakamura and Csikszentmihalyi (2009), who went on to state that "*Staying in flow* requires that attention be held...apathy, boredom, and anxiety, like flow, are largely functions of how attention is being structured at a given time" (p. 92).

The brain shows different activation patterns during flow experiences, even short ones. Researchers set up 3-minute experiences for 23 German men in their 20's via addition problems in which "participants were asked to sum the presented two or more numbers in their mind and to enter the result as accurately and as fast as possible using the on-screen keyboard" (Ulrich, Keller, & Gron, 2016, p. 498). The addition problems were in three categories: boredom (too easy), flow (matched with their skill level which had been assessed previously), and overload (too hard). Each participant experienced all three conditions repeatedly with brief breaks in between. Researchers monitored participants' brain activity with functional magnetic resonance imaging and found that during the flow (fit to skill level) condition, certain brain regions were more active and others were less active than during either the boredom or overload conditions. In other words, participants' brain activity was reliably different during flow in contrast to boredom and overload. And during the boredom and overload conditions, participants showed the similar patterns of brain activity. This is referred to as an inverted U pattern.

They checked to make sure that mathematics interest and accuracy were not factors, and neither of them were. "The flow experience did not depend on participants' task performance, and not on their preference for mental arithmetic. In the brain, differences between conditions following an inverted U-shaped pattern were detected in several mostly lateral frontal and posterior parietal areas, the thalamus, the basal ganglia and in the midbrain. In contrast, MPFC, posterior cingulate (PCC), lateral temporoparietal, and medial temporal regions including the amygdala, were less active during the flow condition compared with control conditions (U effect). Moreover, the U-shaped response profiles of the MPFC and the amygdala under flow were robustly related to participants' experienced degree of flow, as expressed by the flow index" (p. 502). Participants' functional magnetic resonance imaging results matched their reported experiences when they were surveyed right after their testing sessions. Particularly pertinent to people in recovery from an eating disorder, who are likely to have experienced uncomfortable and possibly intrusive levels of self-awareness, the participants' brain activity increased in the areas associated with mental demands, but decreased in the areas associated with self-referential processing that are linked to "unhappiness, negative affectivity, and increased depressive self-focus associated with increased attribution of negative emotions to oneself" (p. 503). Who wouldn't want to have flow experiences if they reliably involved release from self-referential thinking for a time?

In order to have a flow experience, it is important to find an activity that is mentally challenging, but not so hard that it will create a lot of personal anxiety. In fact, flow is a counterpoint to anxiety. Flow happens when a person has a high level of skill in a particular area and also a high level of challenge (Nakamura & Csikszentmihalyi, 2009). Anxiety, on the other hand, occurs when a person has high challenge but low skill. The other two options are low challenge/low skills, which is apathy or boredom and high skill/low challenge, which is relaxation. It also can't be so easy that it is likely to bring about boredom. Sometimes people feel that they cannot engage in meditation – it's too frustrating, their minds wander, etc.

If this is the case, then why not let go of attempts to meditate and instead attempt to create flow experiences? Intense concentration, which might be a big challenge, could also be easier than meditation for some people. Anyone who feels like a failure at meditation might want to give flow experiences a try. In order to identify an activity in which flow is likely, choose something with which there is already a fairly high degree of skill. Learning a new task is not a good flow experience candidate. It can be something simple, like reading or drawing. And one's reading or drawing skill doesn't have to be fantastic, just enough to focus on the doing of the activity, the process of it, with intense concentration.

Contemplative Practice

Contemplative practices can help us to slow down long enough on a regular basis that our brains are able to reach some clarity that they have trouble doing when we are constantly barraged with external inputs. It is not required that contemplation occur in silence. It can be contemplative to listen to music, if listening to music is the main activity – really listening. And then at least the way my brain works, there will come a moment when I realize that I am not listening. My brain has wandered away from the object of contemplation. It can do in two directions. One direction is the concrete problems and issues of my life, "oh I can't believe I said that," "don't forget to pick up some masking tape at the store," etc. The other direction is an opening, a thoughtless and receptive state that is the goal of all meditators. This can happen the first time one engages in contemplative practice, but it is unlikely to happen every time, and it is certainly unlikely to happen in a sustained way as frequently as I would like. Still, even the resting and letting my mind clear is a valuable use of my time.

When I was early in recovery, it was the 1980's and the Walkman had just been put on the market by Sony. I remember buying a very cool pink one and listening to cassette recordings of nature sounds and zoning out. It was incredibly helpful to me during those times when I was needing a mental break. Prior to that, I had relied on binge eating for mental relief. Zoning out was not a new thing to me, but doing it in a healthy way felt revolutionary.

I have found great solace in the practice of centering prayer. I prioritize and protect my time in the morning so that I will have time to engage in centering prayer or some other form of contemplative practice. More information is available about centering prayer from http://www.centeringprayer.com/ It is a decidedly Christian practice, but may feel less Christian than some other familiar prayer practices. I have also practiced Buddhist chanting, and I love it as well. Every religion has some form of contemplative heritage and it is worth investigating to find out what suits each individual. There are also many non-religious contemplative practices. They all have value.

There are many kinds of meditation and many good books out there about meditation. A common technique is to focus on one's breath. Sit quietly, eyes downcast or shut, and focus on the breath for a few minutes and see how that feels. It can often feel surprisingly refreshing. In thinking about how breathing is part of meditation, I am struck by how often we use expressions related to the breath to describe what is going on in our lives. If someone is "coming up for air" they have been very busy with some intense activity and that busyness is passing.

We have so many expressions that use the breath. Obviously we must breathe, but once I started thinking about the many sayings that refer to the breath, I started realizing how much we do relate to life through the breath. Here are some sayings I remembered, I'm sure there are more:

Breathe a sigh of relief …

Breathing down my neck …

Catch my breath …

Breath of fresh air …

Full of hot air …

Don't hold your breath …

Save your breath …

Take a deep breath …

Speaking under one's breath …

Yes, the breath is very important, and it's easy to forget that.

Mindfulness

Mindfulness is both an attitude and a form of meditative practice that has been incorporated into eating disorder and other treatment approaches. Mindfulness "involves observing thoughts nonjudgmentally in the present moment" (Yang, et al., 2016, p. 1) or, put another way, "mindfulness is a nonjudgmental, receptive mind state in which individuals observe their thoughts and feelings as they arise without trying to change them or push them away, but without running away with them either," (Neff, 2003, p. 224). Attitudes and behaviors that are supportive of mindfulness according to groundbreaking researcher and practitioner Kabat-Zinn (1990) are: non-judging, patience, beginner's mind, self-trust, non-striving, accepting, and letting go.

In mindfulness mediation, practitioners often focus on their breath and then when they are distracted, repeatedly re-focus on the breath. This sounds a lot easier than it is. Try it for five minutes. Focusing on one's own breath without inner distraction is possible for a shockingly short period of time. The key is not to avoid distraction because that is impossible, but rather to non-judgmentally observe the distraction and to let it go while re-focusing on the breath. "This observational stance has also been referred to as a metacognitive skill characterized by a decentering from environmental and internal psychophysiological stimuli or processes to produce a reflective space in which new ways of perceiving and responding become possible, rather than enacting habitual automatic or ruminative patterns" (Grecucci, Pappaianni, Siugzdaite, Theuninck & Job, 2015, p. 2).

Among therapeutic approaches that incorporate mindfulness are Acceptance and Commitment Therapy (ACT; Hayes, Strohsal & Wilson, 1999) and Dialectical Behavior Therapy (DBT; Linehan, 1993). There are also therapeutic approaches that use mindfulness as their base and main focus, starting with the seminal Mindfulness-Based Stress Reduction (MBSR; Kabat-Zinn, 1990) and building from there. There almost isn't a problem that hasn't been addressed by a variation of Kabat-Zinn's MBSR. Mindfulness-based Relapse Prevention (MBSR; Bowen, Chawla & Marlatt, 2010). "MBRP practices emphasize intentional awareness and acceptance of all experiences, including those that are uncomfortable or unwanted, and teach skills to better relate to these experiences. MBRP clients are taught to practice a curious and nonjudgmental approach to discomfort, learning to investigate emotional, physical, and cognitive components of experience as they occur in the present moment, rather than attempting to suppress or ameliorate the discomfort, fostering approach- versus avoidance-based coping. It is important to note that these skills can be practiced regardless of the underlying cause of negative affect" (Witkiewitz, Lustyk & Bowen, 2013, p. 352.). The idea of all this mindfulness is that a person can have a bad moment or a bad day and not turn to their negative coping technique. In MBSR, when a person encounters one of her bad moments or days, she is taught to: stop, observe, breathe, expand awareness and respond mindfully (these combine to the acronym SOBER). DBT is also full of acronyms, so many of them in fact that I can't even begin to recall one. They are too long and too involved for me to keep them in my brain. However, the basic concept that when something is negative, instead of mentally running away (avoiding), it is a much more functional strategy to get curious, to approach and interrogate the feeling or issue. Not only does this approach work, it seems to have such profound long term effects that researchers speculate that it actually causes multiple positive changes in the mesolimbic and mesocortials systems of the brain (Witkiewitz, Lustyk & Bowen, 2013). The whole myth that a habit can be changed in 21 days has been disproven by many people in recovery from eating disorders. It's completely possible to binge or restrict after 21 days of not doing so and have it feel almost exactly the same as it did 21 days previously. The reason it feels the same may be that the brain has not changed; only the behavior has changed. In order for the brain to change, one's mental activity around the behavior must change also. A completely new approach has to be introduced and unlike willful self-control, mindfulness is actually a completely different approach.

Regardless of the many possible causes of eating disorders, mindfulness training at its base posits that maladaptive behaviors such as eating disorders are learned and can be unlearned. The twist or secret is that the unlearning means truly shifting one's approach. It's not like using subtraction instead of addition; it's like introducing multiplication to address what seemed to be an addition problem. And as we all may remember from elementary school, multiplication problems are in fact addition problems, but the multiplication solution is a great qualitative improvement over addition.

There are research-based explanations as to why mindfulness has been so successful as an intervention for people with a variety of challenges. One research team reviewed mindfulness interventions and proposed that "the different facets of mindfulness meditation (intention, attention, attitude, body awareness, reappraisal, and changes in perspectives on self) employ both cognitive and experiential mechanisms that enable internal experience of self and the situation to be regulated" (Grecuicci, Pappaianni, Siugzdaite, Theuninck & Job, 2015, p. 4). Researchers asked the quite interesting question, "does mindfulness have an effect primarily using a cognitive mechanism or an experiential mechanism"? (p. 5) and they conclude with one of my favorite responses, which is: it depends. It depends in part on whether the person is experienced in meditation, or a new meditator. Beginners relied more on top-down, cognitive mechanisms, whereas more experienced meditators utilized bottom-up, experiential or perceptual mechanisms. "Mindfulness is a skill and the emotional regulatory mechanism it deploys therefore appears to depend on the degree of meditation practice rather than purely on the application of the mindfulness method" (p. 5) but even the beginners used more experiential and perceptual brain mechanisms than controls who relied entirely on cognitive processes. Additionally, "one of the unique components of mindfulness practice is to enable emotional regulation through the practice of intimate detachment that relies on bottom-up neural activations and pathways" (Grecuicci, Pappaianni, Siugzdaite, Theuninck & Job, 2015, p. 6), so that practice in mindfulness meditation can help a person be able to separate from thoughts, worries, anxieties and so forth in an effective way.

A study of 13 men and women who participated in 40 days of mindfulness meditation for 10 minutes per day found that brain scans were different for the participants before and after the training as well as while meditating vs. while at rest (Yang, et al., 2016). "Short term meditation training yielded lowered acute feelings of tension at the time of scanning in our study. Likewise, our results emulate previous reports of the effects of meditation on well-being in anxiety trait and depression self-reports" (p. 9). Although practice may be important, even 10 minutes per day for 40 days can make a positive impact.

Non-judgmental stance. An important component of mindfulness is a non-judgmental stance. This can be applied to so many things, but let us focus for now on our bodies, food, and eating. The book *Overcoming Overeating* (Hirschman & Munter, 1998/2008) is a particularly good non-Buddhist take on this non-judgmental stance. Observing one's body in the mirror and describing it without judgment is an exercise that they strongly recommend in *Overcoming Overeating*. Using a neutral, non-judgmental attitude toward one's body can be very powerful. Similarly with food and eating, there is no need to judge a particular eating behavior or food as good or bad. Snacking is snacking. Eating a piece of cake is eating a piece of cake. Finishing the vegetables is finishing the vegetables. Candy, cauliflower, and cantaloupe are all foods that may or may not be eaten, without judgment. This is a very tricky because clearly a pound of candy and a pound of cantaloupe are likely to have different effects on one's body and while one does not have to be good and the other bad, it is completely acceptable to say, "no thanks, that's enough," when it comes from a place of inner wisdom and bodily experience rather than from the finger wagging voice in our heads that says, "no so fast, kiddo!" I have heard normal eaters say about candy "that makes my teeth hurt," which I never have personally experienced, but is an interesting concept. I have personally experience both eating too much candy and too much cantaloupe. Too much cantaloupe makes me feel bloated and gassy. Too much candy makes me feel buzzy and lethargic at the same time. Because of my conditioning, I have tended not to judge the bloated/gassy experience as negatively as the buzzy/lethargic feeling because everyone knows that candy is a less nutritionally-sound food than cantaloupe. But neither bodily experience felt very good.

Survival Mode or Mindful Mode?

Living in the present moment is one aspect of mindfulness that is very powerful. This is different from "survival mode," or is it? In a way, they seem very similar, because when I'm in survival mode, I'm really only dealing with what's in front of me. The difference for me is that when I'm being mindful, I have a peace about what I'm not doing, or not attending to, that I don't have when I'm in survival mode. I am setting aside other concerns, not avoiding them, when I'm being mindful. I will get to them – I will have time for them later. This sounds all well and good but there is definitely overlap. When I get back from a work trip or a family vacation, there is more for me to do than there are hours in the day. Laundry gets done, but not put away. I might flag emails to get back to, but I don't clean out my inbox in one day. This is not the way I prefer to live. I prefer to have laundry put away and emails answered and when I get in this "mindfully surviving" mode, I feel uncomfortable enough to be motivated to deal with the details as I can so that I can get back to not having things hanging over my head, waiting to get done.

Survival mode	Mindfulness
Overwhelmed	Calm
Difficulty prioritizing	Prioritized
Avoiding everything	Attending to what's in front of me
Not sure what I'm not attending to	Knowing what I can accomplish

I have gotten a lot of inspiration from David Allen's *Getting Things Done* (2001/2015) approach. I highly recommend his book or TED talk. He has a lot of ideas and tips but for me the most important part is getting everything out there, written down, and organized in a way that doesn't rely on my unreliable brain to be "oh, right, I need to…" It's a more planful and peaceful way of living that he doesn't so much present as mindfulness, but is in fact a component of mindfulness for me. In his writing and online talks, David Allen tells of his background in karate and how when he was a karate student, he learned to aspire to have a "mind like water," which he describes as a mind that has the appropriate reaction to each situation. The analogy is a rock being thrown into a body of water – small rock, small reaction; bigger rock, bigger reaction. I can't say that this is something I have learned in any of my Tae Kwon Do training (yet!), but I do think that he is exactly right in terms of collecting our to-do items, organizing them in such a fashion as to leave nothing to chance, and then to march through our priorities at a pace that feels manageable to ourselves.

Possibly the paradox of completely being in the present moment is that I have two ways of being with regard to life experience: I want them over and done with and I want them to never end. I feel both of these ways about the same experiences. As I think about my upcoming week, I have the competing attitudes of just getting through it and wanting the beauty of each moment to be less fleeting, more concrete and enduring. I want something that I could take a picture of to actually be the picture, instead of being the rich and complex experience that it is – fraught with things I like about it and things I dislike about. Of course, time does not bend to my wishes, and it marches on despite my complicated and competing desires. And I do much better in that surrendered, accepting space where I can enjoy life for what it has to offer and not stress too much about getting to tomorrow, next month, or whatever date it is that I have identified in which life will be less stressful for me. Whatever that date is, it will come and go and I will be no better and no worse for it. It's great to stop and smell the roses, to appreciate what is true in each moment, but I also know that each rose will only be in bloom for a limited period of time.

Contemplation in Religion and Spirituality

The contemplative tradition is present in many religious institutions and spiritual traditions. Religiosity, can be defined as "a system of organized beliefs, practices, rituals and symbols designed to facilitate closeness to the transcendent," and spirituality, which can be defined as "the personal quest for understanding answers to ultimate questions about life, meaning, and a relationship with the transcendent" (Akrawi, Bartop, Potter & Touyz, 2014, p. 2). In a review of the power of mindfulness interventions, researchers noted that "you can find forms of mindfulness and meditation in almost all of the world's religions, such as yogic meditation in the Hindu tradition, kaballah meditation in Judaism, contemplative prayer in Christianty, and Sufi meditation in Islam" (Grecuicci, Pappaianni, Siugzdaite, Theuninck & Job, 2015, p. 2). Specific to the Christian tradition, Jackson (2017) offered "To contemplate the historical human acts of Jesus as acts of an embodied God challenges the eating disorder. To disregard the body is to disregard Jesus. To deny the body is to deny that God said "yes" in Jesus" (p. 266). This may or may not be relevant to people in recovery from eating disorders, but I think it is important to acknowledge that contemplation is consistent with many religious and non-religious traditions.

Reviewing 22 articles published between 2001 and 2014 that examined the linkages between religiosity or spirituality and eating disorders or body image concerns in non-clinical samples, researchers found that "strong and internalized religious beliefs coupled with having a secure and satisfying relationship with God were associated with lower levels of disordered eating, psychopathology and body image concern" (Akrawi, Bartop, Potter & Touyz, 2014, p. 7). Although meditation was never mentioned as religious or spiritual practice of potential value, the practices of prayer and reading body-affirming religious material were found to have beneficial effects.

Contemplative movement practices

I got involved in Tae Kwon Do when my husband and I told our then-10-year-old son that he had to pick some physical activity in which to be involved – soccer, gymnastics, martial arts, they were all physical activities in which he had previously participated and they were all up for grabs. I told him that if he chose Tae Kwon Do, I would attend class with him. He chose it, and I went. I actually cried on my way to the first class, sure that I would make a fool of myself. Little did I know how many times I would make a fool of myself over the subsequent few years, but also little did I know that I would learn to appreciate the process of learning such that the small and not-so-small humiliations would become less of a concern than mastery would be. I had taken ballet as a middle and high schooler. Ballet has a strong component of appearance-focus, despite the concomitant emphasis on technique. Tae Kwon Do has a stronger emphasis on technique and function than I ever experienced in ballet. The joy of feeling my body get stronger and learning how to break boards and empowered me in a way that I had not anticipated. Tae Kwon Do helped my body image because it helped me to recognize the importance of what my body can do over my body's appearance.

I have personally experienced the recommendations of scholars to focus on body function rather than appearance via Tae Kwon Do. "When women emphasize the functionality of their bodies more so than their appearance, they are more likely to hold positive feelings toward their bodies and eat according to their bodies' internal hunger and satiety signals. This finding stresses the importance of encouraging women to adopt a functional orientation toward their bodies (e.g., by focusing on how their bodies feel and what they can do, by wearing comfortable clothing) in lieu of habitually monitoring their appearance to appear attractive for others" (Avalos & Tylka, 2006, p. 495).

Yoga is another contemplative movement-based practice that "allows for the experience of embodiment (i.e., fully inhabiting one's body, experiencing one's body from the inside-out, body attunement and clarity of needs and internal states, feeling "at one with one's body)…With regard to prevention, we have the choice of (a) incorporating eating disorders prevention into yoga classes; or (b) incorporating yoga into eating disorder prevention programs" (Neumark-Sztainer, 2016, p. 32), the latter of which has been happening in many instances, although "when considering the role of yoga within a residential program for individuals with eating disorders it is important to reflect on the fact that yoga was never intended to treat illness. Yogic theories of psychology are concerned with how to reach our full human potential" (Douglass, 2011, p. 89). In a way, yoga is a perfect fit for either prevention or treatment of eating disorders because it offers an embodied solution to an embodied problem. "Eating disorders are, in their simplest form, as set of embodied, physical acts that function to negotiate what are perceived as overwhelming internal and external stresses and demands (Cook-Cottone, 2016, p. 98). And yoga can help. "Yoga interventions involve three primary mechanisms:

mind and body integration, self-regulation and attention, and nonjudgmental awareness of experience. Yoga interventions seek to change one's relationships to daily experiences, building capacity for awareness, and decreasing reactivity thereby helping youth develop self-regulation skills that can be applied across settings and contexts" (Cook-Cottone, 2016, p. 102).

Sometimes I think that the merits of yoga are overblown. At the same time, it can definitely have a positive role in recovery. Yoga can be seen as a form of embodied mindfulness. "Recent research shows that the body-based practices of yoga have the potential to positively shift our embodied experience, making it more receptive to healing" (Douglass, 2009, p. 127). There are different styles of yoga available, but the kinds that are usually used to support eating disorder recovery are slow and meditative. Although yoga is ideally an activity through which one develops a deeper appreciate for and attunement to one's body, in the past I fell so easily into the "comparing and contrasting" my body with others' bodies that for the longest time I was not able to attend yoga classes. I saw myself or others as good/better at yoga than others rather than seeing us all as students/learners of yoga, or as participants in a class where we were learning more about how to connect to our own bodies. I know this did not come from my yoga instructors, but I do think that yoga can reinforce body image dissatisfaction as well as combat against it. "It's a tricky thing, because while the group leaders is trying to increase body awareness, if they focus too much on body awareness or body parts it can be kind of overwhelming and irritating" (Douglass, 2009, p. 130). It is important for both the yoga teacher and the yoga student, especially if that student is recovering from an eating disorder, to have the right attitude about what yoga can and cannot do. "I do not see the yoga class I teach as "therapeutic" for my goal is not to provide or assist in a cure. I teach embodied learning. Together, the clients and I systemically engage in the process and action of thinking through the body (Douglass, 2011, p. 85).

Ideally, yoga classes can help people in recovery find an oasis and an opportunity to re-connect their minds and bodies. "Yoga does not try to change anything; it is not therapy in the conventional sense of moving from a state of disease to east. Yoga is a set of somatic practices to be explored by the practitioner and tested for their veracity; they are starting points for getting to know one's self. The aim of yoga is to experience the present moment" (Douglass, 2009, p. 129). In this way, yoga is a "meditation in motion" and for people who might want to try sitting meditation but do not have the patience or fortitude to withstand silence in a seated position for any length of time, yoga is a highly accessible contemplative movement practice that gives practitioners something to focus on while stilling the mind from its normal chatter.

Here is a very concrete yoga technique, an elaboration of the well-known bridge pose, which is offered by a scholar of yoga who teaches yoga classes in a residential eating disorder treatment center:

> "One of the most effective means I have found for quieting a particularly restless client in the yoga class I teach is to engage in interoceptive learning. I do this by engaging the student's mind in the physiologically sensations of a yoga posture that relieves pressure in the abdomen (many of our clients suffer from gas, constipation, and cramping and desire some relief from these negative sensations). For example, in *setu bandhasana* or bridge pose, students lie on their back and bring their feet close to their hips. Pressing their feet into the floor, they lift their hips from the ground. I follow this movement with the suggestion that they let their hips drop down one inch from their highest position and reach their knees to the front wall. This lengthening of the abdominal cavity creates a perceived sense of "space" and "lightness" that 1) teaches individuals that they have some control over interoceptive stimuli, and 2) the short moment in which they are holding the pose and exploring interoception, they are experiencing the present moment fully,

free of critical thinking or a mind-set that habitually moves to the past or future" (Douglass, 2011, p. 89).

Experiencing one's body in the bridge pose in this way can be a powerful experience that helps with body awareness and reduced anxiety.

CHAPTER 9
Review possible maintaining factors as needed

When (not if) things aren't going as well as they might, consider what personal maintaining factors may be at play. What might be decreased (such as self-weighing, over-planning, or perfectionism) and what might be increased (such as support, sleep, movement, self-compassion, down time, or mentally engaging activities) to foster a greater sense of personal integration, connection, and/or coherence?

Defining Relapse

Relapse is usually considered something that happens after a period of recovery. It is different from not completing treatment, which is a huge issue in eating disorder research, where attrition from treatment studies reaches 33-37% during the treatment phase and then increases from there depending how long the follow up is (even over 75% with an 18-month follow-up) (Stein, Wing, Lewis & Raghunathan, 2011). While dropping out of a study during long-term follow up could be related to relapse, dropping out of a study during treatment phase is usually not considered relapse because the participants did not have enough time to experience consistent recovery of any kind. Among those dropping out from eating disorder treatment, "Findings show a diverse array of differences associated with dropout including higher levels of bulimic cognitions, body weight concerns, comorbid psychiatric disorders, family background, self-conceptions related to problem solving abilities, personality traits, impulsivity, and treatment characteristics including longer treatments. Although studies reveal a long list of correlates of treatment attrition, little convergence among the studies has been found" (p. 358). Researchers acknowledged that "it may be that only those who experience some positive effect were motivated to complete treatment, while those who experienced no relief fled" (p. 365). Alternatively, they also observed that participants for whom the intervention was successful tended to drop out in the follow-up phases. Lots of people quit – people for whom treatment was not successful and people for whom it was successful. It is hard to stick with things. It is hard for all of us. We give up when the going gets tough, and we give up when it seems that we have been successful. So how does a person carry on? That is the question undergirding the issue of avoiding relapse. Whatever the answer is for each individual, it is unlikely to be easy. Because quitting is easy. Sticking it out is hard.

I am not immune to relapse, nor is anyone else, no matter what they say. It is hubris (the opposite of humility) to think that we are better than anyone else, and that is what saying that "I will never relapse" amounts to. But I am protected from relapse, just as I am protected from other unfortunate choices in my life. Just like every other human on the planet, I am vulnerable to all sorts of negative influences. I could hurt someone else or myself, steal something, or commit almost any despicable act. The thing is that I am not tempted in any way to be despicable, so the chances of me succumbing are very, very slim. But relapse is a bit different. At first, in early recovery, the gap between recovery and relapse is so small, it almost seems invisible. Over time, there develops a wide swath of habits, thoughts, attitudes, and behaviors that now protect me from saying "the heck with it – I'll be at the donut place, scarfing down whatever they've got."

A binge for me is a call for help, a cry in what feels like the wilderness, a way of saying:

Help!

I feel alone;

I don't know what to do;

This has to stop;

I am not getting what I need;

I want something to change;

This is actually really serious; or,

Quite simply: Whoa.

What brings on these cries is some sort of situation followed by an inner paralysis. I may or may not recognize the situation, but I have not or cannot do anything about it, possibly because I have not taken the time to acknowledge whatever is bothering me. If I can take stock and get clear about whatever is bothering me, I can usually come up with some sort of action or attitudinal shift that is likely to be helpful in resolving the situation. When I do that, I do not need to binge. I may realize that the something is bothering me once the idea crosses my mind that Oreos now come in a lot more flavors than they used to and I should really purchase and eat an entire package immediately. What now? I can either engage with that particular impulse or I can step back and say, "Catherine, sweetheart, are you okay? Something seems to be bothering you!" My problems are not big or bad or so unusual. Sometimes it is as simple as: "I am exhausted," or "I am running around like a crazy person trying to fulfill all my commitments and I feel like I am not getting the help I need to get everything done." Ok, then. What am I going to do about it? I can ask for help, give myself a break, give myself permission to extend a deadline or to miss an event, or, my favorite, schedule a stay-at-home day – usually a Saturday when I do not leave the house, which does wonders for my soul.

Predictors of relapse

In one of their many pleas for including a psychological component in the definition of full recovery from eating disorders, Badone-Cone and her colleagues (2010) made this strong argument: Without psychological recovery, relapse is more likely. "Most often missing from 'recovery' is the psychological component of eating disorders, especially how individuals think about their bodies, food, and eating. Not assessing for psychological recovery may produce a 'pseudorecovery' state where individuals are 'walking the walk' but internally 'talking' the same eating disorder talk. The presence of lingering eating disorder attitudes is not trivial, since elevated anorexic attitudes and residual concerns about weight and shape predict relapse" (p. 195). At the same time, the 20 fully recovered participants that this research team studied were not perfect. They noted that "it was surprising that 12%

of the fully recovered group reported that aspects of the eating disorder had interfered with psychological functioning in the past three months. However, this percentage is markedly less than the 40% for the eating disorder group. For a minority of the otherwise fully recovered individuals, there may be some scar effects of the eating disorder" (p. 200).

Another research group studied predictors of relapse and found that among 32 women who had experienced abstinence from binge eating disorder at the end of 20 weeks of treatment, 9 of the 32 had relapsed by six months after the end of treatment. The most robust predictors of relapse at six months identified by researchers were (1) onset of binge eating disorder before 16 years of age, and (2) higher eating restraint scores on the eating disorder examination (Safer, Lively, Telch & Agras, 2002). Fifty-four percent of people who started binge eating before age 16 had relapsed, whereas 12 percent of those who started binge eating at a later age had relapsed. This is a strong argument in favor of early intervention, on two fronts. First, the longer a problem persists, the harder it is to change. But also, age matters. If two people had binge eating disorder for 10 years and one developed it at age 10 whereas the other developed it at age 20, the person with later onset would be more likely to have many other successful coping mechanisms, whereas the person who started eating at age 10 may not have had the chance to develop many additional coping mechanisms and therefore would have more – or at least a different kind – of work to do than the person who had developed binge eating later. So in case there is anyone out there who thinks that a child might "grow out of it," it seems wise to assist that growing process by helping the child immediately, rather than waiting.

With regard to eating restraint, study participants who had relapsed scored an average of 1.8 on the restraint subscale of the EDE-Q, whereas the study participants who had maintained binge eating abstinence scored an average of 1.0 on the restraint subscale of the EDE-Q. These questions are scored 0-6 with 0=no days; 1=1-5 days in the past four weeks; 2= 6-12 days in the past four weeks; 3=13-15 days in the past four weeks; 4=16-22 days in the past four weeks; 5=23-27 days in the past four weeks; 6=every day. Community norms for the restraint subscale are 1.25 (Mond, Hay, Rogers & Owen, 2006), higher than the average for those who were still binge-free, but lower than those who relapsed.

Eating restraint is the exact opposite of unconditional permission to eat. This is consistent with Tylka and Wilcox's (2006) findings that unconditional permission to eat is the one component of intuitive eating that directly opposes eating disorder symptomology. One could argue that if a person is still engaged in restricting food, then that person is not actually in recovery, but especially for people with binge eating disorder, it is easy to slip into dietary restraint and to get caught up on a focus on weight, not realizing that these behaviors put them at very high risk for binge eating again. The relapse sequence is likely to start with restricting and yet the person may not see restricting as problematic, or at least not as problematic as binge eating.

As a reminder, the restraint subscale of the EDE-Q (attached as Appendix A) includes:

Question #1 Restraint over eating. Have you been deliberately trying to limit the amount of food you eat to influence your shape or weight (whether or not you have succeeded)?

Question #2 Avoidance of eating. Have you gone for long periods of time (8 waking hours or more) without eating anything at all in order to influence your shape or weight?

Question #3 Food avoidance. Have you tried to exclude from your diet any foods that you like in order to influence your shape or weight (whether or not you have succeeded)?

Question #4 Dietary rules. Have you tried to follow definite rules regarding your eating (for example, a calorie limit) in order to influence your shape or weight (whether or not you have succeeded)?

Question #5 Empty stomach. Have you had a definite desire to have an empty stomach with the aim of influencing your shape or weight?

Body image dissatisfaction and continued weight/shape concern at the end of treatment has also been found to be a strong predictor of relapse (Cogley & Keel, 2003). The most powerful strategy that I have identified to reduce weight/shape concern and to positively impact body image is to cease and desist all self-weighing behavior. I tried only weighing once per week, but what I found was that I was just delaying the information, but the focus was there as long as I knew that I would be weighing myself on some identified date in the future. That's why I had to let go of the idea of weighing myself at the end of my 30-day "no weigh" experiment. The idea that I would weigh myself, still kept enough of a focus on my weight that I was unable to replace my weight focus with a more positive focus on my health and well-being.

Possibly the main take home message is that even though eating disorder recovery is supposed to involve a letting of "all or nothing" thinking, those in recovery would do well to consider "all" of their eating disorder in order to protect against relapse. The eating disorder includes the thoughts, the behaviors, the fears, the all of it, and not just the easier-to-identify behaviors of binge eating or purging. Binge eating or purging are clear, but they might come at the end of a long chain of events, and that chain could have been broken/stopped at a much earlier point if anyone had recognized the signs for what they were. Best never to engage in any of the eating restraint behaviors, and yet those binge eaters who had maintained abstinence were not all in the "never" camp – on average they were experiencing these problematic behaviors 1-5 days out of the past 28; that is, on 4-18 percent of days. The group experiencing relapse were at a 1.8, which puts them somewhere around 4-8 days out of the past 28, or 14-29 percent of days. I don't mean to imply that one has to be perfect – it's certainly not "all or nothing!" But one could benefit from being more inclusive and look at the entirety of the eating disorder behaviors, including safety or maintenance behaviors, because it's pretty hard to engage in certain aspects of an eating disorder and not others. In particular, if one is engaging in eating restraint (and not practicing unconditional permission to eat), then binge eating is likely right around the corner. Please take a wide look at whatever is going on and don't ignore any of it.

When researchers examined the eating disorder recovery trajectories of people diagnosed with eating disorders over a six-year period, they learned a lot, including the fact that the best predictor of relapse was a stressful life event (Grilo, Pagano, Stout, Markowitz, Ansell, Pinto, Aznarini, Yen & Skodol, 2012). These scholars referred to the time between active symptoms and relapse as "remission," which is an interesting way to describe what might have been behavioral but not psychological recovery. They clarified that remission "was defined as eight consecutive weeks with psychiatric status ratings on the Longitudinal Interval Follow-Up Evaluation less than two" (p. 188) where a score of one indicates no symptoms and a score of two indicates subthreshold symptoms with up to moderate functional impairment. "Relapse was defined as eight consecutive weeks with psychiatric status ratings of two or greater (reflecting any eating disorder)" (p. 188). Participants identified their stressful life events from a list of 82 possibilities. Thirty-five to 41 percent of participants relapsed. Participants who had a higher number of stressful negative life events were more likely to relapse earlier. "Specific types of stressful life events that predicted eating disorder relapse were elevated work stressors and social/friendship stressors" (p. 189) and researchers recommended that "clinicians working with these eating disorder patient groups consider integrating relapse prevention and coping skills methods for dealing with stressful life events" (p. 190).

Possibly this goes without saying, but relapse does not usually come up and surprise a person. First there is the urge to binge or restrict or purge, what some people call craving. Then there is an inner fight which may not last a long time, but it does occur. This is the "should I or shouldn't I?" stage of relapse and it is the last opportunity for positive intervention. An analogy for this stage would be the "catch it before it falls" analogy. Say I notice something on a table that is about to fall off. If I do nothing, the thing will fall of the table. If I reach over and move the thing closer to the center of the table, it will not fall off. If I am in an environment where the table is being jostled or shaken, I may need to reach up and re-place the thing frequently. If the table is in an undisturbed environment, the re-placing does not need to happen very often. I feel like I am that thing sometimes. I get closer to the edge than makes me feel comfortable. Certainly, if I am thinking about bingeing, I am too close to the edge. What can I do to re-place myself, get more centered? First I have to determine whether this urge to binge is physical. Often, the urge to eat a lot of food is actually a deep hunger. I truly need to eat more. I've been too restrictive with my food. I'm not eating enough or I'm not eating often enough. If that is the situation, eating more and/or more frequently is an easy fix or re-placement. Other times, I feel deprived but I am not physically hungry. Maybe I said no thanks to a treat and now it's two hours or two days later, and I want some of that treat. If I can figure this out, then the remedy is also eating: find that food, or something close to it and eat it and be done with it. Yet other times, I want to binge because it is a habit that I have when I get uncomfortable. I am doing something scary or about to do something scary and it would feel much more comfortable if I weren't so anxious about whatever it is, but instead was mad at myself for overeating. This is when bingeing or restricting or purging can become a distraction, a way to funnel the otherwise uncomfortable experience into a more familiar uncomfortable experience, one that I can predict and does not involve taking new risks.

When I have had experiences of recovery in the past, after a few months I have been tempted to binge and on the times when I gave into the urge, my recovery halted in its tracks. I am not saying that a binge should halt recovery, but I am saying that is how I used the binge. It's scary to be fully recovered. There are no guarantees. It's uncharted territory. To recognize that sometimes my urge to binge is a sign that I'm uncomfortable and that sometimes discomfort is a good thing is another way to disarm the binge, to intervene and recognize that although part of me wants to binge, the fully recovered part of me is okay in recognizing the discomfort and moving ahead anyway.

Safety behaviors

Times of high anxiety can also contribute to relapse risk, especially when that anxiety centers around one's body and how others might judge one's body. Weddings seem to be a perfect set up for this. One person is wearing a tight fitting white gown and is pretty much the center of attention. If she is recovering or recovered from an eating disorder, just having all eyes on her could be enough. If she has fallen for the "shedding for the wedding" concept, then she has recently been restricting her food and is in an even more vulnerable spot. Whether it is a family reunion, a class reunion, or some other reuniting event, it is easy for any of the attendees to feel on display. Guests at these events are highly likely to say "wow, you look great – you've lost weight" or some such other thoughtless comment. And while that may be the coveted comment, it can also be triggering. People do not run up to others at these events and say "It's so great to see you! What have you been reading lately?" No, they go directly for appearance commentary, and it can be hard to remember that we have value other than our body weight or shape in those moments.

If a person has in the past used safety behaviors (including restricting, bingeing or purging but also body checking, weight checking, monitoring calories, etc.) to try to reduce anxiety, it is important to remember their counter-productive nature. "The persistence of eating disorders is related to how symptoms allow patients to be deeply connected to their bodies within the context of challenging inner experiences they try to avoid (e.g., overwhelming feelings, cognitive challenges, and physical sensations) and an ostensibly invalidating and objectifying external world. That is, patients are doing two seemingly contrary things. Psychologically, patients are working extremely hard to *leave* themselves thereby avoiding the authentic experience of their bodies, thoughts, and feelings. Ironically, their eating disorders actively employ them in an intense, unremitting, cognitive, emotional, and most certainly pathological engagement with their bodies" (Cook-Cottone, 2016, p. 98). Safety or maintenance behaviors seem so logical, and feel so normal to people attempting to recover from eating disorders. But they keep the eating disorders alive, or they re-activate them if they have been dormant for a time. There really is no way around it but, bit by bit, to face life straight on and to deal with all the overwhelming feelings, cognitive challenges, and physical sensations instead of allowing eating disorder behaviors or attitudes to distract us so that we can continue to avoid what feels hard, or at times, impossible.

If I am nervous about how people I have not seen in some time might judge my body when I see them next month, my ineffective but predictable solution to this anxiety might be to check my weight to make sure I am okay. The weight checking, regardless of what the scale tells me, may spiral into me deciding to restrict my food intake in some way over the upcoming month before I see these people so that I can make sure that when they see my body they will have something positive to say. There are so many things wrong with this series of thoughts that it's hard to break it down, but here is an attempt at what I really believe to be my truth:

1. My body is part of me, certainly, but I am so much more than my body;

2. I would not judge an old friend or a family member solely on their appearance, so why do I think others would do that to me?;

3. What does it matter what another person's opinion of my body is, especially if I don't see them regularly (but even if I do see them regularly)?;

4. Checking my weight to make sure that I have not gained serves both to increase my fear of gaining weight and also to drive a wedge in between my mind and my body so that it makes it harder for me to stay in tune with the amounts and types of foods that will truly nourish me;

5. I am okay no matter what my weight is, and sometimes I am not okay no matter what my weight is – my okay-ness and my weight are not inextricably linked;

6. Restricting my food is completely counter-productive. Every single time I have restricted my food in the past, the period of restriction

has ended badly (Geneen Roth has been credited with coining the very apt phrase: for every diet there is an equal and opposite binge).

7. Whatever people say about my body, although they can make me feel temporarily victorious or wounded, they do not get at the part of me that is tucked way inside, the part that wants to know that she is worthy no matter what. I truly believe that all human beings are worthy no matter what, and as a human I thereby qualify as someone who is inherently worthy. I don't have to earn my worthiness. I have it by virtue of my existence. Deep breath. This is where I want to spend my time, contemplating these truths, and living my life from them.

Cognitive challenges

Could it be that there is altered brain activity in women recovered from bulimia? Yes! What is not known is the cause/effect nature of bulimia and differences in brain activity. In a small study using MRI brain scans, researchers found that women who had been in recovery from bulimia for a year or more still had less brain response to glucose than control women despite the fact that all of the participants reported that the glucose tasted sweet and pleasant (Frank, Wagner, Achenbach, McDonaha, Skovira, Zizenstein, Carter & Kaye, 2006). "It is not known whether alterations after recovery were present before the onset of bulimia, were a "scar" caused by the illness, or were an adaptive process related to recovery. Taste experience is strongly influenced not only by biological processes but also by conditioned processes" (p. 78).

At one time the child development world was engaged in a nature vs. nurture debate. That debate has clearly shifted because the current answer to "is it nature or nurture?" is "yes – it's both, and they influence each other." What has happened over the past 25+ years is that brain research has clearly demonstrated that genes and environment are interwoven in a much more complex way than the nature vs. nurture "debate" could ever capture. Repeated behaviors cause brain changes which in turn influence subsequent behaviors. The brain is much more flexible than was previously thought. Our capacities may have genetic limits, but they are surprisingly susceptible to environmental influences. And as our environment shifts, so does our brain. It is both a bit scary and incredibly hopeful. We are not doomed. What feels like something that we "must" do because our brain feels hijacked may be arguably true at the time, but it can be changed through different environmental conditions, including better nutrition, practice and learning, increased acceptance by others, and so forth.

It is important to note that there are cognitive distortions associated with many mental health challenges, and people with eating issues are not necessarily any worse than others who suffer from different challenges. In a study of 111 people, 58 of whom had morbid obesity and 53 of whom did not, there were no statistically significant cognitive distortion differences between the two groups when the researchers took participants' mental health status into account (da Luz, Sainsbury, Hay, Roekenes, Swinbourne, da Silva, & Oliveira, 2017). The main difference identified between the two groups was that the "participants with morbid obesity showed significantly higher scores on anxiety symptoms in comparison to participants of normal weight" (p. 6). There were no differences between the groups on other mental health measures such as depression or stress.

Cognitive distortions are not to be discounted, but they likely are related to mental health issues rather than weight status. That is, unless a person is underweight and severely nutritionally deprived, in which case there can be all kinds of cognitive challenges directly related to weight because it's really hard to think when in an undernourished state. Once a person is getting enough to eat, then there are some cognitive dysfunctions that may occur that are less likely to be weight-related and more likely to be mental-health related, although they can affect how a person deals with food, eating, body and weight. "These distorted thoughts occur, for example, when someone thinks that the desire to eat is irresistible ("magnification"), that they are "losers" because they are obese ("labeling") or that people reject them because they are overweight ("mind reading")" (da Luz, Sainsbury, Hay, Roekenes, Swinbourne, da Silva, & Oliveira, 2017, p. 2).

Global Processing

People with eating disorders have inefficient cognitive processing, in particular displaying poor global processing (Lang, Roberts, Harrison, Lopez, Goddard, Khondoker, Treasure & Tchanturia, 2016). Normal global cognitive processing describes the thinking process whereby the big picture whole is perceived first and is used to comprehend details. In the Rey Osterrieth Complex figure test used by researchers, participants were asked to copy a complex figure as carefully as they could, and then they were scored based on (1) their preference for global or detailed elements and (2) whether their attempts were coherent or fragmented. Researchers found both active and recovered eating disorder patients as well as their non-eating-disordered relatives to be detailed and fragmented, therefore implying that there is a genetic cognitive component to eating disorders. However, not all participants with poor global processing were affected by eating disorders (e.g. all those non-eating-disordered relatives in the study). Just because something runs in families does not make it genetic. But still, it is an interesting finding, because it speaks to an inborn personality trait or characteristic that might be common to people with eating disorders and their family members.

Set Shifting

Set-shifting is more difficult for people with rigid and inflexible thinking patterns. Most people have heard of multi-tasking, but not everyone has heard of set-shifting. "Set shifting" is defined as "the neurocognitive ability to shift back and forth between mental sets and perform a new task in light of interference and priming from a previous task," (Harney & Bardone-Cone, 2014, p. 440) which I think the average person would label "multi-tasking." "Even if it is a potential trait characteristic of anorexia, studies suggest that set shifting may be elastic with the capacity to improve, or worsen, under certain conditions. Although the causal link between set shifting and anorexia remains inconclusive, what is clear is that set shifting ability appears to be impaired in anorexia and warrants further investigation" (p. 440). Findings of Harney and Bardone-Cone's (2014) study looking at body dissatisfaction and set shifting ability among 146 college women did not find a statistically significant impact of body dissatisfaction above and beyond general negative affect (such as depression) on participants' set shifting abilities.

Focusing

One of the aspects of my eating disorder that was most distressing to me was an inability to be mentally present with family and peers, which at the time I thought of as "hanging out." I had a heck of a time just hanging out. I felt that I had to be doing something all the time, and if I was merely sitting still, my mind did not stop. I was doing mental gymnastics even when I appeared to be at rest. I have not become a slouch, and I am often engaged in activity, but I am able to concentrate now, to sit and watch a movie or sports event on TV or in person and to give those activities my full attention, which I did not seem to be able to do while I was active in my eating disorder.

Perfectionism

[Note that the section on personality also includes a discussion of perfectionism, as it is sometimes identified by researchers as a personality trait.]

Perfectionism is a characteristic that can contribute to the development and maintenance of an eating disorder. Perfectionism is not compatible with full recovery. The primary reason that I see for this is that perfectionism does not allow for learning. We might be able to produce a peak performance which we can label "perfect," and maybe that is appropriate in some circumstances such as taking a test or performing in a piano recital, but beyond "I did the best I could do and made no discernible mistakes," on a daily basis, perfectionism only serves to limit us. It takes too long and it keeps us from taking risks and from growing. I have been told that at one point in history, quilters made purposeful mistakes in their quilts in order to show that they had been handmade and not machine-wrought. This is very likely a myth, but it is the kind of myth that is compelling and that is possibly why it has persisted. Purposeful mistakes are obviously not really mistakes. But anyone who feels that she must be perfect might want to start experimenting with purposeful mistakes. It might be smoother to ease into greater humility if errors are planned, or possibly noted and willfully ignored. There will come a day when a mistake is truly that – a small accidental error. The smaller the error, the less humiliating. But big errors do occur and if they are accidental, who are we to beat ourselves up mentally or to berate others for forgetfulness, or inattention, or for mere humanity? Mistakes truly do make us human. We are not machines and it can be a great celebration of our humanity to recognize that and to see it as a strength and not a moral failing.

The characteristic of perfectionism also comes into play in the process of body trust vs. body distrust. It is probably not completely accurate to say that developing hunger signal trust is exactly the same as letting go of perfectionism, but the two are highly related. If I want to eat "perfectly" then I am using some external measure to judge my eating; I am not relying on my internal hunger signals. Young children rely on their internal hunger signals and they have not yet developed the capacity to be self-destructive perfectionists. Letting go of the counting and the sharp lines of perfectionism opens up the possibility of embracing the one's own beautiful human body. To love one's own body and to lovingly care for it is quite different from living with an active eating disorder. One way to let go of perfectionism is to temporarily block out the past and the future and fully experience this very moment – right now – the sounds, sights, smells, and feel of now. The feel of air on skin, the ambient sounds of the environment, its smell, and so forth. That is the quickest way I know to pop out of eating disordered thinking.

Perfectionism means different things to different people, and it may mean different things to the "experts" vs. the people who are labeled as perfectionists. A group of 15 women in treatment for eating disorders described their experiences of perfectionism in ways that researchers were not expecting (Petersson, Johnsson & Perseius, 2017). The recovering women described perfectionism as a strategy that they employed to deal with uncomfortable feelings at the same time as they found perfectionism impossible and exhausting, and saw that it made their eating disorders worse and not better. Some of the women experienced perfectionism with regard to their bodies as well as other aspects of their lives (housecleaning) and saw striving for perfection as a way of seeking validation. But all of them saw it as a double-edged coping strategy, a game that is impossible to win. Researchers concluded, "The results showed that measures like the EDI-P do not always capture a patient's conception of perfectionism. Regarding that perfectionism may serve as a means to regulate affects, and may lead to an exacerbation of the eating disorder, and to the development of obsessive-compulsive symptoms (which is an aggravating factor in eating disorder development)" (p. 9).

In Tribole and Resch's (2012) iconic book *Intuitive Eating*, the first recommendation is to reject diet mentality. As many times as I attempted to read that book, I got stuck on this principle. I remember thinking, "yeah, easy for you to say." And to give myself credit, rejecting diet mentality is a lot more complex than it seems at first blush. Essentially the first chapter could be "recover from your eating disorder," followed by what to do after that. When I finally saw that my perfectionism was the puzzle piece that I was missing here, keeping me from moving on to the next chapter, it made my life a lot easier. I can purge my diet books and feel a great sense of relief, but that does not actually change my thinking or my way of being around food or eating. It only made me a perfectionist without a plan, which is a mighty uncomfortable place to be. But just recognizing that perfectionism was an issue helped me to move on.

Mindset

Growth vs. Fixed mindset is a well research concept introduced to many people through the book *Mindset: The New Psychology of Success* (Dweck, 2006).

A person with a growth mindset believes that a person can always become more intelligent through effort. A person with a fixed mindset believes that intelligence does not change, even though people can learn new things. Thinking about intelligence in a malleable way is not a traditional view of intelligence, but it is one that has a lot of scientific support. Children are learning about growth mindset in schools, but adults haven't always caught up with this new way of understanding the brain's capabilities. It would serve a person recovering from an eating disorder well to adopt a growth mindset about full recovery. It may take effort, but it is definitely possible. There was definitely a time when I did not believe that full recovery was possible. Then I was introduced to the concept, and I had hope. But then I tried to be fully recovered and I didn't get it right away. The logical, rational, prideful part of me said, "I guess I was wrong – it really isn't possible." I had hopes, but they were dashed. I didn't know that effort and perseverance were going to be so useful to me. I think a lot of people in partial eating disorder recovery have a frustrating experience and conclude prematurely that it's not possible to reach full recovery. For whatever reason, although I've had those thoughts many times, I always seemed to come back to thinking, "this has to be possible," partly because I saw other people being successful and even though I wasn't there yet, I knew that I could get there if I kept trying.

It's the persistent effort part of growth mindset that is really helpful to people wishing to make the transition from partial to full recovery. It may not be pretty – it's almost guaranteed not to be pretty – but it can happen. One person may struggle months or years longer than another person, but that's not a good reason to give up the struggle! Yes, it's hard. Keep at it. The goal is attainable.

Mindset can also be seen as something that one has in an eating disorder and must change in recovery. Instead of growth vs. fixed mindset, one might think of this as disordered vs. recovered mindset, or possibly disordered vs. healthy mindset. See a comparison of the two as outlined by Dakanalis, Favagrossa, Clerici, Prunas, Colmegna, Zanetti and Riva (2015).

Eating Disorder Mindset	Recovered/Healthy Eating Mindset
Body dissatisfaction - Drive for thinness and/or muscularity	Body acceptance
Frequent body checking ("includes any behavior aimed at gaining information about one's shape/size, such as mirror checking, pinching one's fat or feeling muscles for size/density, social comparison, and seeking reassurance	Less frequent body checking – healthy eaters are in the "never" or "very infrequently" range.

from others about one's body" (Dakanalis, Favagrossa, Clerici, Prunas, Colmegna, Zanetti, & Riva, 2015, p. 88).	
Perfectionism	Flexibility
Restrained Eating	Eating to satisfaction
Emotional dysregulation (Emotional eating)	Finding ways of responding to strong emotions that are not impulsive or self-destructive and/or finding ways to prevent strong emotion.
Basing self-worth on body size or shape	Conscious rejection of media standards of attractiveness
Attachment insecurities (fear of rejection, intense need for approval, and need to keep significant others close by) that drive long-term interpersonal difficulties	Secure attachments – developing comfort with independence, closeness and separation Also, protecting oneself by emotionally distancing from others so as to desensitize from societal ideals or expectation of beauty. In other words, finding other means than body shape/size to gain others' acceptance and to reduce fears of rejection.

Both men and women can experience eating disorders related to body dissatisfaction. In women, the desire to change one's body is often referred to as a "drive for thinness," but in men the parallel phenomenon is labeled the "drive for muscularity." "Drive for muscularity is closely associated with rigid dietary regimens and inflexible rules regarding the type and amount of food to be consumed (i.e., taking food supplements and a meal every couple of hours regardless of hunger), over-exercise, use of anabolic-androgenic steriods, and related appearance and performance-enhancing substances (Dakanalis, Favagrossa, Clerici, Prunas, Colmegna, Zanetti, & Riva, 2015, p. 86). Body dissatisfaction may put college men in the U.S. at risk for eating disorders on both fronts – the drive for thinness and the drive for muscularity-- which are evidence by men's dissatisfaction with the amount of fat and muscle on their bodies (Mayo & George, 2014). The 339 men in this study took the EAT-26, an eating disorder risk inventory that is measured in the three subscales of dieting, bulimia and food preoccupation, and oral control. Those with higher EAT-26 scores, indicating higher eating disorder risk, were also more likely to be dissatisfied with the amount of fat (too much) and muscle (not enough) on their own bodies. Another interesting finding of the study was that men chose a higher amount of muscle mass that they thought women would find attractive, compared to what the 441 women in the study reported to find attractive. So, men lost two ways – they were dissatisfied with the amount of muscle mass on their bodies because their ideal did not match their reality, and they chose a higher level of muscle mass as an ideal for men's bodies than women had chosen for men's bodies. This of course assumes that women's judgements of men's bodies are important, which could be debated but is nonetheless noteworthy. Researchers concluded that among their community sample there was both a high level of body dissatisfaction and a high level of eating disorder risk. "We found that a particularly high percentage (13%) of these male students were at risk for eating disorders, and 28% of males would be recommended to seek evaluation from a mental health professional to address eating disorder risk" (Mayo & George, 2014, p. 413).

Self-fulfilling prophecies. Another component of mindset is that we all will try our best to make our beliefs come true. If I believe "I can't do it," then almost certainly I won't do it. If I believe "I can do it," there is a possibility that I won't be able to do it, but at least I won't be the one standing in my own way. This is something that I have learned a great deal about through my practice of Tae Kwon Do. When I started attending Tae Kwon Do classes, I was in fairly good shape regarding stamina (I went to the gym regularly and exercised on the stair stepper) but I did not have much strength, and I was particularly challenged in the area of upper body strength. For instance, I could not complete one entire sit up or one push up. It did not take much time in Tae Kwon Do before I could complete 10 sit ups and 10 pushups, and then I moved on to 20 sit ups and 20 pushups. Practice really does make better, and I saw the results of that first hand. But when it came to breaking boards, especially the hand breaks, I did not think I could do that. I did not feel that I had the upper body strength to break a board with my hand. And of course, I was right. Because a person who does not think she can break a board definitely cannot break that board. On my leg breaks, where I felt pretty confident, I was not always successful, but on the second or third try, I was usually able to break the board. The knife hand strike however, and other hand breaks, were beyond my capabilities, or so I thought. I heard from enough people, my teacher most particularly, that it was all in my head. So, after a time, I was willing to believe that they believed that I could do it. And lo and behold, I could in fact do it. I found I could break one board with a knife strike, and then later, for my temporary black belt test – with much coaching and encouragement from others in addition to practice and visualization – I broke two boards with a knife strike on the first try. Was it a miracle? Not at all. I had practiced. I had gotten advice and encouragement. I had seen it in my mind. I knew I could do it. And I did it.

Recovery is not so different from board breaking. It's really hard to imagine oneself living a life of recovery before that reality happens. But it's important to be able to see it happening before it happens. It is important to believe that full recovery is possible in order to make full recovery possible. I used to imagine myself saying truthfully, "no thanks, I've had plenty," and "sure, that sounds great, I'd love one," "I'm full," and "I'm still hungry," and other normal-around-food comments that I heard others unselfconsciously utter. And, like board breaking, I gave myself credit for trying. Like board breaking, I sought out others' advice. But no matter how much wisdom or advice another person might have, I know in board breaking and in recovery that it was something I had to believe in and do on my own. All the social support, coaching and education in the world was not going to matter if I did not own it.

Still now sometimes when I get that thought that maybe I could just spend the evening bingeing, I have to own my belief in full recovery. Yes, I could spend my evening bingeing. I always have the choice. But I don't want to do that because I don't want to go back to that way of life. I want to move forward, to stay connected to myself and my body, to live free of binge eating and of all the associated thoughts and feelings that go along with it. There is a price, though, and the price is that I sometimes struggle with myself to stay on the path. I have to basically refuse to get off the path sometimes. Most of the time, it's not hard, but when it is, the struggle is internal and it is at the level of my beliefs about what is possible and what is important and it takes courage and steadfastness and wisdom that are sometimes hard to find but are always there when I put forth some effort.

Getting Support

For research Study 1 and Study 2 participants, supportive social relationships were key to their recovery. Alex reported *"There was a year when I was going to a therapist, nutritionist, and doctor every week…I was also part of a 4 person support group…we were all starting to recover."* Beth explained that her relationships with other women who were also recovering from anorexia and her new romantic relationship with a man were pivotal to her recovery. Caroline found her relationship with her boyfriend, then fiancé, was invaluable in developing a sense of personal worthiness and establishing an identity separate from her family of origin. Despite many previous interactions with treatment and therapists, he was the first person that she was truly honest with about the abuse she had experienced and about her anorexia. She felt that he was the first person to show Caroline *"unconditional love,"* and with his help, she began to recover and is still making progress. Ella developed a life apart from her mother but then struggled with whether or not she should separate from her boyfriend. She recognized her need for human connection. *"I worry that I wouldn't see anyone for days, besides my work, if I broke up with him. I'm too social and too connected with people to do that to myself."* She saw recovery as *"learning new ways of being"* and became committed to self-care, to authenticity, and to strengthening her personal identity development through nurturing relationships.

Alice was glad to talk to her brother in law, who had been through recovery himself, *"talking to him was a lot more helpful because he's been through it."* Natalie received support from multiple sources, *"The counseling center was very important to make myself realize what was going on…I'm getting encouragement from others who see me."*

Alex attended a support group that she found very helpful. *"We had a therapist, but the group support was probably the most helpful."*

Relational Cultural Theory

Relational cultural theory posits that women need to experience mutually empathetic and mutually empowering relationships for optimal development (Jordan, 2001; Miller & Stiver, 1997). This is a theory just for women. In contrast to traditional, male theories of psychological development that emphasize the development of a separate self, relational cultural theory emphasizes the development of a connected self. Relational cultural theory sees relational isolation or disconnection as a problem and growth-fostering connection as a solution. It also readily acknowledges that everyone experiences disconnection in relationships on a continuum from commonplace lack of validation in a brief exchange to ongoing traumatic sexual abuse. When disconnection occurs, people form ways to cope with this uncomfortable experience, some of which are adaptive and some of which are not.

What is known as the "central relational paradox" (Jordan, 2001; Miller & Stiver, 1997) states that a chronic level of self-disconnection can be formed out of relational disconnection when people feel that they need to wall off part of themselves in order to maintain existing relationships. We disconnect (from ourselves) in order to connect (with others). Eating disorders can be a way of coping with relational disconnection, and may be particularly prominent when one has become disconnected from oneself as an interim relational coping mechanism.

Relational cultural theory at its heart is a theory of women's development and healing. It highlights the need for supportive relationships, which have been found to be important to the process of recovery from eating disorders. While lack of mutuality is related to eating disorder symptoms, researchers have found that developing supportive relationships was very important to the recovery from anorexia of women who had successfully maintained a healthy weight one year after treatment (Frederici & Kaplan, 2008). In another study, women interviewed six months after treatment for eating disorders pointed to social support as helpful in maintaining recovery and preventing relapse but when they felt isolated or disconnected from others, they were more likely to return to bingeing or restricting (Cockell, Zaitsoff, & Geller, 2004). Relational cultural theory may help explain why it seems nearly impossible to recover from eating disorders alone. Whether it is a therapist, friend, family member, significant other, or a support group, it is really important to involve others in our journey to full recovery.

Social Support

Getting support from friends, family, or a partner was most helpful to 40 women recovered from bulimia and support from others recovering from bulimia was the second most helpful thing during their recovery process (Rorty, Yager & Rossotto, 1993). After reviewing 20 non-diet interventions that focused on teaching participants to eat according to internal cues, "The authors caution that social support runs the risk of some members spreading inappropriate dietary messages and encouraging maladaptive behaviors. As a result, they recommend that a social support group be implemented after a nondiet intervention to enhance sustainability of effects and behaviors" (Schaefer & Magnuson, 2014, p. 757), which can be tricky when a group is led by a professional facilitator. As a person who has attended many professionally facilitated groups on a variety of topics over the years, I have noticed that the group dynamic develops to include the facilitator and if that facilitator steps out at the end while wholeheartedly encouraging the group to continue meeting for social support, more often than not, the group cannot survive without the facilitator because of its history of reliance on that person.

Feeling like I am part of a group of likeminded individuals is really, really important to me. I'm what some people might call "a joiner," because I like to join organizations, to be "one of the gang." But I am also an introvert at heart and find other people exhausting. I do not like to be lonely, but I do like to be alone. I want to affiliate with others, but I don't actually want to spend a lot of time with them.

The time when I was actively bulimic were perhaps the loneliest years of my life, because I was actively hiding part of myself and much of my behavior from others. I was living a double life, or trying to, and I was the main casualty. I certainly didn't feel like I could be honest with others, I wasn't sure if I should even be honest with myself. There was nowhere that I belonged, or that's what it felt like anyway.

Each person in recovery must choose whether or not to affiliate with various groups, and if so, whether these groups are focused on recovery, or more generally supportive of personal growth and development.

A counselor, or better yet, a treatment team (which usually means a counselor, medical doctor and dietitian at a minimum) is recommended to help a person escape the strong grip of any eating disorder. But after a time, even with a team, the person in recovery will need to adopt some personal agency and decide if and where to find support outside of paid professionals. Some individuals get better without professional intervention (Vandereycken, 2012), but when this is the case, they still rely on others for support, most often in the form of close friends, parents, or partners. Going it alone is never a great way to live life, but even going without any professional treatment for an eating disorder assumes a certain level of mature ability to analyze one's own situation critically. "If people lack this kind of critical self-reflection, they risk becoming easy victims of the never ending stream of "new" methods with the seducing promise of a simple and quick fix, be it in the new commercialized market of self-help, alternative healing, or so-called professional help. A serious risk, then, is that the search for adequate treatment is needlessly postponed or-even worse-that the disillusioned self-changer has lost all hope even in the available health care system" (p. 94).

Even without formal group affiliation, some kind of support is often a critical part of recovery. Finnish women who had been through treatment five years earlier reported "As the most important factors for recovery, the participants mentioned insight, treatment, and love and support from partners and family. A few also mentioned becoming a mother as important for recovery. A strong connection between insight and motivation to change was reflected in these answers" (Isomaa & Isomaa, 2014, p. 571.)

12 step groups offer a lot to a person in recovery. They offer peer support, a pre-determined way of going through the process of recovery, a spiritual basis that is not religious, and possibly best of all, there is no charge (other than a free will donation which is completely optional). In one study of women in the Overeaters Anonymous (OA) 12 step group, which is but one of many food-related 12 step groups out there, researchers found that one of the positive benefits of participation in OA was the opportunity to establish secure relationships with others in the group (Hertz, Addad & Ronel, 2012). "The interpersonal theory of binge-eating disorder, originally developed from research on the depression literature, places emphasis on the role of affect, including helplessness and anxiety, in the development and maintenance of binge eating…Studies have affirmed OA's claim that the social network, with its emphasis on social acceptance, plays a major role in the self-transformation that members go through: The experience of being unconditionally welcomed and the absence of any judgmental element, as well as the principle of anonymity that disregards distinguishing personality traits among participants, enable a process of recovery" (p. 111). The story they told from interviews with 20 women recovering in OA was positive and hopeful. The women who were interviewed experienced a new-found permission to share their truths with others and to develop supportive relationships with peers and sponsors. Researchers commented that the OA functions as a "mother figure, one who is there and present for her dependent and needy child" (p. 115) and that the basic archetype is also carried out on a member-to-member basis, particularly with sponsors acting as archetypal mothers for their sponsees. This reliable and nurturing human interaction, combined with a 12-step view of a loving, compassionate father-type God can help women develop healthy secure

attachments that the OA participants interviewed reported not having experienced in their families of origin.

When I was first introduced to 12 step programs, I was completely blown away by how much I felt that I belonged. I quickly made a commitment to a food plan and a group of people who adhered to that food plan and I was "home," I had a place where I fit. I felt completely accepted, but it was an overtly conditional acceptance, one predicated on my continued adherence to the food plan. This did not start to feel oppressive to me until 7 years later when I was introduced to the concept and possibility of full recovery via *Breaking Free from Compulsive Eating* (Roth, 1993/2004). I had been a committed member of my particular recovery tribe for 7 years and once I started to question the assumption that I was never going to get better, all of a sudden I didn't feel like I belonged any more. I wanted to go out and test the waters, to see if I could maybe truly recover. I tried and tried and tried again and found that actually, full recovery as I had imagined it was unlikely to be at the end of my particular rainbow. But I also didn't go back to my group. My eyes had been opened and I just couldn't, or at any rate wouldn't, go back. I joined almost every single food- and eating disorder-related 12 step group but eventually left each one of them. I did not personally have the experience that the 20 women interviewed by Hertz, Addad and Ronel (2012) reported. I have probably worked with 20 different sponsors over the years and each one of them was a caring, generous woman. But each one was also a fellow sufferer, someone who was willing to help me but also someone whose job it was to remind me that I had a disease and would never get better and that the best possible outcome was to keep working a 12 step program for the rest of my life and to maintain abstinence from bingeing, restricting and purging. Not that abstinence is a bad goal, it just did not go far enough for me. My time in 12-step programs were in some ways emotional holding patterns, not times of great emotional or spiritual growth. It took me a long time before I found other, more loosely organized communities where I could feel like I belonged. I have never been able to replace that tight-knit feeling I had in my first 12-step group, and I'm not sure at this point in my life that

I would even want to. My goal is no longer years of back-to-back abstinence from compulsive eating. My current goal is to be connected with my body and to take the best care of myself that I can.

In a review of the literature studying relapse from alcoholism, scholars reported that personal investment in social support networks is particularly important in avoiding relapse (Hunter-Reel, McCrady & Hildebrandt, 2009). This can be a dicey thing because for me; it cuts both ways. On the one hand, when I have been most invested in social relationships that strongly and directly supported my recovery (coaches or 12 step sponsors and 12 step groups), I was least likely to stray into eating disorder behavior, most clear about what I needed to do to maintain abstinence from binge eating, and most able to maintain long term, back-to-back abstinence from binge eating. On the other hand, when I received all that social support, I was also least well connected to myself, as most of my efforts were invested in meeting the expectations of my social support person or group. In particular, when I have left 12 step food groups I have felt that they did not prepare me well for life outside of 12 step food groups. Either you are a "lifer" or you are on your own. On my own, I could be successful, but it took an inordinate amount of time because I didn't know what I didn't know. Mostly what I didn't know was the attuned/intuitive/mindful stuff. I didn't know that connection with my body was even important, let alone the thing that would sustain me. There are many challenges when translating the 12 steps of Alcoholics Anonymous to eating disorders, but the main one is also the one that I think separates partial from full recovery: body acceptance. Without body acceptance work, it is really hard to reliably connect with hunger and satiety, to consistently trust in our body's signals, to eat to satisfaction whenever possible, to take the best, loving, nurturing care of ourselves that we can. These factors can grow at the same time, but there was nothing about the 12 step eating programs I participated in that involved learning how to trust my own body. Often people in 12 food-related programs say that the difference between alcohol- and drug-related 12 step programs and food-related programs is that alcohol and drugs can be completely eliminated, but we all still have to eat three (or more) times per day. While this is true, 12 step programs often treat food as an addictive drug that one must take in controlled amounts in order to survive, so that the stated problem is resolved through enforced limits and a basic sense of distrust toward the food and toward one's own body. And that works, as long as distrust is maintained. But as soon as the idea is accepted that actually, my body is completely trustworthy and the problem is that I either haven't trusted it or haven't even listened to it, all of a sudden, the managed/controlled/distrustful system breaks down. And, for me, what I would do for a sponsor (bypass hunger, eat when I was not hungry, write essays on my own moral failings) became unbearable. I trusted the sponsor because I didn't trust myself. When I started to trust myself, I no longer fully trusted the sponsor, or at least I started running whatever the sponsor was saying through my own filter and could not be as blindly obedient as before. It didn't take long before I wasn't a member of that 12-step group any more.

Eating disorder professionals – those who assist others who are recovering – have sometimes also personally battled eating disorders. The insights of those who have not only recovered from an eating disorder themselves but also have helped others to recover can be particularly insightful. In interviews with 13 recovered eating disorders professionals, researchers found that the conception of recovery can go well beyond the psychological minimums mentioned above (Bowlby, Anderson, Hall & Willingham, 2015). Six themes discussed by recovered professionals as characteristics that are essential to the recovery process were:

"(a) recovery is a nonlinear process;

(b) recovery is comprehensive, including both external and internal components:

(c) recovery involves the process of learning to understand and value the self;

(d) recovery involves coming to an understanding that the eating disorder is separate from one's identity as a person;

(e) recovery involves finding purpose and meaning in life; and

(f) recovery requires the development of healthy and meaningful relationships" (p. 5).

The therapists in this study preferred the term "recovering" over "recovered" to describe their own experiences. "Their narratives did not indicate an ongoing sense of seeing themselves as sick, as in the addiction model. Nor did they see ongoing struggles as primarily the result of encountering objectifying social pressures. Rather, they saw the process of recovery as blending into a more normative developmental path of continuing maturity and confronting on an ongoing basis the "issues that everyone on earth has"" (p. 8), which in my view fits squarely into the "recovered" category.

But what if a person has outgrown the need for regular counseling appointments and has rejected the 12-step approach? What social support is available then? Of course, family and friends can be supportive. But often family and friends don't really "get it" unless they have been in recovery themselves. Things that can be difficult for a person with a history of an eating disorder are quite different from things that others might find stressful. Lots of travel and unpredictable meals and can be difficult, shifts in hormones affecting appetite (pregnancy, peri-menopause, certain medicines) can be difficult, special or celebratory meals can be difficult, and so forth. It can be very reassuring to know that there are others who face the same challenges and to hear or read their success stories as they navigate them. I have not found face-to-face groups that fit this description. There are numerous online options that I have describe below in the tech support section.

Tech support

It seems that everything happens online these days. Social media is a combination of technological and social and so could be ideal in helping a person support full eating disorder recovery. It does not always work that way, so it's good to think about how it does work. Instagram may work against people recovering from an eating disorder (Ridgway & Clayton, 2012; Marcus, 2016). But many websites have sprung up, in particular those intended to help people early in recovery. One Australian website is a great example: at www.himh.org.au/navigatingedhealth. People with eating disorders and those who care for them can download useful resources (News, June, 2017).

The internet can be used for both prevention and treatment. In a review of 20 online eating disorder recovery-focused treatment programs, researchers found that compared to no treatment, people participating in online programs significantly decreased body dissatisfaction, internalization of the thin ideal, shape and weight concern, dietary restriction, negative affect, and bulimic symptoms, with drive for thinness being the only factor studied that did not reach statistically significant difference on average between the online intervention groups and the control groups among the ten studies in the meta-analysis that included it as a factor (Bauer, Franko, Moessner, Ozer, Chabrol & Rogers, 2016). Each of the 20 studies reviewed included a similar-sized control group, so it was possible in each study as well as in the meta-analysis to determine the effects of online interventions, but not all of the studies included each factor analyzed in the meta-analysis. The online programs targeted different populations, and the meta-analysis showed that online programs can be effective with different groups of people, including those with eating disorder symptoms and those who wanted to improve their body image but did not necessarily have eating disorder symptoms.

One online eating disorder prevention program named StudentBodies™ has been found to be successful, both in the U.S. and in Germany (Beintner, Jacobi & Taylor, 2012). Fourteen studies including 990 female high school and college students from the U.S. and Germany participated in this online eating disorder prevention program and were found overall to have improved scores in the areas of disordered eating and weight and shape concerns, which were maintained after program ended during follow-up data collection. "StudentBodies™ is a structured cognitive-behavioural online programme for adolescent girls and women that addresses a number of factors that are presumed to lead or to allay eating pathology. These include cognitive and affective factors (e.g., nutritional and exercise knowledge and attitudes, body image, drive for thinness, self-efficacy, perceived social support), sociocultural and peer norms (thinness ideal, dietary and exercise practices) and behavioral factors (coping, goal setting, food preparation and exercise patterns)" (p. 2). In 8 weeks, the following topics were covered:

1. Beliefs about my body and self-esteem;

2. Cultural images of beauty, changing how I feel about my body, eating disorders, body image journal (threaded throughout many of the following sessions);

3. Exercise, nutrition;

4. Why diets don't work and commitment not to diet;

5. Media, dealing with critical comments, more on exercise and nutrition;

6. Knowing when you're full, more on eating disorders;

7. Goal setting and achievements, more on nutrition;

8. Review of body image, self-esteem, exercise, nutrition, and eating disorders.

All of these topics of course could be delivered in face-to-face meetings but an online format allows for more convenience as well as more confidentiality among participants. It is unlikely that eating disorders were prevented among all 990 participants, but that would be true in face-to-face programs also, and face-to-face programs would have been less convenient and less confidential. Especially as more and more adolescents are interacting online around a variety of topics, it seems wise and even natural to offer eating disorder prevention programs online as well.

I find it quite helpful to follow like-minded people on Twitter. I look for people whose descriptions include key words such as non-diet or anti-diet, intuitive eating, #HAES or health at every size, body positive, and so forth. Then when I need inspiration or if I just have a few minutes of downtime, I can scroll through my Twitter feed and be reminded of what I value and how I want to live in this world, because it's darned easy to forget, and let's not pretend that it isn't!

Instagram can be a landmine of body-image messages, both positive and negative. In a survey of 420 Instagram users, it was found that body image satisfaction predicts selfie posting, which in turn predicts Instagram conflict and negative romantic relationship outcomes (Ridgway & Clayton, 2016). While at first blush it seems like a good thing that people who are more satisfied with their bodies are more likely to post images of themselves on Instagram, the act of doing so can have negative results, which researchers refer to as "dark side" effects. "Research has shown narcissism, psychopathy, and insularity to be associated with sharing of images of one's self to social networking sites. Additional research posits, however, that social media sites help empower users by serving as a platform for self-representation" (p. 3). One of the complications is that it depends which community a person is involved with on Instagram. There are both body positivity and body negativity communities on Instagram and they serve to reinforce very different body image standards. In a study of the pro-anorexia and the fat acceptance communities on Instagram, researchers found that "The communities within this study indicate overlapping tactics to convey affiliation, reinforce solidarity, raise esteem, and distinguish against outsiders. Both groups used the strategy of labeling themselves through hashtags…Additionally, each community compared their own group's physical characteristics, attitudes and values with outside groups in order to assert their worth…For example, both groups engaged in conflict with outsiders on whether their body types should be considered beautiful…Fat acceptance posts showed disagreements about whether a large body size was healthy, while pro-anorexic posts showed disagreements about whether an emaciated body was healthy" (Marcus, 2016, p. 13). All of this is to note that while social media can be extremely supportive, just as in face-to-face peer groups, one has to be careful about with whom one becomes involved. Each group is insular, reinforcing and supporting its own belief system, and if it is one that does not lead to eating disorder recovery, then it is one that should be avoided. I think it is tempting to go "social media free," but is that realistic? Is it realistic to say to a high schooler, upon discovering that there is an unsavory group of kids at the high school who are promoting anti-social behavior that the high schooler should go friend-free? No! Generally, we try to encourage adolescents to be wise about the people with whom they spend the bulk of their time. The same should be true on social media. One caveat, however, is that the posting of selfies brings and added body image vulnerability to social media sites and one should be aware of the possible "dark side" effects of posting pictures of oneself to any social media site. This is not to say that it should never be done, but it is something that one might want to be careful about, due to the possible negative emotional consequences.

Other popular social media sites, such as Facebook, have not been as helpful for me regarding eating disorder recovery and support. I have been a member of a number of private groups and in the short term some of them have been quite helpful, but over time they seem to fade in interest. I find Facebook more useful for keeping in touch with friends and family with whom I do not frequently interact.

There are many cool apps out there now that help people keep track of what they have eaten. A great free one for people in recovery from eating disorders is one called RR, which stands for Recovery Record. Tracking food can be accomplished in writing or by taking a picture of each meal or snack. It is certainly is faster to snap a picture before digging in (or while digging in) than to track intake through writing. The point here is not to be perfect, not to say 3.5 ounces of whatever, but literally to keep track, not to lose track, to stay on top of, to be aware of, to observe, to monitor, to get a handle on, to record, to document, to chronicle. Tracking can help a person to be more mindful, even though I think that most mindfulness teachers would hesitate to prescribe writing things down in order to enhance one's mindfulness. Most mindfulness practices do not involve writing, but rather fully experiencing the moment, which is hard to do while also writing. But still, writing or otherwise tracking food intake can increase one's awareness and provide some accountability without becoming oppressive. If I write it down, it really did happen. Yes, I really ate, or really didn't eat, that item or those items. Tracking can help keep a person honest. Another big benefit is that once food is written it down, it can be forgotten. No need to obsess about it if it's written down. Weight Watchers has an all-encompassing and very popular app for logging food which has a closed social media component called Connect. It's very popular and used by literally millions of people, but it's also almost 100% weight focused. They aren't called Weight Watchers for no reason. Weight Watchers does not allow people with active eating disorders to become members. Possibly people in recovery from eating disorders may wish to stay away also.

CHAPTER 10
Move on

Keep a hand in recovery by helping someone else or making the world a better place for all bodies, but make commitments in other areas of life; pursue other interests.

Identity

In Study 2, participants addressed their developmental stage of eating disorder recovery. Maria was in a transitional identity stage. She said, *"I feel like a big fat woman after I eat…It's hard to go to a new self when you don't even know where you are and what you have."* Anna similarly stated, *"I'm still forcing myself to be more comfortable…I've made a good start, but it'll go beyond that."* Alex was farther along in recovery. She poignantly stated: *"It's no longer who I am, although it helped define who I became. It took a long time to get to that."* Natalie did not see her eating disorder as part of her true self. She said, *"I've divided myself from it, seeing it as a part of me but it's not me."*

Debbie, a participant in Study 1, wrote about a cathartic experience of separating herself from with her eating disorder identity. Here is the story in her own words:

"I handed my therapist a bag of clothes. Clothes that I knew I needed to get rid of in order to take the next step in recovery. She asked me if I wanted to do anything else with the clothes such as cut them up. "No, please just take them" I said. I desperately wanted to give these to her, so they no longer had power over me. It had taken so much to surrender these clothes. These clothes symbolized the darkest places of my eating disorder--clothes that could have been worn by a small child. Giving them to my therapist meant never going back to the place that felt so safe.

Later that week, I thought about what I really wanted to get rid of: my wedding dress! No, I thought, I want to destroy it! I could not get the thought out of my head. I knew that it sounded crazy. I wondered what I would do if anyone ever asked why I no longer have my wedding dress. I was really good at lying by this point in my eating disorder and I decided that if anyone ever asked, I would tell them that I gave it to Goodwill. I got home early from work one day and took that giant white dress out of the closet. I laid it in the living room and grabbed a black Sharpie. I wrote all over that stupid dress. "Counting calories; FEAR; alone; loss of control; growing up; too thin; looking like I'm 12; This isn't me; I hated you from the day I bought you; run, run, run; skeletal; SEX; I don't understand" these phrases and more covered the dress. When I had finished, I cut out what I had written and threw the rest of the dress away.

I look back at that day, now close to three years ago, and see how taking a risk, doing something that a 'good little girl' would never do jumpstarted my recovery."

Who am I?

Identity shifts as we grow and develop. Are we our eating disorders? No, of course not, but can I separate my "self" from my eating disorder? Yes and no, but mostly no because that it's all part of me. It feels self-rejecting to me to try to lop off that part of me and call it "Ed." I think the key is to start not just to see myself differently, but to reexamine my idea of the concept of identity. This statement by Neff (2003) made me realize how much I needed to change the way I look at identity. Self-esteem is out and self-compassion is in. "People with unstable, contingent high self-esteem often feel shame when they don't meet their desired self-validation goals and may express anger towards others in an attempt to externalize blame. They may also react with aggression towards those who threaten the ego" (p. 4). Eek. That cut a little too close to the bone for my liking. It's not a very flattering picture, but it is an accurate one of the way I have operated at times, and the way I see others operate – others who I do not want to be my role models. Leading with the ego is like asking for trouble. I want something more enduring. "Self-compassion confers many of the same benefits as self-esteem in that it provides positive self-affect and a strong sense of self-acceptance. However, these feelings are not based on evaluating the separate self or on comparing personal performances to those of others. Rather, they stem from recognizing the shared nature of the human condition, so that the self can be seen clearly and extended kindness without the need to feel superior to others" (p. 8). Sign me up.

There are a lot of people in this world who define themselves by what they eat. Some of those people are in recovery. It has been a struggle for me to not let what I eat or what I weigh define who I am. I have been through almost every modern food approach known to women, including low carbohydrate, low fat, vegan, and paleo, to mention just a few. This approach to identity, based on behaviors rather than a more enduring sense of self-worth, put me in the vulnerable situation of constantly needing to defend my identity with my behaviors. "Ironically, a person with high self-esteem is in a vulnerable position because even slight failure (e.g. an A student who receives a B) can feel like a self-esteem blow, while the excitement of a self-esteem boost may require near perfection (e.g., an A student needs to receive an A+ to feel anything special). Because it is not always possible to meet personal goals and expectations, even people with high trait self-esteem may have state self-esteem that fluctuates a great deal. Unstable state self-esteem often occurs when perceived self-worth is highly contingent on success in particular domains – getting that desired job, grade, date, competition trophy, and so on" (Neff, 2008, p. 3), or in the case of a person who has struggled with an eating disorder, achieving or maintaining that weight, following that food plan perfectly, staying on target regarding calories or other food counts. Identity as a vegan or paleo person is contingent on certain behaviors that, at least for me, were too easily violated. And where did that put me? It put me back in a situation where I wasn't sure about my identity any more. Fortunately for me, the whole concept of self-compassion came to the rescue, which allowed me to see myself as less different than other people, less in need of a distinguishing characteristic to put out into the world and defend to the death. I can be kinder to myself, more aware that I am one among many, and less identified with my thoughts and feelings (for more detail on self-compassion, review the section on this topic near the end of Chapter 7).

If self-compassion does not appeal, then another approach is to improve one's self-schemas. In an effort to target changes in identity related to eating disorder recovery, researchers developed an intervention designed "to alter the underlying array of self-related cognitions, referred to as self-schemas, as the mechanism underlying changes in eating disorder symptoms and health" (Stein, Wing, Lewis, & Rughunathan, 2011, p. 358). In other words, they saw self-schemas, or a person's sense of identity, as a driver of eating disorders rather than a consequence of eating disorders. And their intervention attempted to shift a person's self-schemas, or sense of identity, in order to alleviate their eating disorders. They went on to write, "The intervention program is based on findings that show a highly interconnected collection of few positive and many negative self-schemas is predictive of eating disorder symptoms in clinical and community-based samples and this effect is mediated through availability of a fat self-schema" (Stein, Wing, Lewis, & Rughunathan, 2011, p. 358). Their efforts were aimed not at dismantling this "fat" self-schema, but rather at adding positive self-schemas in other areas that were unrelated to body weight or shape.

Much has already been discussed about self-worth and the possible damage to one's eating of appearance contingent self-worth. There is a difference between identity and self-worth, but they do overlap. Identity answers the question "who am I?" whereas self-worth answers the question "how do I know that I am worthy?" Brené Brown (2013) has made a huge contribution in the area of self-worth, which I like to think of as inherent self-worth. By this way of thinking, which is consistent with many religious views, every single human on the planet is inherently worthy. There is nothing that any of us can do to become more or less worthy as human beings. Certainly we can do good and evil, to contribute or take advantage, but each individual person is basically worthy. I find this way of thinking to be a great relief. I don't have to "hustle for my self-worth," (Brown, 2013) because I am already worthy. If I start with the assumption that I am worthy, then it becomes a lot easier to consider my identity. Who am I? I can consider my roles: mother, wife, daughter, friend, colleague, professor, church member; I can also consider my accomplishments: tenured full professor, black belt; or my loves: reader, dog lover; or I can identify myself by the characteristics I value: honesty, grit, wisdom, and so forth. But every time I come out with an "I am…" statement, I have learned to ask myself these questions:

1. Does this aspect of my identity (my "I am…") separate me from others – does it lead me to feel superior to or inferior from anyone else? Because if so, then I need to question whether this is more reflective of my ego than of a sense of enduring self-worth.

2. Is this aspect of my identity (my "I am…") contingent on certain behaviors? Because if I have to continue to do something in order to maintain my identity, then it's probably not very enduring and is more likely an ego thing than a true sense of who I am inside.

3. Is this aspect of my identity (my "I am…") related to food, eating, body, or weight? Because if I am using food, eating, body, or weight to define myself, then most likely I am operating out of my anxiety-driven eating disorder.

When I ask myself who I am, I often come up with either descriptive or contingent answers. This is how I have been taught in my culture to define myself. But now that I know more about self-compassion and its relationship to identity, I have started to shift the way I think about identity. Self-Compassion includes the increase of self-kindness, common humanity, and mindfulness, as well as the reduction of self-judgment, isolation, and over-identification (Neff, 2003). So really maybe all I need to ask is:

4. Does this aspect of my identity (my "I am…") increase my self-kindness, common humanity and mindfulness and decrease my self-judgment, isolation, an over-identification? Because if it does, then I am well on my way to a self-compassionate identity.

Each of us is a rich combination of many parts. Our bodies do play a role in who we are – the color of our skin, the shape of our eyes, and many other aspects of our bodies. Full recovery from an eating disorder does not mean that we leave our bodies behind. It means that we no longer let our bodies' shapes and weights unduly affect our sense of ourselves. I am partly my body, partly many other things that all add up to my unique self. And yet, if I put my accomplishments and my commitments and my values out there and let them define me, I cringe at how vulnerable that makes me. Yes, I have earned a black belt in Tae Kwon Do. Yes, I have raised two children. Yes, I have been married for a long time. Those accomplishments will not be taken away from me. But I risk losing any enduring sense of self-worth and miss the whole concept of self-compassion if I identify either with my eating disorder or with a food plan, or even as a person in full recovery. Basing my identity on behaviors is a risky proposition. Why can't I see myself as yet one more human being who is doing my very best to be my very best? I want to be one among many, a person who works hard to fulfill my commitments and to be kind to myself and others and to weather the storms of feelings – including the hurts and the slights as well as the glowing praise and the love – without being blown completely off course by them.

Commitment

Early on in my recovery, when I was very involved in a food-plan-based 12 step group, we talked about bringing our cups, our scales, and our commitments with us when we stepped out into the world. I don't judge people who weigh and measure their food. I did it for seven years and it helped me a lot at the time. I don't do it now, though. I still have a strong commitment. The thing that has changed is what I am committed to. During the time that I was weighing and measuring my food, I was committed to following my food plan no matter what. And as long as I maintained that commitment, I could follow the food plan. As soon as it occurred to me that maybe I could stop following the food plan and still be okay around food, it became almost impossible for me to follow the food plan any more. I had lost my commitment. Now I am more committed to my whole self than I am to any particular doctrine or approach or group of people. I think it is important to get clear about our commitments. We all want to make promises we can keep. But to whom/what are those promises made? I am somewhat committed to eating healthfully, but I am more committed to taking care of myself, to eating in response to my physical, emotional and spiritual needs. Sometimes that might not fit the "healthy eating" description of another person, but to me it's healthy because it involves responsive self-care. I am committed to taking care of myself around food and eating, to paying attention to my body, mind and spirit and to responding as appropriately as I can.

Pride and Humility

Pride is not an entirely bad thing. It is really important to feel good about our accomplishments. But there is unhealthy pride, and it is almost guaranteed to lead to disaster, at least that is my experience. The minute I start thinking, "I'm done," "I am a success," or "I've got this," I risk straying into an ego-pride that feels fantastic for a while, then almost depressingly predictably activates a part of me that insists that I stay humble. If I don't wake up to the fact that I am strutting around feeling too me-me-me for my own good, then I quickly find myself doing what I suppose might be considered self-sabotage but I have come to realize is a way of me remembering how important it is to stay humble. To stay recovered is to stay humble, for me. I am not better than anyone else. I am not even a better person that I used to be. I am the same person, thinking differently and acting differently as a result, but I am not better in a superior/inferior way. I am also not worse than anyone else. I am not worse than a person who never had an eating disorder. I am not worse than someone who has not struggled as much as I have. I am not worse than someone who has a beautiful tan, or is six feet tall, or has any other physical attribute or any other kind of attribute. I am just another human being, doing the best I can to operate as maturely as I am able. It's not that I don't want to feel good about all of the hard work that I've put in, or give up because who even cares. What I want to do is to recognize that when I put my ego in charge of how I feel about myself, I'm on slippery ground.

Prevention Efforts

Prevention is always better than intervention. With regard to body image, there are many people both with and without eating disorders who are suffering from body dissatisfaction, so whatever can be done to prevent or decrease that suffering, whether or not the person is at risk for developing an eating disorder, is likely a worthwhile investment of time and energy. "Eating disorder prevention should address the doorway to pathology – the individual's relationship with the body. To recover, or avoid illness in the first place, individuals must learn to be with, and in, their bodies in a healthy and effective way…From an early age, we can teach children positive self-care practices and ways of being that go beyond prevention toward what it takes to live a life full of embodied self-regulation and body appreciation… To effectively prevent and treat eating disorders, children and adolescents must learn how to negotiate life without leaving themselves or turning against the body" (Cook-Cottone, 2016, p. 99).

There are myriad wellness professionals with whom a person interacts over the course of her lifetime. This includes a physical education teacher, who is usually a regular fixture of elementary students' lives, as well as a health teacher, who may not come on the scene until middle school, but who can have a profound effect on students' understanding of healthful attitudes around food, eating, exercise and their bodies. Just because a person is put in a position of health or wellness power, however, does not mean that they are well informed about eating disorders. It also does not mean that they do not have a current, active eating disorder themselves. When researchers surveyed 596 teacher education students in Australia (Yager, Gray, Curry & McLean, 2017), they found that those who were preparing to become health and physical education teachers were more likely to be engaging in excessive exercise than other teacher education students. These findings are consistent with other research regarding professionals in the food and exercise industry who are put in a position of trust to help the children of our world develop sustainably healthy attitudes and behaviors but may themselves be caught in a situation where they experience high levels of pressure to be thin (women) or muscular (men). So please do not expect others to do all the prevention work. They honestly may not be up to it. This is a shared responsibility of us all.

School-based eating disorder prevention programs give a chance for every student in a school to consider how they approach food, eating, body, and weight, which are certainly issues that touch us all. "School-based eating disorder prevention programs (including those within university settings) have advanced greatly in the past decade in that, in addition to the availability of different programs, we are witnessing larger funding opportunities, increased effectiveness, and greater dissemination of evidence-based programs" (Neumark-Sztainer, 2016, p. 30). This is hugely encouraging. When done right, obesity and eating disorder prevention can be conducted at the same time, because, really, the message should be the same (even though obesity prevention messages often are harsh and shaming, they have the opportunity to be more supportive and encouraging – more consistent with a Health at Every Size ® approach).

One approach to prevention is to try to aim healthy messages to all. Another approach is to target higher-risk individuals. The three major risk factors have been theorized to operate in a causative way, "starting with preoccupation with body weight and shape, which leads to excessive self-control and body anxiety, which in turn predicts using various methods of weight loss, such as dieting," (Zarychta, Mullan, Kruk, & Luszczynska, 2017, p. 2), but these researchers determined that it's all a vicious cycle whereby each of the three elements lead to and predict the other elements. Any person who is over-concerned with their body weight and shape or who is engaging in excessive self-control, or who is anxious about their body or is attempting weight loss through dieting or other means is at risk for developing an eating disorder, because each of these elements are both causes and effects of each other. Adolescents can enter the vicious cycle at any point: appearance orientation, appearance worry, or dieting. Prevention efforts must include more than the easy-to-repeat mantra "diets don't work," because the message behind this, which is true, is that diets don't result in long term weight loss. But the part that is completely missed is the appearance component. We must protect children against appearance orientation and appearance worries. Maybe there needs to be an addendum to the mantra: Diets totally work if the goal is: constant worry about appearance, thinking that how a person looks is what is most important about that person, and/or the possible development of an eating disorder.

Communication

Many problems in life are communication problems. Most people could benefit from improved communication. Someone who restricts or binges or purges may be trying to "say" something indirectly through her eating disorder. Helping children and adults to communicate directly can help prevent the need to use food and eating to serve a communicative purpose. Just as in real estate the thing to consider when buying a house is "location, location, location," the thing to consider in human relationships, in a family or at school or at work, is "communication, communication, communication."

I have found that it is very helpful for me to journal in order to get to an appropriate level of self-understanding before I attempt to communicate with others about what is going on with me. Sometimes I find that I can figure out what is going on with me in conversation with people I trust, but I seem to be more effective at this when I write it out. Once I know what's going on with me and what I need or want to say, then saying it directly to others is both terrifying and a huge relief.

Just the idea of truly speaking my truth makes me want to crawl under the table and hide, but some courage and faith that I am doing the right thing can catapult me to say whatever it is that I need or want to say, and all of a sudden life starts looking up. Even then, just because I've said something once or may many more than once does not mean that it has been effectively communicated. But even my botched attempts to share my truth in a caring and direct manner can alleviate my need to use my food, eating, body or weight to indirectly communicate what is going on with me. Refusing to eat or eating too much does not effectively communicate my hurt, anger, resentment, or anything else. And I am the one to suffer, not the person to whom I should have said something.

Parents

Parents play can play an important role in prevention. According to groundbreaking scholar Neumark-Sztainer (2016), Four "cornerstones" that parents can use to help their children have a positive body image and a healthy weight "include the following: (a) model healthy behaviors for your children (e.g., eat a piece of cake, not the whole cake, and express enjoyment, rather than sentiments of guilt); (b) provide an environment that makes it easy for your children to make healthy choices (e.g., family meals); (c) focus less on weight, instead focus on behaviors and overall health; and (d) provide a supportive environment with lots of talking and even more listening" with the overall message being "talk less, do more…meaning parents should talk less about weight and do more to model behaviors that they want their children to emulate and to provide a home environment in which healthier choices are the easier choices" (p. 31).

In reviewing 20 reports of interventions to prevent body dissatisfaction and eating disorders that involved parents between 1992 and 2013, researchers found that although parents' roles have not been extensively investigated, when they are retained and engaged, parents can have a significant positive impact on preventing children's negative body image and eating problems (Hart, Cornell, Damiano, Paxton, 2015). It is a complex situation, like many parenting challenges. The idea is for parents to support children's positive body image so to avoid their children's future body dissatisfaction, because "Body dissatisfaction predicts the development of disordered eating patterns (i.e., dieting behaviors, binge eating, and using food for emotional regulation), higher body mass index (BMI), less physical activity, poor dietary quality, low self-esteem, depressive symptoms, and clinical eating disorders in children and adolescents" (Hart, Damiano, & Paxton, 2016, p. 458).

The window of time to positively impact children in a prevention (as opposed to an intervention) way is relatively short and must be accomplished fairly early in life. Whatever parents do when their children are young really sets the stage for later parenting as well as later independent living. "Child body dissatisfaction, unhealthy eating patterns and parental feeding practices, have all been highlighted as targets for obesity prevention. A review of prevention interventions for weight-related problems in children concluded that effective interventions should be approached from a health-centred rather than a weight centred perspective, with the parents as central agents of change" (p. 459). Researchers developed a positive body image program for parents to implement with their preschool aged children.

"Confident Body, Confident Child (CBCC) is a new universal prevention resource, providing parenting strategies to promote body satisfaction and healthy eating in 2- to 6-year-old children. CBCC includes booklets, a poster, a children's book, website and parent workshop, which were developed from research evidence" (p. 459). Researchers randomly assigned 345 parents to (1) CBCC resources and 2-hour workshop, (2) CBCC resources only (no workshop), (3) printed nutrition resource, and (4) waitlist control (no materials provided during the study). Not surprisingly, the first group of parents of 2- to 6-year old children who received the materials and participated in a workshop showed the most impressive gains, followed by those who received the CBCC resources only, those who received the printed nutrition resource, and those who did not receive any information at all. All parents would no doubt benefit from knowing the power that they have over their children's positive body image. By focusing on health and not weight, avoiding weight-related teasing, not using food as a punishment or as a reward but instead sharing family meals with the TV off, parents can have a profound positive impact on their children's physical and mental health.

Other researchers "have observed that younger children appear to benefit from the concrete, embodied components of prevention programs that address self-regulation and self-care (e.g., active yoga practice, relaxation strategies, feeling identification and coping). These observations are consistent with research suggesting self-regulation can be taught to and practiced by children prior to the full emergence of metacognitive skills with studies showing improvement among children as young as in the first grade" (Cook-Cottone, 2016, p. 100-101). Embodied self-care and self-regulation can be used at the treatment or prevention level, so why not start early in hopes that our children will grow up more resilient and able to manage their lives without developing eating disorders? Cook-Cottone (2016) specifically suggested what she named Mindful Self-Care. "Mindful self-care is actionable, accessible, and addresses both the internal and external experiences of the self. Practices that address internal or intrapersonal experience include: self-awareness, (e.g., I have a calm awareness of my feelings), self-compassion (e.g., I kindly acknowledged my own challenges and difficulties) and physical practices (e.g., healthy eating, hydration, moderate exercise, and rest). Mindful self-care practices that address the external experience of the self include cultivating supportive relationships, creating a body positive environment, and setting personal boundaries" (p. 101).

Regarding supporting parents in children's food choices, there are so many things out there for parents, but the main thing that I have learned it (1) not to assume that adults know better than a child about how hungry the child is or is not, and (2) not to shame a child's body, or anybody's body for that matter. As with all parenting, we are actively trying to work our way out of a job. So how do we want our children to act around food when they are out of our presence? We certainly do not want our children so starved for cookies or other treats that they raid the neighbor's cabinets whenever they get the chance. We also want them to be open to trying new foods and to be willing to eat non-preferred food when necessary. We can introduce new foods and offer sweets and treats and generally show positive, healthy behaviors around food that we model to our children and to others.

Another role that parents may be able to play is to help foster children's self-compassion. This involves a protective set of attitudes that can help young people immensely. "The feelings of self-acceptance and self-kindness entailed by self-compassion should lead to fewer harsh judgments when adolescents confront disliked aspects of themselves. The ability to frame one's experience in light of the common human experience should provide a sense of interpersonal connectedness that can help teens cope with fears of social rejection. The mindful aspect of self-compassion should help prevent adolescents from obsessively ruminating on pessimistic thoughts and emotions, a process that often leads to psychological dysfunction" (Neff & McGee, 2010, p. 226). How to do this is to be as responsive as possible when the child is an infant, so as to foster a secure attachment bond, to continue to support children as they grow, and to function as effectively as possible as a family unit by talking about issues without blaming or shaming. "An adolescent with a secure attachment bond, supportive mother, and functional family is likely to have more self-compassion than one with a problematic family environment, given that care and compassion have been appropriately modeled by others" (p. 227-228). But possibly more important is modeling, and if necessary directly teaching, the concept of self-compassion, because it adds something over and above all the other positive parenting behaviors. Neff and McGee's (2010) study of 235 adolescents and 287 young adults revealed that "self-compassion partially mediated the link between the predictors of maternal support, family functioning, attachment, and the personal fable and the outcome of wellbeing" (p. 233). By itself, "self-compassion was a significant predictor of mental health among adolescents as well as young adults. Those with more self-compassion reported less depression and anxiety as well as greater feelings of social connectedness" (p. 235). How to foster greater self-compassion among adolescents and young adults? Neff and McGee (2010) found that greater maternal support (as opposed to maternal criticism) was predictive of greater self-compassion. The more an adolescent or young adult reported harmonious, close families with warm, caring and supportive parents, the more likely there were to have higher self-compassion scores. This is possibly because self-compassion was modeled to them by their parents, and possibly because their parents had directly taught them self-kindness, common humanity, and de-identification with negative emotions.

It is important to note that eating disorders are not completely preventable. "Parents are an important piece of the puzzle and can help in the prevention, early detection, and successful treatment of their children. However, families operate within broader systems, including individual dispositions, friends, schools, communities, societal values, and physical environments. Therefore, while parents can decrease the risk of eating disorders developing in their children, there are other factors at play and even if parents do "everything right" an eating disorder may develop" (Neumark-Sztainer, 2016, p. 32).

Body acceptance

When Avalos and Tylka (2006) studied 597 college women, they found that "lack of body acceptance by others may encourage women to spend more time attending to their outer appearance than the functioning of their bodies" (p. 494) which has long been theorized by scholars to be true. They also found that general acceptance was not relevant as a predictor of undue attention to appearance – only body acceptance messages helped to deflect this focus on physical appearance. This is important for those of us who hope to positively influence the next generation. They went on to write that, "the better way to encourage women's positive attitudes and respect toward their bodies is via communication of acceptance of their bodies rather than via hints, suggestions, and/or criticisms that they need to lose weight" (p. 494).

Greetings

One thing that I started practicing a number of years ago was to forego as many comments as I could about other people's appearance. I refrain as much as possible from saying "oh what a cute shirt," or "your hair looks fabulous," or whatever else people say to bond with each other around appearance, usually in greeting. What convinced me to do this was the argument that all judgment, whether negative or positive, is still judgment. If a particular shirt is cute/good then what about the other shirts that person has worn in my presence? Are they ugly/bad? I certainly learned at an early age that it was unacceptable to greet someone with the comment with "wow, that shirt is really ugly," so why is the reverse completely appropriate? It leaves unsaid the negative and then makes it necessary to say something positive in order to allay people's fears of my possible negative judgment. I do not want anyone worrying about what I might say about their outfit while they are getting dressed. If they like it, they should wear it. If it's uncomfortable to them for some reason, they should not wear it. My opinion, or anyone else's opinion, is not something that anyone should worry about. That is almost the definition of objectification – when we see our bodies through others' eyes. I think that comments about others' appearance is objectification, short and simple. As I have refrained from these comments over the years, I have noticed a number of things. First, I have noticed how many people engage in this form of social commentary, even those who I think should "know better," even people who I have "educated" about the possible harmful nature of physical commentary. They persist and nothing I think will stop them. I say things like, "it's so great to see you," or "it's been too long," or "thanks for coming," or some kind of other positive social greeting that avoids the need to make physical commentary. And yet, I get physical commentary in response. Mostly I try to be polite and say, "thanks so much," but I don't really feel grateful, and if it's someone I see on a regular basis, then I might say something. I told a co-worker once, "no more comments about my body or my clothing, ever." He stopped. All of his comments up until that point about my body and clothing had been completely socially appropriate, but they also made me uncomfortable. Somehow it was easier to say that to a man than to a woman. I have tried to say it to women, but they have engaged in discussion about it and justified it and don't stop. Men have the good sense to see the boundary set by me as a woman, and to abide by it without argument. Women, or at least some of the women I know, use physical commentary as capital and cannot envision other ways of relating to each other. Or something. All I know is that they do not stop even after I ask. I am probably also not as clear with women either, so I should probably take responsibility for that.

Imagine my glee when I read this in a research review article: "*Complimentary weightism*, or appearance-related compliments (e.g. Telling a patient, "You've lost weight…looking good!), is stigmatizing because although seemingly positive on the surface, it still marks people as good or bad based on their weight" (Tylka, Annuziato, Burgard, Danielsdottir, Shuman, Davis & Calogero, 2014, p. 5). Aha! There is a term for my pet peeve! I will now avoid complimentary weightism whenever I can. According to these researchers, the negative effects of complimentary weightism include internalized weight stigma. "*Internalized weight stigma* refers to the degree to which individuals personally adopt negative weight-based societal stereotypes and judge themselves based on these stereotypes. This self-judgment may foster body blame and body shame (e.g., "If only I wasn't so large, I would not be teased—I am therefore ashamed of my body") and appearance monitoring (e.g., vigilant about wearing slimming clothing to prevent others' from stigmatizing her body). Internalized weight bias is not related to BMI; thus, a person of any weight can experience and internalize weight bias and discrimination" (Tylka, Annuziato, Burgard, Danielsdottir, Shuman, Davis & Calogero, 2014, p. 5).

Possible things to say in greeting other than commenting on a person's body or clothing:

It's great to see you!

It's been too long.

How are you?

I've missed you.

How are you feeling after such a long trip?

Hi or Hello.

Good to see you again.

Use the person's same and say it happily – ex: "Susan!"

I challenge us all to try this and to see what happens. There should be nothing offensive about it, and yet it is somehow bucking the system to avoid physical comments. I really opened my eyes.

Vision

In Study 2, we asked participants, "If you were to imagine your life without an eating disorder, what would it look like?" I think this is a good exercise for people who are in partial recovery. Really the question is not that different from "what is your vision of full eating disorder recovery?" Below are what women in the study shared. These are beautiful visions, capturing both where each woman was in her journey to full recovery as well as the types of challenges (or maintenance factors) with which she is struggling.

Natalie: *"Overall it wouldn't be a lot different…everybody has their stuff that they have to deal with…I wouldn't be so self-conscious, less apt to blame my weight on things…more accepting of myself…more confident."*

Alex: "*It would look a lot different because right as I was done recovering I met my now husband and I clung to that relationship so much that I didn't take the time to figure out my own goals and what I wanted to do. Had I not been so focused all through high school and college, I might have been able to figure out me before I just jumped into a relationship with someone because he liked me. I didn't really enjoy college – I was immersed in food and calorie counting. I didn't have a lot of friends and such. I also think that I am who I am because I went through that. I am an understanding person.*"

Alice: "*I'd have a lot more time to do other stuff that I want. Not such much anymore, but I was always preoccupied by it. I couldn't go out to dinner, and stuff like that.*"

Maria: "*It would be wonderful. I worry too much about clothes and how I look. Health-wise it would be awesome too because I am so concerned about health and my looks. It would be an awesome thing if I didn't have an eating disorder.*"

Cathy: "*My habits wouldn't be that different because I eat most meals and I don't think about food that much.*"

What?

For full recovery from eating disorders, it is important to pinpoint where one's vision of what constitutes full recovery might need to be readjusted. For years, I thought that that the goal was to never crave sugar or sweets. If I didn't crave sugar or sweets, I wouldn't eat them, and therefore I wouldn't binge on them. Although that is certainly logical, I wasn't helpful in the long (or even in most cases short) run because in fact I did crave sugar and sweets at times. It took me a long time to figure out that I had been focusing on the wrong link in the chain of thoughts and behaviors that led to a binge. I came to learn that everyone craves sugar or sweets sometimes. The difference between someone without an eating disorder and me was that they craved sugar or sweets, had a bit or a bit more than a bit, and were satisfied. How did they do that? In part, they did that because their thinking was different than mine. They thought "gosh I really want some ice cream, some really good ice cream." Then they went to their freezer or the store, had some, ate until satisfied (and didn't need to eat the whole pint to get to satisfaction)

217

and then felt and possibly said "ah...that really hit the spot," and went on with their lives. My thinking was something like "I could really go for some ice cream....no...can't...no...don't....no....oh, f-it, yes...gimme, lots...shouldn't have done that...more...get more...now...ugh...yuck, wish I hadn't done that."

Why?

When I was in the depths of my eating disorder, my why was a number on a scale, and behind that why was social acceptance – among family, friends, myself, future love interests, and so forth. I thought I would be more acceptable, more okay, if I weighed a certain amount. There is certainly a lot of data out there that people of average or low weight are more accepted in society, but of course no one person is any more worthy or unworthy of love, attention, and acceptance than any other person, no matter their weight or skin color or hairstyle or grades or job or income or any other factor that distinguishes one person from another. Yet as much as I know that in my heart, the weight thing is still present in me to some extent and in American society as well. Just the fact that this is a shallow and socially unjust goal did not and probably would not have deterred me from pursuing it. What deters me now from focusing so strongly on weight is that I want to feel good in my body, to feel satisfied, to feel the best that I can feel on any given day. But why? Because I feel fantastic when I feel connected to my own body, when I am trusting it, responding appropriately to its messages. It just feels great. Possibly I have an overblown reaction to this experience of inner connection due to my years of mind-body disconnection, but also perhaps others in recovery have the same celebratory reaction to feeling connected as I do. Plus, the alternative is really unattractive. I am motivated by not wanting to feel like I'm at war with my body. I don't want to hate my body or any other part of myself. Those area great whys. I have both positive (carrot) and negative (stick) motivations, as most people do. Mainly I want to move on. I don't want to live in my eating disorder. I'm moving on.

Some of my friends who are recovered from eating disorders describe their number one recovery motivation as "Freedom." They want freedom from dieting, from obsession, freedom to eat spontaneously, freedom to be whoever they want. My number one motivation is "Wholeness." I value freedom, don't get me wrong, but I am willing to sacrifice some freedom if I can feel connected internally. I want to feel good, but I know that I don't and won't always feel good. Even on the days that I feel bad, I want to feel connected to all parts of myself. I also know I don't and won't always be as responsive to all parts of myself as I would like. That's normal. But I want to try; I want to have that as my goal, and to do the best I can on any given day. So that's my primary motivation, but I have others also. Here's my more comprehensive list:

1. To feel whole by being connected within myself – mind-body-spirt – and to be as responsive as I can be to/with all parts of my being;

2. To be a good role model;

3. To feel as good as I can physically (energetic), mentally (clear-minded), emotionally (even-keeled), and spiritually (connected);

4. To fulfill my purpose on the planet, whatever that is;

5. To prove that I can, not just survive an eating disorder, but that I can overcome it;

6. To be healthy enough (physically, mentally, emotionally and spiritually) that I can be there for my children's life events (graduation, marriage, etc.) and eventually, possibly, my grandchildren's events.

Wholeness

Synonyms to "connected" that I like are: allied, attached, together, linked, united, bonded, associated, partnered, and joined. Antonyms (opposites): disconnected, dissociated, separated, alienated. Partly it's fun to play with words but it's also helpful to me to explore what I mean by "connected." If it's going to be my entire goal of recovery, then what do I mean by it? I remember quite clearly in college when I was not diagnosed with anorexia but should have been, and I was reading Karl Marx for an economics class. One of Marx's ideas is that in industrial factories, workers were alienated from their work product, in other words, disconnected from the product they were helping to create. I remember focusing on that word "alienated" and realizing how much it applied to me, and how far beyond factory work it went. I felt alienated from almost everything, but most importantly I felt alienated from my body and myself. What I want now is truly the opposite of feeling alienated. I want to feel connected, true to myself, and doing the best I can to care for my body and myself in a responsive or attuned way.

I notice that wholeness is basically the opposite of dissociation. And dissociation is what I felt both during my eating disorder and also during some early parts of my recovery. Following all the rules felt awful to me, but it wasn't just because I am a rebel who doesn't like following rules. It was in part because the rules were not consistent with my inner signals. It's like I was following a plan that said "go to bed every night at 10 pm" but I wasn't tired at 10 pm. Sometimes I was tired at 9 pm, sometimes at 10:30. And yet, I had to follow the 10 pm rule in order to… in order to what? To get my gold star, to be a good girl, to feel okay about myself. Well I finally realized that my exact bedtime isn't the point – the point for me is paying attention to my needs, to generally have a bedtime that fits my own physical needs but to be able to be flexible and to take care of my own needs without apology or guilt, in fact, with pride and confidence.

I am not alone in this desire to be whole. One recovered eating disorder therapist captured the complexity of both the problem and a path to the solution when she said to researchers: *"With eating disorders, so many live in their head. People are disembodied and talking about therapy. The problem is that they are not in their bodies…I think there is a way to model an embodied stance that has a lot to offer with eating disorders…The scariest thing for people I think is to be sexual, sensual, aggressive. Yet that is exactly what they want, in a way. I don't know at what point they become two-dimensional in their mind, but in the eating disorder they are just a visual image to themselves. It is just tragic because they are living on the fringes of themselves…Recovery is an incarnation of the whole body and getting in touch with those drives"* (Bowlby, Anderson, Hall & Willingham, 2015, p. 6). Researchers described this process in part as "moving from a place of self-hatred and self-betrayal to a place of self-love and acceptance" (p. 6), although the embodiment component adds another layer of wholeness to that.

Quality of life

Another reason to recover fully from an eating disorder is improved quality of life. Low quality of life is a vulnerability factor for and a result of eating disorders, and improved quality of life can both spur recovery and be a result of recovery. Quality of life, as defined by 19 research participants who were suffering or recovering from eating disorders included (in order of most often to less often mentioned): intimate and family relationships, physical health, mental wellbeing, work/study, friendships and leisure (Mitchison, Dawson, Hand, Mond & Hay, 2016). Who does not want all of those? I think it is a helpful motivator to be reminded, as in this study, that people with eating disorders report much lower quality of life than those who have moved on. For me, the more I move on, the better my quality of life. I am more able to be present in my relationships, my physical health is not compromised by questionable eating practices, I feel better about myself and am more able to handle challenges that come my way, I can concentrate more on my work and on learning new things, I can show up for my friendships more effectively and I can organize leisure activities and show up for them too. One of the things I learned in 12-step programs was to think through the possible consequences of acting on the urge to binge, restrict, or purge. While the immediate consequences of binge eating, restricting or purging may not be as severe as I was led to believe they would be during my years 12 step programs, there are definitely immediate consequences to every aspect of my quality of life, starting with my mental well-being and extending to all other areas that the study participants mentioned. I want all of those areas of my life to flourish. It's probably not enough to keep me walking on the path of recovery every day to know that my head is clear and I want it to stay that way, but it is good to remember every once in a while how foggy I used to be and how now I have a level of clarity that I want to keep as long as I possibly can. Whatever mental fogginess I experience I would like to be a symptom of ageing rather than eating or not eating (although of course I want to put off the mental fogginess of age as long as I can!).

Eating expectancies

Along with a broad vision, each person has certain expectations of what is likely to happen when she eats. One thing I learned a long time ago about expectations with regard to movies is that I want to keep my expectations in check. If I think "oh, this is going to be the best movie ever; I've heard such good things about it," I am almost guaranteed to be disappointed. But if I think "this might be good; let's see!" with a slightly positive but mostly neutral expectation, then I am much less likely to be disappointed. Eating expectancies are possibly similar to my experience with movies, but more likely they become self-fulfilling prophecies. If I expect something to be terrible, I can pretty much make it terrible and then I can at least feel that I was correct in my expectations. If I expect something to be satisfying, then it doesn't automatically become satisfying, but I can manage the situation so that I am more likely to confirm my expectations.

There is a measure of eating expectancies (what a person expects about eating) called the Eating Expectancy Inventory. It includes these five subscales: (1) eating helps manage negative affect; (2) eating alleviates boredom; (3) eating is pleasurable and useful as a reward; (4) eating enhances cognitive competence; and (5) eating leads to feeling out of control (EEI; Hohlstein, Smith, & Atlas, 1998). When comparing non-eating disorder controls to people who were fully recovered, partially recovered, and active in their eating disorder, researchers found interesting difference by group (Fitzsimmons-Craft, Keatts & Bardone-Cone, 2013). As hypothesized and replicating previous findings, the control group scored more similarly to the fully recovered group and the partially recovered group scored more like the active eating disorder group. Of particular interest is that the partially recovered group was most likely to expect that eating would lead to feeling out of control. Their scores were actually higher than those in an active eating disorder. And it makes sense, because they were in a period of transition and they were scared. Fully recovered participants were least likely to expect feeling out of control after eating, whereas non-eating disorder controls were in the middle. It's normal to expect to feel a little bit out of control around eating. This is another example of where perfectionism stands in the way of normalcy. Normal people are not perfect, by definition. If they were perfect, they would not be normal! The non-eating disorder controls were least likely to expect that eating helps manage negative affect or alleviates boredom and most likely to expect that eating enhances cognitive competence. The non-eating disorder controls and fully recovered group had about the same expectations that eating is pleasurable and useful as a reward, and on this sub-scale they were quite a bit lower than the partially recovered and active group, who scored about the same as each other. I provide all these details because I think it can be helpful in seeing where it is that a non-eating disorder person is in relation to someone with an eating disorder, what to shoot for, and how to be realistic in one's vision.

Inventory/Review

One thing that I notice about what I have learned is that I forget things. I'm talking about more than walking into a room and wondering what it was that I was looking for in that room. I'm talking about things that I know to be true for myself. Whatever I know to be true to myself has to be on some kind of self-reminder system for me, or I drift away from what I know to be true and fall into the same old behaviors that I thought had put behind me long ago. I learned about this review system from David Allen's (2001/2015) *Getting Things Done* approach. He argued that our brains are not good at keeping track of things. We need to set up reminders for ourselves so that we don't forget. These reminders extend to checklist items (call for an oil change) as well as for other, hopefully more meaningful, personal inventories. One way to do this is a weekly inventory on Saturday mornings to see how I'm doing on the things that I know work for me. It's not a pass/fail test. It's a check to see how I'm doing. Am I straying from what I know to be good for me? How far am I straying? What if anything might I want to adjust to stay on track?

Based on the topics in this book, here are the questions I suggest for a weekly inventory:

1. Have I been eating regularly?

2.   Have I been eating to satisfaction?

3.   Have I really believed that full recovery is possible?

4.   Have I practiced body acceptance and appreciation?

5.   Have I practiced body-led eating?

6.   Have I kept my thinking about food, eating, body and weight to a minimum?

7.   Have I been thinking mostly about other aspects of life (beyond food, eating, body or weight)?

8.   Have I been in the zone on a daily – or at least regular - basis?

9.   Have any of my personal maintaining factors snuck back in? (Have I been anxious about anything? Have I been uncomfortable about my body's appearance and not processed that feeling by journaling or talking to someone about it? Have I weighed myself? Have I been counting calories? Have I been restricting my eating, even subtly?)

10. Have I contributed to the greater good by helping someone else or by making the world a better place for all bodies?

These questions work well for me because I wrote them, but I think it is a good exercise for each person to come up with individualized weekly inventory questions. The point is not to be judgmental, but rather to use the questions as a way of staying on track, a way of reminding myself what I want to be doing, a way of staying in full eating disorder recovery.

Below is a blank weekly inventory form for whatever questions might be helpful. Consider it one more way to move on. And best of luck. We are all capable of full eating disorder recovery, and worthy to achieve it.

Weekly inventory questions	Space to write out answer
1. Have I been…	
2. Have I been …	
3. Have I really believed…	
4. Have I practiced…	
5. Have I practiced…	
6. Have I been thinking about…	

REFERENCES

Aguera, Z., Brewin, N., Chen, J., Granero, R., Kang, Q., Fernandez-Aranda, F., & Arcelus, J. (2017). Eating symptomology and general psychopathology in patients with anorexia nervosa from China, UK and Spain: A cross-cultural study examining the role of social attitudes, *PLoS ONE*, 12(3), 1-14.

Alcoholics Anonymous (2001). *Alcoholics Anonymous, 4th Ed.* NY: A.A. World Services.

Allen, D. (2001/2015) *Getting Things Done: The Art of Stress-Free Productivity.* Penguin: NY.

American Psychiatric Association (1994). *Diagnostic and Statistical Manual of Mental Disorders (4th Ed.)* USA: American Psychiatric Association.

American Psychiatric Association (2013). *Diagnostic and Statistical Manual of Mental Disorders (5th Ed.)* USA: American Psychiatric Association.

Augustus-Horvath, C. L., & Tylka, T. L. (2011). The acceptance model of intuitive eating: A comparison of women in emerging adulthood, early adulthood, and middle adulthood, *Journal of Counseling Psychology,* 58(1), 110-125.

Avalos, L.C., & Tylka, T.L. (2006). Exploring a model of intuitive eating with college women, *Journal of Counseling Psychology,* 53(4) 486-497.

Bacon. L. (2008). *Health at Every Size: The Surprising Truth About Your Weight.* Dallas: Benbella.

Bandyopadhyay, A.R. (2017). Eating disorder/and or eating behavior researches from West Bengal, India: Suppressing the facts?? *Asian Journal of Medical Sciences*, 8(2), 14-20.

Bardone-Cone, A.M., Brownstone, L.M., Higgins, M.K., Fitzsimmons-Craft, E.E., & Harney, M.B. (2013). Anxiety, appearance contingent self-work, and appearance conversations with friends in relation to disordered eating: Examining moderator models, *Cognitive Therapy Research,* 37, 953-963.

Bardone-Cone, A.M., Harney, M.B., Maldonado, C.R., Lawson, M.A., Robinson, D.P., Smith, R., & Tosh, A. (2010). Defining recovery from an eating disorder: Conceptualization, validation and examination of psychosocial functioning and psychiatric comorbitity, *Behavior Research and Therapy,* 48, 194-202.

Bardone-Cone, A.M., Schaefer, L.M., Maldonado, C.R., Fitzsimmons, E. E., Harney, M.B., Lawson, M.A., Robinson, D.P, Tosh, A., & Smith R. (2010). Aspects of self-concept and eating disorder recovery: What does the sense of self look like when an individual recovers from an eating disorder? *Journal of Social and Clinical Psychology,* 29(7), 821-846.

Bardone-Cone, A.M. (2012). Examining the match between assessed eating disorder recovery and subjective sense of recovery: Preliminary findings, *European Eating Disorders Review,* 20, 246-249.

Beintner, I., Jacobi, C., & Taylor, C.B. (2012). Effects of an internet-based prevention programme for eating disorders in the USA and Germany – A meta-analytic review, *European Eating Disorders Review,* 20, 1-8.

Bjork, T., Wallin, K., & Pettersen, G. (2012). Male experiences of life after recovery from an eating disorder, *Eating Disorders,* 20, 440-468.

Bloom, L., Shelton, B., Bengough, M., & Brennan, L. (2013). Psychosocial outcomes of a non-dieting based positive body image community program for overweight adults: A pilot study, *Journal of Eating Disorders,* 1(44), 1-12.

Bowen, S., Chawla, N., & Marlatt, G.A. (2010). *Mindfulness-based relapse prevention for the treatment of substance-abuse disorders: A clinician's guide.* NY: Guilford.

Bowlby, C.G., Anderson, T. L, Hall, M.E.L., & Willingham, M.M. (2015). Recovered professionals exploring eating disorder recovery: A qualitative investigation of meaning, *Clinical Social Work Journal,* 43, 1-10.

Brouwers, M. (1990). Treatment of body image dissatisfaction among women with bulimia nervosa, *Journal of Counseling and Development,* 69, 144-147.

Brown, B. (2013). *Daring Greatly: How the Courage to be Vulnerable Transforms the Way We Live, Love, Parent, and Lead.* Penguin.

Burger, A. J., Hoffeditz, L.A., Firmin, M.W., Hwang, C-e, & Wantz, R.A. (2008). The relationship between eating disorder behavior and Myers-Briggs® Personality Type, *Journal of Psychological Type,* 2, 68(2), 11-18.

Byrtek-Matera, A., & Czepczor, K. (2017). Models of eating disorders: a theoretical investigation of abnormal eating patterns and body image disturbance, *Archives of Psychiatry and Psychotherapy,* 1, 16-26.

Cardi, V., Di Matteo, R., Gilbert, P., & Treasure, J. (2014). Rank perception and self-evaluation in eating disorders, *International Journal of Eating Disorders,* 47, 543-552.

Cockell, S. J., Zaitsoff, S. L., & Geller, J. (2004). Maintaining change following eating disorder treatment, *Professional Psychology: Research and Practice,* 35(5), 527-534.

Cogley, C.B., & Keel, P.K. (2003). Requiring remission of undue influence of weight and shape on self-evaluation in the definition of recovery for bulimia nervosa, *International Journal of Eating Disorders,* 200-210.

Cook-Cottone, C. (2016). Embodied self-regulation and mindful self-care in the prevention of eating disorders, *Eating Disorders,* 24(1), 98-105.

Csikszentmihalyi, M. (1990). *Flow: The Psychology of Optimal Experience.* HarperCollins: NY.

Culnan, E., Holliday, B., Daly, B.P, Aggarwal, R., & Kloss, J.D. (2013). Insufficient sleep and weight status in high school students: Should we be focusing on the extremes? *Children's Health Care* 42, 99-115.

Dakanalis, A., Favagrossa, L., Clerici, M., Prunas, A., Colmegna, F., Zanetti, M.A., & Riva, G. (2015). Body dissatisfaction and eating disorder symptomatology: A latent structural equation modeling analysis of moderating variables in 18-to-28-year-old males, *The Journal of Psychology,* 149(1), 85-112.

Da Luz, F.Q., Sainsbury, A., Hay, P., Roekenes, J.A., Swinbourne, J., da Silva, D.C., & Oliveira, M.d.S. (2017). Early maladaptive schemas and cognitive distortions in adults with morbid obesity: Relationships with mental health status, *Behavioral Science*, 7(10), 1-11.

Darling, C.A., Coccia, C., & Senatore, N. (2012). Women in midlife: Stress, health and life satisfaction, *Stress and Health*, 28, 31-40.

Douglass, L. (2009). Yoga as an intervention in the treatment of eating disorders: Does it help? *Eating Disorders*, 17, 126-139.

Douglass, L. (2011). Thinking through the body: The conceptualization of yoga as therapy for individuals with eating disorders, *Eating Disorders*, 19, 83-96.

Dweck, C. S. (2006). *Mindset: The New Psychology of Success*. NY: Random House.

Erguner-Tekinalp, B., & Gillespie, C. W. (2010). Mental health practitioners' professional opinions of etiology of eating disorders: A cross-cultural study. *International Journal of Mental Health*.

Eshkevari, E., Rieger, E., Longo, M.R., Haggard, P., & Treasure, J. (2014). Persistent body image disturbance following recovery from eating disorders, *International Journal of Eating Disorders*, 47, 400-409.

Fairburn, C.G., & Beglin, S. (2008). Eating disorder examination questionnaire. In *Cognitive Behavior Therapy and Eating Disorders*, Fairburn, C.G (Ed.). NY: Guilford.

Fairburn, C.G., Cooper, Z., Shafran, R., Bohn, K., Hawker, D.M., Murphy, R., & Straebler, S. (2008). Enhanced cognitive behavior therapy for eating disorders: The core protocol. In *Cognitive Behavior Therapy and Eating Disorders*, Fairburn, C.G (Ed.). NY: Guilford.

Fee, A., & Gillespie, C.W. (2014). Recovery is developmental: An exploration of Eriksonian psychosocial theory adapted to eating disorder recovery. *Modern Psychological Studies*, 1 (20), 59-78.

Frederici, A., & Kaplan, A.S. (2008). The patient's account of relapse and recovery in anorexia nervosa: A qualitative study, *European Eating Disorders Review,* 16, 1-10.

Fitzsimmons, E.E., & Bardone-Cone, A.M. (2010). Differences in coping across stages of recovery from an eating disorder, *International Journal of Eating Disorders,* 43, 689-693.

Fitzsimmons, E.E., Bardone-Cone, A.M., Wonderlich, S.A., Crosby, R.D., Engel, S.G., & Bulik, C.M. (2015). The relationships among social comparisons, body surveillance, and body dissatisfaction in the natural environment, *Behavior Therapy,* 46, 257-271.

Fitzsimmons-Craft, E.E., Keatts, D.A., & Bardone-Cone, A.M. (2013). Eating expectancies in relation to eating disorder recovery, *Cognitive Therapy Research,* 37, 1041-1047.

Fogelkvist, M., Parling, T., Kjellin, L., & Gustafsson, S.A. (2016). A qualitative analysis of participants' reflections on body image during participation in a randomized controlled trial of acceptance and commitment therapy, *Journal of Eating Disorders,* 4(29), 1-9.

Frank, G.K., Wagner, A., Achenbach, S., McConaha, C., Skovira, K., Aizenstein, H., Carter, C.S., & Kaye, W.H. (2006). Altered brain activity in women recovered from bulimic-type eating disorders after a glucose challenge: A pilot study, *International Journal of Eating Disorders,* 39, 76-79.

Frederici, A., & Kaplan, A. S. (2008). The patient's account of relapse and recovery in anorexia nervosa: A qualitative study. European Eating Disorders Review, 16, 1010.

Fuller-Tyszkiewicz, M., & Mussap, A. J. (2008). The relationship between dissociation and binge eating, Journal of Trauma & Dissociation, Vol. 9(4). 445-462.

Fursland, A., Bryne, S., Watson, H., Puma, M.L., Allen, K., & Bryne, S. (2012). Enhanced Cognitive Behavior Therapy: A single treatment for all eating disorder, *Journal of Counseling and Development,* 90(3), 319-329.

Gilbert, S.C., Crump, S., Madhere, S., & Shutz, W. (2009). Internalization of the thin ideal as a predictor of body dissatisfaction and disordered eating in African, African-American, and Afro-Caribbean female college students, *Journal of College Student Psychotherapy*, 23, 196-211.

Gillespie, C.W. (2013) Structure plus trust equals freedom and peace: A personal journey of recovery from eating disorders, *Critical Dietetics Journal*, 1(3), 36-40.

Gillespie, C.W. (2016). Dealing with relapse. *Critical Dietetics*, 3(1), 11-15.

Godfrey, K. M., Gallo, L. C., & Afari, N. (2015). Mindfulness-based interventions for binge eating: a systematic review and meta-analysis, *Journal of Behavioral Medicine*, 38, 348-362.

Grilo, C.M., Pagano, M.E., Stout, R.L., Markowitz, J.C., Ansell, E.B., Pinto, A., Zanarini, M.C. Yen, S., & Skodol, A.E. (2012). Stressful life events predict eating disorder relapse following remission: Six-year prospective outcomes, *International Journal of Eating Disorders*, 45, 185-192.

Grecucci, A., Pappaianni, E., Siugzdaite, R., Theuninck, A., & Job, R. (2015). Mindful emotion regulation: Exploring the neurocognitive mechanisms behind mindfulness, *BioMed Research International*, 1-9.

Harney, M.B., & Bardone-Cone, A.M. (2014). The influence of body dissatisfaction on set shifting ability, *Cognitive Therapy Research*, 38, 439-448.

Hart, L.M., Cornell, C., Damiano, S.R., & Paxton, S.J. (2015). Parents and prevention: A systematic review of interventions involving parents that aim to prevent body dissatisfaction or eating disorders, *International Journal of Eating Disorders*, 48, 157-169.

Hart, L.M, Damiano, S.R., & Paxton, S.J. (2016). Confident body, confident child: A randomized controlled trial evaluation of a parenting resource for promoting healthy body image and eating patterns in 2- and 6-year old children, *International Journal of Eating Disorders*, 458-472.

Hayes, S.C., Strohsal, K.D., & Wilson, K.G. (1999). *Acceptance and commitment therapy: An experiential approach to behavior change.* NY: Guilford.

Hertz, P., Addad, M., & Ronel, N. (2012). Members of overeaters anonymous who have recovered from binge-eating disorder, *Health and Social Work,* 110-122.

Hirschmann J.R., & Munter, C.H. (1988/2008). *Overcoming Overeating: How to break the diet/binge cycle and life a healthier, more satisfying life.* Addison-Wesley

Hirschmann J.R., & Munter, C.H (1995). *When Women Stop Hating Their Bodies: Freeing Yourself from Food and Weight Obsession.* Random House: NY.

Hohlstein, L.A., Smith, G.T, & Atlas, J.G. (1998). An application of expectancy theory to eating disorders: Development and validation of measures of eating and dieting expectancies, *Psychological Assessment, 10,* 49-58.

Holtkamp, K., Muller, B., Heussen, N., Remschmidt, H., Herpertz-Dahlmann, B. (2005). Depression, anxiety, and obsessionality in long-term recovered patients with adolescent-onset anorexia nervosa, *European Child and Adolescent Psychiatry,* 14, 106-110.

Hunter-Reel, D., McCrady, B., & Hildebrandt, T. (2009). Emphasizing interpersonal factors: An extension of the Witkiewitz and Marlatt relapse model, *Addiction*, 104, 1281-1290.

Isomaa R., & Isomaa, A.-L. (2014). And then what happened? A 5-year follow-up of eating disorder patients, *Nordic Journal of Psychiatry*, 68(8), 567-572.

Jackson, J. (2017) Re-ordering desires: A Trinitarian lens on eating disorders, *Anglican Theological Review,* 255-274.

Jordan, J. V. (2001). A relational-cultural model: Healing through mutual empathy, Bulletin of the Menninger Clinic, 65(1), 92-103.

Kabat-Zinn, J. (1990). *Full catastrophe living: Using the wisdom of your body and mind to face stress, pain, and illness.* NY: Dell.

Kim, K.R. (2010). Sleep disturbances are common in eating disorders, *Eating Disorders Review,* 21(3), 3.

Kordy, H., Kramer, B., Palmer, R.L., Papezova, H., Pellet, J., Richard, M., & Treasure, J. (2002). Remission, recovery, relapse, and recurrence in eating disorders: Conceptualization and illustration of a validation strategy, *Journal of Clinical Psychology,* 58(7), 833-846.

Lamarre, A., & Rice, C. (2016) Normal eating is counter-cultural: Embodied experiences of eating disorder recovery, *Journal of Community and Applied Social Psychology,* 26, 136-149.

Lang, K., Roberts, M., Harrison, A., Lopez, C., Goddard, E., Khondoker, M., Treasure, J., & Tchanturia, K. (2016). Central coherence in eating disorders: A synthesis of studies using the Rey Osterrieth Complex Figure Test, *PLos One* 11(11) 1-11.

Lathia, N., Sandstrom, G.M., Mascolo, C., & Rentfrow, P.J. (2017). Happier people live more active lives: Using smartphones to link happiness and physical activity, *PLoS ONE,* (12):1, 1-13.

Levallius, J., Roberts, B.W., Clinton, D., Norring, C. (2016). Take charge: Personality as a predictor of recovery from an eating disorder, *Psychiatry Research,* 447-452.

Lewis-Smith, H., Diedrichs, P.C., Rumsey, N., & Harcourt, D. (2016). A systematic review of interventions on body image and disordered eating outcomes among women in midlife, *International Journal of Eating Disorders,* 49(1), 5-18.

Linehan, M.M. (1993). *Skills training manual for treating borderline personality disorder.* NY: Guilford.

Logel, C., Stinson, D.A., & Brochu, P.M. (2015). Weight loss is not the answer: A well-being solution to the "obesity problem," *Social and Personality Psychology Compass,* 9(11), 678-695.

Marcus, S.R. (2016). Thinspiration vs. thicksperation: Comparing pro-anorexic and fat acceptance image posts on a photo-sharing site. *Cyberpsychology: Journal of Psychosocial Research on Cyberspace,* 10(2), 1-20.

Matz, J. & Frankel, E. (2006). *Diet Survivor's Handbook: 60 Lessons in Eating, Acceptance, and Self-Care.* Sourcebooks: Naperville, IL.

Mayo, C., & George, V. (2014). Eating disorder risk and body dissatisfaction based on muscularity and body fat in male university students, *Journal of American College Health*, 62(6), 407-415.

McFarlane, T., Olmsted, M.P., & Trottier, K. (2008). Timing and prediction of relapse in a transdiagnostic eating disorder sample, *International Journal of Eating Disorders*, 41, 587-593.

McGuinnes, S., & Taylor, J.E. (2016). Understanding body image dissatisfaction and disordered eating in midlife adults, *New Zealand Journal of Psychology*, 45(1), 4-12.

Melioli, T., Bauer, S., Franko, D.L., Moessner, M., Ozer, F., Chabrol, H., & Rodgers, R.F. (2016). *International Journal of Eating Disorders*, 49, 19-31.

Miller, J. B., & Stiver, I. P. (1997). *The healing connections: How women form connection in both therapy and life*. Boston: Beacon Press.

Mitchison, D., Dawson, L., Hand, L., Mond, J., & Hay, P. (2016). Quality of life as a vulnerability and recovery factor in eating disorders: a community-based study, *BMC Psychiatry*, 16, 328.

Mond, J.M., Hay, P.J., Rogers, B., & Owen, C. (2006). Eating Disorder Examination Questionnaire (EDE-Q): Norms for adult young women, *Behaviour Research and Therapy*, , 44(1), 53-62.

Nakai, Y., Nin, K., Sun'ichi, N., Hamagaki, S., Takagi, R., & Wonderlich, S.A. (2014). Outcome of eating disorders in a Japanese sample: A 4- to 9-year follow-up study, *European Eating Disorders Review*, 2, 206-211.

Nakamura, J., & Csikszentmihalyi, M. (2009). The concept of flow. In Snyder, C. R., & Lopez, S.J. (Ed.). *Oxford Handbook of Positive Psychology*. Oxford University press, USA, 89-105.

Neff, K.D. (2003). Development and validation of a scale to measure self-compassion, *Self and Identity*, 2, 223-250.

Neff, K.D. (2008). Self-compassion: Moving beyond the pitfalls of a separate self-concept. In J. Bauer & H.A. Wayment (Eds.) *Transcending Self-*

Interest: Psychological Explorations of the Quiet Ego (95-105). APA Books: Washington, D.C.

Neff, K.D. (2011) *Self-Compassion: Stop Beating Yourself Up and Leave Insecurity Behind*. HaperCollins.

Neff, K.D., & McGehee, P. (2010). Self-compassion and psychological resilience among adolescents and young adults, *Self and Identity,* 9(3), 225-240.

News (June, 2017). Help for those with an eating disorder, *Australian Nursing & Midwifery Journal,* 24(11), 8.

Neumark-Sztainer, D. (2016). Eating disorders prevention: Looking backward, moving forward; looking inward, moving outward, *Eating Disorders,* 24(1), 29-38.

Nilsson, K., Engstrom, I., & Hagglof, B. (2012). Family climate and recovery in adolescent onset eating disorders: A prospective study, *European Eating Disorders Review,* 20, e96-e102.

Noordenbos, G. (2011). When have eating disorder patients recovered and what to the DSM-IV criteria tell about recovery? *Eating Disorders,* 19, 234-245.

O'Connor, S.M., Klump, K.L., VanHuysse, J.L., & Iacono, W. (2016). Does parental divorce moderate the heritability of body dissatisfaction? An extension of previous gene-environment interaction effects, *International Journal of Eating Disorders,* 49, 188-192.

O'Reilly, G. A., Cook, L. Spruijt-Metz, D., & Black, D. S. (2014). Mindfulness-based interventions for obesity-related eating behaviours: a literature review, *Obesity Reviews,* 15, 453-461.

Pannowitz, D. (2015). Clinical applications of mindful eating, *Journal of the Australian Traditional-Medicine Society,* 21(3), 168-171.

Petersson, S., Johnsson, P., & Perseius, K-I. (2017). A Sisyphean task: Experiences of perfectionism in patients with eating disorders, *Journal of Eating Disorders,* 5(3), 1-11.

Richards, P. S., Crowton, S., Berrett, M.E., Smith, M.H. & Passemore, K. (2017). Can patients with eating disorders learn to eat intuitively? A 2-year pilot study, *Eating Disorders: The Journal of Treatment and Prevention*, 25(2), 99-113.

Ridgway, J.L, & Clayton, R.B. (2016). Instagram unfiltered: exploring associations of body image satisfaction, Instagram #selfie posting, and negative romantic relationship outcomes, *Cyberpsychology, Behavior, and Social Networking*, 19(1), 1-7.

Roane, B.M. Seifer, R., Sharkey, K.M., Reen, E.V., Bond, T.L.Y., Raffray, T., & Carskadon, M.A. (2015). What role does sleep play in weight gain in the first semester of university? *Behavioral Sleep Medicine,* 13, 491-505.

Rorty, M., Yager, J., & Rossotto, E. (1993). Why and how do women recover from bulimia nervosa? The subjective appraisals of forty women recovered for a year or more, *International Journal of Eating Disorders,* 14(3), 249-260.

Roth, G. (1993/2004) *Breaking Free From Emotional Eating.* NY: Plume

Safer, D.L., Lively, T.J., Telch, C.F., & Agras, W.S. (2002). Predictors of relapse following successful dialectical behavior therapy for binge eating disorder, *International Journal of Eating Disorders,* 155-163.

Satter, E. (2008). *Secrets of Feeding a healthy Family.* Kelcy Press.

Schaefer, J.T., & Magnuson, A.B. (2014). A review of interventions that promote eating by internal cues, *Journal of the Academy of Nutrition and Dietetics*, 114(5), 734-760.

Shohet, M. (2007). Narrating anorexia: "Full" and "Struggling" genres of recovery, *Ethos*, 35(3), 344-382.

Stein, D., Kaye, W.H., Matsunaga, H., Orbach. I., Har-Even, D., Frank, D., McConaha, C.W., & Rao, R. (2002). Eating-related concerns, mood, and personality traits in recovered bulimia nervosa subjects: A replication study, *International Journal of Eating Disorders,* 32, 225-229.

Stein, K.F., Wing, J., Lewis, A., & Raghunathan, T. (2011). An eating disorder randomized clinical trial and attrition: Profiles and determinants of dropout, *International Journal of Eating Disorders*, 44, 356-368.

Stice, E., & Shaw, H. (2002). Role of body dissatisfaction in the onset and maintenance of eating pathology: A synthesis of research findings, *Journal of Psychosomatic Resarch*, 53, 985-993.

Strien, T.V., Engels, R.C.M.E., Leeuwe, J.V., & Snoek, H.M. (2005). The Stice model of overeating: Tests in clinical and non-clinical samples, *Appetite*, 45(3), 205-213.

Tribole, E. & Resch, E. (2012). *Intuitive Eating: A Revolutionary Program that Works*, 3rd. ed. St. Martin's Press: NY.

Trottier, K., Wonderlich, S.A., Monson, C.M., Crosby, R.D., & Olmsted, M.P. (2016). Investigating posttraumatic stress disorder as a psychological maintain factor of eating disorders, *International Journal of Eating Disorders*, 49, 455-457.

Tylka, T.L., Annunziato, R.A., Burgard, D., Danielsdottir, S., Shuman, E., Davis, C., & Calogero, R.M. (2014). The weight-inclusive versus weight-normative approach to health: Evaluating the evidence for prioritizing well-being over weight loss, *Journal of Obesity*, 1-18.

Tylka, T.L., Calogero, R.M., & Danielsdottir, S. (2015). Is intuitive eating the same as flexible dietary control? Their links to each other and well-being could provide an answer, *Appetite*, 95, 166-175.

Tylka, T.L., & Kroon Van Diest, A.M. (2013). The intuitive eating scale-2: Item refinement and psychometric evaluation with college women and men, *Journal of Counseling Psychology*, 60(1), 137-153.

Tylka, T.L., & Wilcox, J.A. (2006). Are intuitive eating and eating disorder symptomatology opposite poles of the same construct? *Journal of Counseling Psychology*, 53(4), 474-485.

Uchoa, F.N.M, Lustosa, R.P., Rocha, M.T.M, Daniele, T.M.C., Deana, N.F., Alves, N., & Aranha, A.C.M. (2017). Media influence and body dissatisfaction in Brazilian adolescents, *Biomedical Research,* 28(6), 2445-2451.

Ulian, M.D., Benatti, F.B., de Campos-Ferraz, P.L., Roble, O.J., Unsain, R.F., de Morais Sato, P., Brita, B.C., Murakawa, K.A., Modesto, B.T., Aburad, L., Bertuzzi, R., Lancha, A.H. Jr., Bualano, B., & Scagliusi, F.B. (2015). The effects of a "Health at Every Size®"-based approach in obese women: a pilot-trial of the "Health and Wellness in Obesity" study, *Frontiers in Nutrition* 2(34), 1-12.

Ulrich, M., Keller, J., Gron, G. (2016). Neural signatures of experimentally induced flow experiences identified in a typical fMRI block design with BOLD imaging, *Social Cognitive and Affective Neuroscience*, 496-507.

Vandereycken, W. (2012). Self-change in eating disorders: Is "spontaneous recovery" possible? *Eating Disorders*, 20, 87-98.

Waller, G., & Marcoulides, O.K. (2013). Safety behaviours in eating disorders: Factor structure and clinical validation of the brief safety behaviors scale, *European Eating Disorders Review*, 21, 257-261.

Wanden-Berghe, R. G., Sanz-Valero, J., & Wanden-Berghe, C. (2011) The application of mindfulness to eating disorders treatment: a systematic review, *Eating Disorders*, 19, 34-48.

Warburton, D.E.R., Nicol, C.W, Bredin, S.D. (2006). Health benefits of physical activity: The evidence, *CMAJ*, 174(6), 801-809.

Watson, H.J., Torgersen, L., Zerwas, S., Reichborn-Kjennerud, T., Knoph, C., Stoltenbert, C., Siega-Riz, A.M., Von Holle, A., Hamer, R. M., Meltzer, H. M., Ferguson, E. H., Haugen, M., Magnus, P., Kuhns, R., & Bulik, C. M. (2014). Eating disorders, pregnancy, and the postpartum period: Findings from the Norwegian mother and child cohort study (MoBa), *Norsk Epidemiologi*, 24(1-2), 51-62.

Witkiewitz, K., Lustyk, M.K., & Bowen, S. (2013). Retraining the addicted brain: A review of hypothesized neurobiological mechanisms of mindfulness-based relapse prevention, *Psychology of Addictive Behaviors*, 27(2), 351-365.

Yager, Z., Gray, T., Curry, C., & McLean, S. (2017). Body dissatisfaction, excessive exercise, and weight change strategies used by first-year undergraduate students: Comparing health and physical education and other education students, *Journal of Eating Disorders*, 5(10), 1-11.

Yaguang, Z., Klem, M.L., Sereika, S.M., Danford, C.A., Ewing, L.J., & Burke, L.E. (2015), Self-weighing in weight management: A systematic literature review. *Obesity*, 23(2), 256-265.

Yang, C-C., Barros-Loscertales, A., Pinazo, D., Ventura-Campos, N., Borchardt, V., Bustamante, J-C., Rodriguez-Pujadas, A., Fuentes-Claramonte, Balaguer, R., Avila, C., & Walter, M. (2016). State and training effects of mindfulness meditation on brain networks reflect neuronal mechanisms of its antidepressant effect, *Neural Plasticity, 1-14.*

Zarychta, K., Mullan, B., Kruk, M., & Luszczynska, A. (2017). A vicious cycle among cognitions and behaviors enhancing risk for eating disorders, *BMC Psychiatry*, 17(154), 1-10.

Zaman, K., & Humaira, J. (2016). Body image dissatisfaction and disordered eating behaviors in mothers during lactation period, *Pakistan Journal of Psychological Research,* 31(2), 609-634.

Appendix A

The EDE-Q is the Eating Disorder Questionnaire, by Fairburn and Beglin (2008) published in *Cognitive Behavior Therapy and Eating Disorders*, edited by C.G. Fairburn.

ID: **Date:**

EATING QUESTIONNAIRE

Instructions: The following questions are concerned with the past four weeks (28 days) only. Please read each question carefully. Please answer all of the questions. Please only choose one answer for each question. Thank you.

Questions 1 to 12: Please circle the appropriate number on the right. Remember that the questions only refer to the past four weeks (28 days).

0= No days; 1=1-5 days; 2=6-12 days; 3=13-15 days; 4=16-22 days; 5=23-27 days; 6=Every Day

On how many of the past 28 days…

1.	Have you been deliberately <u>trying</u> to limit the amount of food you eat to influence your shape or weight (whether or not you have succeeded)?	0 1 2 3 4 5 6
2.	Have you gone for long periods of time (8 waking hours or more) without eating anything at all in order to influence your shape or weight?	0 1 2 3 4 5 6
3.	Have you <u>tried</u> to exclude from your diet any foods that you like in order to influence your shape or weight (whether or not you have succeeded)?	0 1 2 3 4 5 6
4.	Have you <u>tried</u> to follow definite rules regarding your eating (for example, a calorie limit) in order to influence your shape or weight (whether or not you have succeeded)?	0 1 2 3 4 5 6
5.	Have you had a definite desire to have an <u>empty</u>	0 1 2 3 4 5 6

.	stomach with the aim of influencing your shape or weight?	
.	6 Have you had a definite desire to have a <u>totally</u> <u>flat</u> stomach?	0 1 2 3 4 5 6
.	7 Has thinking about <u>food, eating or calories</u> made it very difficult to concentrate on things you are interested in (for example, working, following a conversation, or reading)?	0 1 2 3 4 5 6
.	8 Has thinking about shape or weight made it very difficult to concentrate on things you are interested in (for example, working, following a conversation, or reading)?	0 1 2 3 4 5 6
.	9 Have you had a definite fear of losing control over eating?	0 1 2 3 4 5 6
0.	1 Have you had a definite fear that you might gain weight?	0 1 2 3 4 5 6
1.	1 Have you felt fat?	0 1 2 3 4 5 6
2.	1 Have you had a strong desire to lose weight?	0 1 2 3 4 5 6

Questions 13-18: Please fill in the appropriate number in the boxes on the right. Remember that the questions only refer to the past four weeks (28 days).

Over the past four weeks (28 days)...

3.	1 Over the past 28 days, how many <u>times </u>have you eaten what other people would regard as an <u>unusually large amount of food</u> (given the circumstances)?	....
4.	1 On how many of these times did you have a sense of having lost control over your eating (at	....

241

	the time that you were eating)?	
5.	1 Over the past 28 days, on how many **DAYS** have such episodes of overeating occurred (i.e. you have eaten an unusually large amount of food and have had a sense of loss of control at the time)?	....
6.	1 Over the past 28 days, how many <u>times</u> have you made yourself sick (vomit) as a means of controlling your shape or weight?	....
7.	1 Over the past 28 days, how many <u>times</u> have you taken laxatives as a means of controlling your shape or weight?	....
8.	1 Over the past 28 days, how many <u>times</u> have you exercised in a "driven" or "compulsive" way as a means of controlling your weight, shape or amount of fat or to burn off calories?	0 1 2 3 4 5 6

Questions 19-21: Please circle the appropriate number. <u>Please note for these question the term "binge eating" means</u> eating what others would regard as an unusually large amount of food for the circumstances, accompanied by a sense of having lost control over eating.

0= No days; 1=1-5 days; 2=6-12 days; 3=13-15 days; 4=16-22 days; 5=23-27 days; 6=Every Day

9.	1 Over the past 28 days, how many days have you eaten in secret (i.e., furtively)? ...Do not count episodes of binge eating	0 1 2 3 4 5 6

0=None of the days; 1=A few of the times; 2=Less than half the time; 3=Half of the time; 4=More than half the time; 5=Most of the time; 6=Every time

	2 On what proportion of the times that you have	0 1 2 3 4 5 6

0.	eaten have you felt guilty (felt that you've done wrong) because of its effect on your shape or weight? … Do not count episodes of binge eating	

0=Not at all; 2 =Slightly; 3-4=Moderately; 6=Markedly

	2 Over the past 28 days, how concerned have	0 1 2 3 4 5 6
1.	you been about other people seeing you eat?... Do not count episodes of binge eating.	

Questions 22-28: Please circle the appropriate number on the right.

Remember that the questions only refer to the past four weeks (28 days)

0=Not at all; 2 =Slightly; 3-4=Moderately; 6=Markedly

On how many of the past 28 days…

	2 Has your <u>weight</u> influenced how you think about (judge) yourself as a person?	0 1 2 3 4 5 6
2.		
3.	2 Has your <u>shape</u> influenced how you think about (judge) yourself as a person?	0 1 2 3 4 5 6
4.	2 How much would it have upset you if you had been asked to weigh yourself once a week (no more, or less, often) for the next four weeks?	0 1 2 3 4 5 6
5.	2 How dissatisfied have you been with your <u>weight</u>?	0 1 2 3 4 5 6
6.	2 How dissatisfied have you been with your <u>shape</u>?	0 1 2 3 4 5 6
7.	2 How uncomfortable have you felt seeing your body (for example, seeing your shape in the mirror, in a shop window reflection, while undressing or taking a bath or shower)?	0 1 2 3 4 5 6
	2 How uncomfortable have you felt about others	0 1 2 3 4 5 6

8.	seeing your shape or figure (for example, in communal changing rooms, when swimming, or wearing tight clothes)?	

What is your weight at present? (Please give your best estimate).

....

What is your height? (Please give your best estimate).   ....

If female: Over the past three-to-four months have you missed any menstrual periods? ....

        If so, how many?   ....

        Have you been taking the "pill"? ....

THANK YOU

Subscale items of the EDE-Q

Restraint

1 Restraint over eating

2 Avoidance of eating

3 Food avoidance

4 Dietary rules

5 Empty stomach

Eating concern

7 Preoccupation with food, eating or calories

9 Fear of losing control over eating

19 Eating in secret

21 Social eating

20 Guild about eating

Shape concern

6 Flat stomach

8 Preoccupation with shape or weight

23 Importance of shape

10 Fear of weight gain

26 Dissatisfaction with shape

27 Discomfort seeing body

28 Avoidance of exposure

11 Feelings of fatness

Weight concern

22 Importance of weight

24 Reaction to prescribed weighing

8 Preoccupation with shape or weight

25 Dissatisfaction with weight

12 Desire to lose weight

ABOUT THE AUTHOR

Dr. Catherine Wilson Gillespie earned her B.A. from Wellesley College, her M.Ed. from Lesley University, and her Ph.D. from the University of Tennessee at Knoxville. She is a Professor at Drake University School of Education in Des Moines, Iowa, where she has worked since 1996. Dr. Gillespie has struggled with and recovered from her own eating disorder. She has published research in eating disorder recovery as well as in other areas including early childhood education. She is married, has two children, and lives in Iowa. She has also earned a black belt in the martial art of Tae Kwon Do.

Made in the USA
Middletown, DE
26 June 2019